Politics and  World

D0345917

Attempts by Third World regimes to develop adequate political institutions and foster popular legitimacy are often unsuccessful, resulting in recurrent instances of repression, political instability, and at times even revolutions. These political dynamics occur within, and in turn affect changes in, the social and cultural milieu of Third World nations.

Political institutionalisation often takes place side by side with industrial development, which is itself inherently urban based, and encourages imports of goods and technology, neglect of the agricultural sector, and rampant growth of urban centres. The industrial and economic development policies adopted, coupled with the political characteristics of the regimes involved, foster specific social and cultural conditions. Most notably, there is social change, which first results from and then accentuates the variation from existing social norms – a process that can dramatically alter the prevailing political culture. These characteristics, when combined, provide the social and political circumstances that give rise to revolutions or, at least, chronic episodes of political instability and social upheaval.

Politics and society in the Third World is an accessible and stimulating text that provides a multi-disciplinary approach to the study of the Third World, examining the region politically as well as socially and culturally.

Mehran Kamrava holds a PhD in Social and Political Sciences from Cambridge University and is Assistant Professor of International Studies at Rhodes College, Memphis, Tennessee. He is also the author of *Revolution in Iran: the Roots of Turmoil, Political History of Modern Iran* and *Revolutionary Politics*.

Politics and society in the Third World

Mehran Kamrava

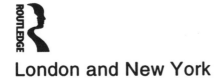

London and New York

First published 1993
by Routledge
11 New Fetter Lane, London EC4P 4EE

Simultaneously published in the USA and Canada
by Routledge
29 West 35th Street, New York, NY 10001

© 1993 Mehran Kamrava

Typeset in Bembo by LaserScript, Mitcham, Surrey
Printed and bound in Great Britain by
Mackays of Chatham PLC, Chatham, Kent

British Library Cataloguing in Publication Data
A catalogue record for this book is available from the British Library

Library of Congress Cataloging in Publication Data
Kamrava, Mehran, 1964–
    Politics and society in the third world/Mehran Kamrava.
    p. cm.
    Includes bibliographical references and index.
    ISBN 0–415–09047–4: $59.95. – ISBN 0–415–09048–2 (pbk.): $15.95
    1. Developing countries – Politics and government. 2. Developing
    countries – Social conditions. 3. Developing countries – Economic
    conditions. I. Title.
    JF60.K34   1993
    306.2'091724 – dc20   92-32057
                    CIP

ISBN 0–415–090474   ISBN 0–415–090482 (pbk)

Contents

Preface

Some years ago, I found myself troubled by my inability to find a satisfactory answer to the question of 'why is democracy absent from the Third World?' The harder I searched for an answer, the more puzzling the enigma grew. One after another, what on the surface appeared as satisfactory answers – greedy leaders, warped heritages, authoritarian cultures, etc. – became exposed as the tautologies which they were. I searched in the political, but found the social as compellingly important; I analysed the social, and found the cultural inseparable; I examined the cultural, but found it void without the other two.

Admittedly, it was this intellectual confusion which gave birth to the present work. In my search for dynamics which have chased democracy out of the Third World, I found the Third World itself a victim of much academic and scholarly neglect. While British scholars retain a seminal interest in the study of the region, the Third World as a whole has in recent years aroused the curiosity of few American observers. Once the preserve of such giants of the field as Samuel Huntington and Lucian Pye, the Third World has since the end of the 1960s been progressively pushed onto the academic backburner, no longer the fashionable subject that it once was, having become marginalized into something of a doctrinal toy for a few ideological diehards who find its peculiar characteristics supportive of their agendas. There is indeed a paucity of recent serious scholarship on the region, although, again, a few impressive works have come out of England.

It was within this vacuous atmosphere that I felt compelled to write this book, not necessarily to right the academic wrongs of recent years but to at least try to once again bring the subject to the fore of analysis and debate. For now, this seemingly elementary task appears much more pressing than the question of why democracy and the Third World have for so long been diametrically opposed.

I have examined the subject within a multidisciplinary frame-work, analysing the Third World not only politically but socially and culturally as well. The book analyses the processes of political and industrial development, their numerous consequences on social forms and societal actors, their implications for political culture, and, finally, their endemic contribution to political instability and revolutions. Chapters 1 and 6 examine the political phenomena of state-building and revolutions respectively. These political developments, the following pages argue, occur and are invariably conditioned within the social and cultural milieux in which they evolve. To this end, chapters 2 and 3 each examine industrial development and urbanisation. Both chapters entail considerably more analysis on the *social* consequences of modernisation and demographic shifts than on their micro- and macroeconomic aspects, examining economic factors only in so far as they affect social and political life. Chapters 4 and 5 are devoted specifically to these two spheres. Chapter 4 examines the varied and far-reaching affects of social change, while chapter 5 discusses characteristics inherent in Third World political cultures which in turn shape the contours of political conduct and social interaction. Throughout, I have attempted to emphasise the interconnected nature of these seemingly diverse developments. The political and social lives of the Third World cannot be understood in isolation from one another, and any attempt to separate the two is bound to result in what can at best be only an incomplete and partial understanding of the subject.

Through the long and arduous task of writing this book, I was helped by numerous friends, associates, and family members. They are too many to individually name, but a few were true saviours. The warmth and constant support of my mother and my brother kept my sanity intact during the many times that both the task of writing the book and its subject seemed insane. Melih Sindel provided invaluable insight with his views on the question of ethnicity in the Third World and beyond. My colleagues and students at the International Studies Department of Rhodes College, where the final pages of this book were written, also provided invaluable support and assistance during the last hectic days of work on the manuscript, when the end at times seemed as distant as when the book was a mere confusing idea. I gratefully acknowledge their help. The book's mistakes and shortcomings are, of course, my own responsibility.

M. K.

Memphis, Tennessee.

List of terms

barriadas, barrios	squatter settlements (Latin America)
barung-barongs	squatter settlements (Philippines)
bidonville	squatter settlement (North Africa, especially in Algeria)
bustees	squatter settlements (India)
callampas, colonias	squatter settlements (Latin America)
dependistas	supporters of dependency theory
descamisados	the shirtless ones (in Peron's regime, the underprivileged)
favelas	squatter settlements (Latin America)
gecekondu	squatter settlements (Turkey)
gourbiville	squatter settlement (North Africa, especially in Algeria)
halab-abads	squatter settlements (Iran)
kampongs	squatter settlements (Malaysia)
lumpen proletariat	rural migrants and unskilled workers
mostazafan	the disinherited (in post-revolutionary Iran)
personalismo	a personality cult
proletarias	squatter settlements (Latin America)
ranchos	squatter settlements (Latin America)

Chapter 1

Political systems and processes

An overwhelming majority of developing countries embody restrictive political structures and non-democratic institutions. There are only a few Third World governments that are more receptive to the needs and the demands of their peoples through free elections, independent judicial systems, and the rule of law. Democratic political institutions have been taking roots in an increasing number of Third World countries, especially those in Latin America. However, such examples of Third World democracies are strikingly few, and in most cases, as in India and Kenya, a strong argument can be made concerning the essentially restrictive nature of their polities.[1] In most parts of the Third World, authoritarian systems dominate the political landscape. What often varies from one country to another is not necessarily the nature of political systems as a whole but rather the details and the precise manner in which dictatorial regimes operate.

The political processes that occur in the Third World can in large measure be summed up as efforts to attain institutionalisation and legitimacy. For reasons enumerated below, these two developments assume crucial importance in Third World countries, where the combined effects of rapid industrial and urban growth, intense social change, and disjointed political cultures have made change and instability as inseparable to politics as authoritarian tendencies are to regimes. In essence, the politics of the Third World is driven by continuous struggles on the part of Third World governments to attain legitimacy and in the process to institutionalise themselves in their respective societies. Different types of governments develop out of these efforts, of course not without the influence of indigenous factors, ranging from personalist regimes to bureaucratic-authoritarian and populist ones.

INSTITUTIONALISATION

Political institutionalisation is one of the dilemmas that Third World governments have long faced. Institutionalisation refers to the effective establishment of governmental authority over society through especially created political structures and organs. In its most elementary form, political institutionalisation is a state-building process. As an unavoidable phase in the process of political development, institutionalisation involves the 'extent to which the entire polity is organised as a system of interacting relationships, first among the offices and agencies of the government, and then among the various groups and interests seeking to make demands upon the system, and finally in the relationships between officials and articulating citizens.'[2] Some scholars view institutionalisation as a linear, evolutionary phenomenon whereby 'a political structure is made operational in accordance with stipulated rules and procedures, enabling more regularised, hence predictable, patterns of political behavior, minimal trauma in power transfer, and a foundation for the effective development of policies as well as the application of justice'. 'Ideally', they argue,

> political institutionalisation enables a movement from the erratic practices and arbitrary decisions stemming from a high dependence on personalized rule. In its success, it also reduces the likelihood of abrupt, drastic change in basic structure, including revolution, since change is made possible in legal, evolutionary manner by established procedures.[3]

Yet such a directional definition of political institutionalisation is applicable only to selective cases, where political actors have made deliberate attempts at engineering specific political institutions and practices in particular directions. That such efforts have resulted in largely failed experiments, as the African continent sadly testifies, stands as testimony to the futility of ascribing to institutionalisation politically evolutionary characteristics. Instead, *institutionalisation* needs to be seen as precisely what it stands for: the penetration, both objectively as well as subjectively, of society by existing political institutions. The degree to which a particular system is institutionalised depends not on the extent of its correspondence to democratic rules and practices but on its success in penetrating the various levels of society, hence resulting in popular compliance with the body politic, whether voluntarily or through an actual or perceived threat of coercion. Thus institutionalisation involves more than the mere mechanical penetration of society by various governmental organs and institutions. It carries with it an implied emotional and ideological acceptance, whether forced or voluntary, of the credibility of institutions which emanate political power.

In essence, institutionalisation determines the extent of the solidity of the nexus between state and society. It is this function, that of a linkage between state and society, that makes institutionalisation so quintessentially central to the political process in the Third World. It is, indeed, as will be shown, the extent of institutionalisation that to a large extent determines the viability of particular political regimes and the measure of their popularity among those they govern. The greater and more in-depth the institutional bonds between state and society, the less likely it is for political alternatives to gain hold among the popular classes. Adversely, the more fluid such nexuses, the higher is the probability of political change and the less permanent are state structures likely to be. The inherently fragile political systems of most Third World countries, and the even more tenuous bonds that bridge Third World political and social actors together, are both products of what is at best skewed and incomplete institutionalisation.

It is important to note that institutionalisation is possible only in societies where there is a clear and dominant centre of power that is capable of overcoming other competing power centres. Institutionalisation cannot take place when political institutions are either not strong enough or do not have a single and identifiable social mass to penetrate. In such societies, deep communal divisions and conflicting allegiances prevent the effective domination of one group over another and result in the emergence of community-exclusive authority structures. Thus in places like Mandatory Palestine, Northern Ireland, Cyprus, and Lebanon, 'political authority is divided between the sovereign political center on the one hand, and the institutionalised or semi-institutionalised political centers of the constituent communities on the other'.[4] In the absence of any overwhelming centres of authority, the rule of the state becomes precarious and highly susceptive to shifts and fluctuations in the economy, demography, and communal balances of power. For institutionalisation to take place, there needs to be a dominant centre of power that is capable of enforcing its authority over other social forces. Without such domination by any one group, political institutionalisation cannot occur and a 'stateless society', similar to that of Lebanon in the 1970s and the 1980s, emerges.

Political institutionalisation in the Third World takes place through several mechanisms and at various levels. Specifically, institutionalisation occurs first in the narrow confines of the political establishment itself. In this sense, it refers to the development of norms and explicit as well as implicit codes of conduct, 'the rules of the game', among principal political actors and institutions. It signifies the routinisation of certain political procedures and the prevalence, whether due to precedent or to legal prescriptions, of certain principles over others. This sort of political institutionalisation is most frequently attempted through the provision of national constitutions, most of which lay down in detail the mechanics of the political system and the relationships of its various components. In a broader level, implicit codes of political conduct and procedural behaviour emerge and dominate the political life of society, frequently sanctioned by the highest levels of political office. A second mechanism through which political institutionalisation is achieved is through various institutions which link the political system to the broader confines of society. These institutions include, most notably, the bureaucracy and other administrative arms of the state such as parastatals, its coercive organs such as the military and the police, and other organisations through which the state solicits popular support and participation.

The most prevalent of these measures, and perhaps the least effective, has been the provision of constitutions that lay down the nature and the characteristics of political institutions in elaborate detail. It is often thought, both by Third World political figures and by intellectuals, that the provision of a constitution is the first and the most fundamental step toward the creation of an ideal state. Constitutions are often intended to serve two diametrically opposed goals. For revolutionaries and national liberation fighters, of the kind that pervaded throughout Africa in the 1960s, constitutions hold promises of institutionally guaranteed civil liberties and political democracy. They are official documents intended to outline the contours of the political establishment and to keep in check the powers of politicians and other public figures. Often, such constitutions are hurriedly put before the public in a national referendum, as the constitution of the Islamic Republic of Iran was for example,[5] in order to enhance their popular legitimacy and supposed sacrosanctity. It was with these aspirations that European-style constitutions proliferated in post-independence Africa, with the hope that the democracies of the former colonial powers could be transplanted on throughout the continent.[6]

But not all constitutions set out to outline democratic systems. In numerous Third World countries, especially those ruled by authoritarian regimes, constitutions are tailor-made to fulfil specific political purposes and to present a mere cloak of legitimacy to norms and practices otherwise considered as unpopular and illegitimate. In the 1970s, Ferdinand Marcos in the Philippines, Kim Il Sung in North Korea, and General Park Chung-hee in South Korea, to name only a few, devised constitutions convenient for their own personal ends,[7] as do to this day successive military governments in Thailand[8] and the new regimes of Africa.[9] Even the libertarian provisions of the first constitution of post-revolutionary Iran have been changed beyond recognition, retaining little if any of their original democratic flavour.[10]

Nevertheless, whether democratic or authoritarian, by themselves constitutions have largely proven to be hopelessly incapable of guaranteeing the longevity of the systems they were intended to create and to safeguard. This unworkability of (democratic) constitutions in the Third World can largely be attributed to their failure to take into account indigenous social and political conditions.[11] To begin with, a lack of existing political infrastructures, organisational cohesion, and a shared political heritage in most Third World countries precludes the evolution of political institutions there based on constitutional models imported from the West. Efforts at wholesale constitutional engineering have met with little success because they blindly attempt to implement an overnight transformation of political attitudes and practices. Political institutionalisation involves piecemeal social engineering and time instead of mere importation of ideas and institutions.[12] In post-independence Africa, for example, the constitutional pattern of the colonial countries were emulated in an effort to superimpose European institutions on African settings.[13] But the predominance of communalism and of tribal loyalties invariably resulted in the breakdown of imported institutions such as parliaments and of concepts such as democracy. Imported European institutions were no more capable of overcoming the centrifugal forces of African societies than were any other institutions.[14]

In Latin America, efforts to import North American and Western European political ideals and constitutional measures yielded equally dismal results. Before the wave of democratisation that appeared in the 1980s, despite the devotion that Latin Americans had traditionally had for constitutionalism, little respect for constitutional mandates could be found in the region and the majority of political leaders there observed constitutional procedures only when suited to their purposes.[15] The element of *personalismo* in Latin American culture and politics has also encouraged the predominance of leaders with strong personalities over political institutions and principles, thus further reducing the practical viability of constitutions.[16] Similar reasons have led to the failure of constitutionalism in the Middle East, whose political culture is marked by a predominance of per-sonalities and strong elements of patrimonialism. In most Middle Eastern countries, dictatorial leaders are often the embodiment of the very political systems over which they rule.[17] The forceful personalities of leaders like Gemal Abdul Nasser, Hafiz al-Assad, Saddam Hussein, and Ayatollah Khomeini, coupled with their distaste for limitations imposed by democracy, have left little or no room for the growth and maturation of constitutional restraints and principles in their countries. Moreover, most Middle Eastern countries share Africa's problems of communalism and ethnic heterogeneity, giving political leaders added purchase in curtailing democratic rights in the name of political stability and national unity.[18]

As a result of the overall failure of constitutionalism in the develop-ing nations, political structures and institutions there have evolved largely independent of constitutional restraints and are instead at the mercy of strong, existing centres of power. Throughout the Third World, the political symmetry and the balance of power provided in most constitutions has been tilted in favour of one of the existing centres of political and/or social power. Political institutionalisation has taken place, though not in accordance with constitutional means and procedures but according to the capabilities and the wishes of those who happen to hold the reins of power. The nature and characteristics of this society-wide powerful group, and the reasons behind its emergence as a power-broker and an institutionalising agent, depend on indigenous factors and conditions, thus varying from one region and country to another. None the less, whereas constitutional measures have failed to act as viable institutionalising agents, political institutionalisation in the Third World has gone full speed ahead at another level: the gap between state and society has often been bridged through the bureaucratic and coercive arms of the state. Untamed and unrestrained by constitutional limitations, or at best selectively interpreting legal restrictions to suit their purposes, most Third World governments have, with varying degrees, come to rely on the military to sustain themselves in power and on the bureaucracy to penetrate the inner echelons of their society.

The role of the bureaucratic apparatus as an agent of political institutionalisation in the Third World is particularly important, in fact so much so that the bureaucracy has come to be one of the most central of state institutions itself. Often the main agents of social change and of political socialisation, Third World bureaucracies are frequently highly involved in the political process and play a major role in implementing political goals.[19] Bureaucracies are, in fact, by far the most omnipresent symbols and extensions of the political establishment. They frequently serve as the sole source of contact between the average citizen and the government and are thus the only forum for political input and participation. Nevertheless, the role of bureaucracy in most Third World countries is often purely administrative rather than one of innovation and policy-making, the latter frequently being the exclusive domain of politicians.[20] In order to carry out the numerous tasks that it has often taken on, the bureaucratic establishment in most Third World countries is enormous in size and its duties are cumbrous. Not only is the bureaucracy seen as the principle agent through which the masses and the state come into contact, it is further viewed as the primary force through which developmental goals are carried through. An overwhelmingly large bureaucracy is thus maintained in most Third World countries, the size of which is perpetuated by a variety of factors. Most frequently, civil service jobs are attractive owing to their inherent social prestige, as is the case in South Korea for example,[21] and, more important, because they offer secure employment to thousands of otherwise redundant high school and university graduates. Even when economic shortcomings result in increased unemployment and redundancies, jobs in the civil service, whose members provide one of the main sources of a regime's powers, are relatively immuned compared with those in the private sector.[22]

LEGITIMACY

By itself, excessive bureaucratisation is no guarantee as to the institutional solidity of a political system. Neither is institutionalisation per se a sufficient requisite for political stability. The Third World is inundated with examples of countries that are overly bureaucratised yet remain hopelessly outside the purview of popular legitimacy and are inherently unstable.[23] A viable, functioning political system needs to not only embody institutions that are capable of enforcing its mandates throughout society, but to also have an ability to give some sort of credibility to those mandates among significant social strata. Somehow, the political system needs to justify its rule, at least among those social actors whose interaction with and support for the body politic makes the latter's survival possible. Without a 'moral authority' to enforce its rule, the polity's institutions remain socially unintegrated and the governing abilities of political incumbents are greatly reduced.[24] Whereas institutionalisation provides the mechanical and structural nexus between state and society, legitimation links the two emotionally and psychologically. The extent of a polity's institutionalisation determines the degree of its functional viability. Nevertheless, for a regime to be viable in the social sphere as well, its political mandate needs to be underwritten by norms and practices that legitimise its existence. Thus the search by developing countries to find and to maintain popular legitimacy is an integral part of the process of political development.[25]

In the Third World, where instability and fragile institutions mark the political landscape, the attainment of popular legitimacy has been a constant and intense factor in the political drama. In the face of a general absence of solid institutions and apparatuses, ingrained traditions, shared experiences and a common political heritage, and the meteoric rise and fall of maverick politicians and their customised regimes, legitimacy, no matter how narrowly based or derived from fallacious premises, becomes crucial to basic political survival. For those even slightly concerned about political longevity, achieving some measure of popular legitimacy becomes just as important as the efficiency of political institutions and the effectiveness of the coercive arms of the state. This pivotal task is achieved through several different means, each of which depends on the particular nature of forces that prevail in society and on the characteristics of the political establishment itself. Specifically, five broad and interrelated mechanisms can be identified through which political legitimacy is acquired and is in turn sustained. They include charismatic authority, patrimonialism, clientelist relations, the appeal to ideology or to emotionally significant historical events, and politically inclusionary policies aimed at expanding a regime's popular support base. To varying degrees, Third World regimes employ one or a combination of these political forms in order to emphasise and to augment their moral authority to rule.

In its purest form, legitimacy signifies a shared conviction by the people of the ruler's unshaken right to rule. This type of legitimacy can be found in instances of charismatic leadership. The charismatic leader is popularly believed to be infallible and endowed with supernatural qualities, qualities that are not inherent to the individual leader but arise out of the relationships which develop between him and his followers. As such, charismatic authority is marked by an absolute and unwavering devotion of the masses to their leader, a relationship reminiscent of the 'peculiar kind of deference . . . paid to prophets', one of 'masters' and 'followers and disciples'.[26] Thus so long as conditions conducive to his image as a charismatic leader prevail, the legitimacy of the ruler is unquestionable. Whether based on magical qualities or on a cunning ability to gratify communal emotional or economic exigencies, the continued perception of the individual leader as charismatic underwrites his legitimacy. This to a great extent explains the unending efforts of Third World leaders at self-edification and to present larger-than-life pictures of themselves to their peoples (see below).

Yet by nature, charismatic leadership is unstable and impermanent. Instances of genuinely charismatic authority are indeed rare and occur only in extraordinary circumstances, when all three elements of charismatic rule – a devoted mass of followers, a leader able to fulfil a charismatic role, and conditions that conduce a leader–devotee relationship – are present. Charismatic leadership is at best a transitory form of political rule that inevitably gives way to routinised and procedurally more sound types of leadership.[27] In the popular eye, the charismatic leader loses his legitimacy when 'his mission is extinguished'.

> The charismatic holder is deserted by his following . . . because pure charisma does not know any 'legitimacy' other than that flowing from personal strength, that is, one which is constantly being proved.[28]

In essence, the charismatic leader needs constantly to live up to his perpetuated image, maintaining a ceaseless drive to fulfil one prophetic mission after another. The vitriolic rhetoric of ancient and contemporary charismatic leaders, from historic worriers to modern-day Hitlers, Castros, and Khomeinis, only attests to their unending struggle to keep the flames that fan their legitimacy from subsiding. In order to maximise their legitimacy, charismatic figures make deliberate efforts to portray themselves as average citizens, concerned with the needs and pains of the downtrodden. They become an uncanny reflection of the man in the street, generating and in turn symbolising a sense of national identity.[29] In the process, they establish a particularly intense one-to-one relationship with at least one segment of the population, among whom their appeal and power reaches unparalleled heights. Practically every charismatic leader has his equivalent of the Hitler Youth, fanatic followers for whom real or concocted causes form the essence of the charismatic leader's self-proclaimed mission. Peron proudly espoused the causes of the 'shirtless ones' (*descamisados*), Khomeini those of the 'disinherited' (*mostazafan*), and Nkrumah became immortal in the eyes of a group of devout followers called the Youth Pioneers. It is among these groups and classes that the leader's charisma becomes a powerful motivating factor, prompting an almost blind devotion to his directives and orders. For the likes of the 'shirtless ones', only the charismatic leader understands and identifies with their miseries, and only he can free them of their seemingly eternal bondage.

Whereas charismatic systems rely exclusively on the bonding force of the political leader's personality, patrimonial polities are based on a resonance of personal loyalties not only between the people and the leader but between political incumbents and their successive echelons of lieutenants as well. Charismatic leadership is inherently a political aberration, void of specialised institutions and procedures that transmit the directives of the ruler to the ruled. It is intrinsically informal. The political system can be summed up in the person of the leader and in the force of his aura, which in turn penetrates the society and mobilises diverse social classes. As such, the legitimacy of the political system rests entirely on the personality of the leader and on his actions. In patrimonial systems, however, while a strong personality continues to dominate the political system, it is not as central to its legitimacy as is the case in instances of charismatic rule. Instead, the political establishment relies on a series of informal networks made up of personal ties, kinship, and loyalty. Even the development of formal institutions such as bureaucracies do not reduce the informality that pervades the decision-making processes of patrimonial systems.[30] The patrimonial relationships that dominate the household and the family are fabricated throughout society and link the person of the ruler to those whose support is of vital political importance. It is through these linkages, between political leaders and their powerful proxies, and in turn between the proxies and their subordinates, and so on and so forth, that the political system acquires its legitimacy. The state and society, informal as the former is, are tied together through an intricate and proliferating web of networks that emanate from the highest political offices and stretch down to the narrow reaches of society.

To this day, patrimonial systems inundate the political landscape of what Max Weber called 'traditional' societies, particularly those found in the Middle East.[31] Nevertheless, the steady transformation of traditional societies into transitional ones due to industrial development and economic change, and the gradual emergence of enclaves of economic and in some instances even political elites within these countries, has forced political establishments to rely increasingly on clientalist relations in order to maintain their legitimacy. The relationship of governments and elites becomes one of patrons and clients: political stability and order depend on the consensus of support for the ruling regime, exhibited by powerful and influential elites. In order to be certain of the greatest degree of elite consensus, a regime must implement and formulate policies that cater directly to the demands of those elites, to their constituencies, and to those whom they represent.[32] The elite in turn grow increasingly more dependent on the state for the preservation of their elite status through special privileges and access to goods. Through its overwhelming control of resources, the state is able to provide various benefits and services to individuals and groups in exchange for their support or at least political complaisance.[33] The state's legitimacy thus rests on its continued ability to provide patronage to politically significant elite groups.

Advanced and institutionally evolved patrimonial arrangements often find expression in the form of clientalist or even corporatist systems. Due to the early and accelerated industrial development of the region as a whole, and also because of the manner in which this development has largely come about, patron–client relations are most readily discernible in Latin America.[34] Successive civilian and military regimes, brutally authoritarian as they were and continue to be, staked their legitimacy on the success of their developmentalist agendas and on the economic fruits of their policies. Gradually, these clientalist relations have matured into corporatist ones, in which the state is answerable not to individuals but instead to organised, corporate groups such as trade unions, industrial conglomerates, military establishments, civil servants, and the like.[35] Corporatist states are usually highly centralised (corporatism originated with the fascist regimes of Italy and Spain), and actively promote political and/or economic programmes, an activism that is as much ideologically motivated as it is necessitated by the need to constantly cater to corporatist groups.[36] Such groups mediate between the individual and the central government, and each generates independent allegiances which will be pooled and reconciled in the common submission to a single government.[37] Similar to clientalist relations, these allegiances underwrite the legitimacy of the political system based on its ability to protect and promote the interests of the corporate groups.

Popular legitimacy is also achieved through the promotion of populist, politically inclusionary policies aimed at reducing the gap between the masses and the governing elite. Most often, such states develop when post-revolutionary regimes successfully perpetuate the popular enthusiasm of the revolutionary experience and channel it toward legitimising new political forms and institutions. Similar to regimes headed by charismatic leaders, inclusionary regimes derive their legitimacy through a direct and intense fusion of the state and society, ostensibly promoting direct mass participation in the political process. However, unlike purely charismatic leadership, the political institutions of inclusionary regimes are well developed and are specifically designed to direct mass participation toward politically sustaining goals. Political legitimacy lies not in the personal appeal of a central figure, or in the viability of patrimonial networks or clientalist or corporatist relations. Instead, the legitimacy of populist, inclusionary regimes rests on their unimpeded capacity to generate mass-based political participation and in directing it toward furthering their own sustenance. Political mobilisation, and the accruement of certain tangible or emotional benefits for the masses in the process, preclude the possibility of political instability and change in regimes with inclusionary polities.[38]

Lastly, political establishments seek legitimacy in the shelter of ideologies, claiming before their citizens to follow moral and theoretical frameworks which for one reason or another are held in high esteem by significant strata of society. In one shape and extent or another, all regimes claim to be the followers and protectors of a certain ideology. Yet some regimes, those whose very genesis can be traced to ideological movements, are decidedly more doctrinaire than others. In post-revolutionary states, for example, any slight deviation from narrowly interpreted, prevailing doctrines is tantamount to heresy and punishable as high crimes and treason. The emphasis on Marxism–Leninism in socialist states or of, say, Islam in post-revolutionary Iran is more than a matter of the forced imposition of doctrinal values over society by its new leaders. It is part of an intense legitimation process which the new leaders embark on, staking their claims on not only immediate and tangible results but also on promises of future betterment and glory. So long as they can deliver the goods that were promised, or to at least convince enough people that their ideology is indeed the right one, then competing ideologies find little purchase among the masses and the legitimacy of incumbents remains intact.

But for regimes to stake their legitimacy on the righteousness of their ideology, an experience as traumatic as that of revolutions is not a necessary prerequisite. Post-revolutionary regimes do indeed tend to be more bombastic in their adherence to and propagation of specific ideologies and doctrines. That is primarily because such regimes are *revolutionary* by nature. Ideological fanaticism is a result of both the still-on-going indoctrination of the masses as well as the need to substitute for institutional exigencies by emotional and extralegal appeals. Yet fanaticism does not mark all regimes whose popular legitimacy is a prime result of their ideological orientations. Once in force and accepted by large segments of population, ideologies lose their strictly doctrinal character and become part of a growing, internalised value system.[39] Ideological orientations, on the part of the elites and the masses alike, become part of a comprehensive world view, free of their once engrossing missionary zeal and instead controlling subtle nuances in thought and behaviour. The rigid confines of ideological interpretation become loosened, the state-sponsored ideology becoming less and less ideological. Even the symbols whose very significance lies in ideological roots – constitutions, monuments, national holidays, etc. – lose their fervently emotional significance and become part of the rituals of everyday life.

The declining importance of ideology as a means of political legitimation is dependent on both the extent to which an ideology already has popular roots and on the degree to which the political establishment is institutionalised. The greater the solidity of prevailing political institutions, and the more routinised the downward flow of power from the upper echelons of the state, the lesser is the need to justify existing political forms by ideological justifications. The most vivid example of Third World countries for whom ideologies have shed much of their doctrinal thrust and have instead become popularly accepted norms can be found in Latin America. Especially in the newly democratised countries of the region, and in isolated East Asian examples such as India and South Korea, those doctrinal principles which underlie the legitimacy of the political system have been ingrained enough not to need active and intense propagation by the governments concerned. Democracy has long been a cherished principle in Latin America, and its shy appearance there in recent years has pushed into the background most other competing ideologies.[40] Moreover, in most Latin American and in a few East Asian countries, political institutionalisation has reached comparative heights in relation to the rest of the Third World. But in much of the Third World ideology continues to be a compelling force. Over-bureaucratisation and inflated government structures, so long hallmarks of Middle Eastern and African governments, have, for the most part, failed to result in routine and institutionally sound processes of decision making and state–society nexus. Thus the rhetoric of ideology, unbending and unwilling to compromise, reigns supreme in these regions and continues to give birth to demagogues and prophets.

Structurally, the institutional characteristics of the various regime types have direct bearing on their search for legitimation: personal appeal legitimises charismatic leadership; informal ties and loyalties help sustain patrimonial regimes, as do in other instances clientalist and corporatist taints; and, to varying degrees, ideologies either are the very justifications for which regimes exist or form a world-view of which existing states are an integral part. The centrality of institutionalisation and legitimation is ignored by few, not least of all by Third World political actors themselves. Yet despite often frantic and concerted efforts, both political institutionalisation and legitimacy in much of the Third World remain at best elusive goals. Gigantic bureaucratic apparatuses thrive and grow uncontrollably, but often in size and inefficiency and waste rather than in their ability to bridge the gap between the state and the narrow reaches of society. At best, only a majority of the urban society becomes subject to the rule of bureaucratic norms and governance, and even then it does so grudgingly and with reluctance. For the most part, civil society remains resistant to the advent of bureaucratised procedures and to the regulative impulses of the bureaucracy, only to be accentuated by the emotional and ideological detachment of bureaucratic 'second stratums' themselves from the political executive.[41] What results are political systems that are run overwhelmingly according to only perfunctory constitutional frameworks, operating largely in a social vacuum and remaining aloof from civil society, and at best only partially successful in carrying through the directiees of their highest executive offices. Popular legitimacy remains a distant dream, unless attained through appealing to personal emotions and manipulating collective sentiments. Within such a context, the political systems that evolve embody highly authoritarian traits, traits that find breathing space and reinforcement in prevailing social, cultural, and economic circumstances. Budding democratic systems remain highly fragile and tenuous, susceptive to the persisting dictatorial tendencies of a wretched history not long past.[42]

TYPOLOGY OF REGIMES

Within the context of skewed institutionalisation and ongoing struggles to attain popular legitimacy, four broad types of political establishments can be found in the Third World. 'Sultanistic' and neopatrimonial regimes, solely dependent on the force of their leader's personality, predominated the Third World's political landscape not too long ago but are now dwindling in number and are rarely found in their pure form. Frequently, personalist regimes develop increasingly specialised agencies and come to rely on more institutionalised procedures and coercive means, such as the bureaucracy and the armed forces, in order to stay in power. The result is authoritarian-bureaucratic regimes, in which the foundations of political power rest on a domestically oriented military and an ever-growing network of government bureaus and institutions. Populist, inclusionary regimes, meanwhile, rely not only on personal appeal and on institutional means to hold on to power but include the additional element of mass collective behaviour. Lastly, a growing number of experiments in democracy have dotted the Third World since the 1980s, especially in Latin America, in which party politics are timidly played out in tenuous and fragile settings.

Personalist regimes thrive in societies where the development of organisations and institutions have been particularly mute.[43] An absence of solid political institutions and of procedural methods facilitate the ascension of ambitious personalities to positions of political power by enabling them to employ non-institutional means in order to attain power. As a result, factors that are otherwise politically insignificant, such as personal willpower and wiliness, connections and loyalties, social prestige, and charisma and oratorical skills assume paramount political importance. The root causes of the paucity of firmly established political institutions are both social as well as political. Institutions and organisations have failed to acquire solidity and strength in large measure owing to their alien nature. This is particularly the case in Africa and in the Middle East, where there have been frequent efforts to superimpose European institutions on incompatible, indigenous social and political settings.[44] Political systems have sprung up based on notions and principles with which the public is only familiar in the abstract, on political practices with little or no precedent in culture or political heritage, and on offices and institutions which have hitherto been nonexistent. Thus politically salient forces like patrimonialism and autocracy frequently manifest themselves in such modern guises as presidency and multiparty systems. Age-old practices and traditions overwhelm and dominate the conduct of modern institutions and offices. Hence 'presidential monarchies' or, whether or not officially so entitled, presidents for life, appear with unabated regularity. Moreover, the political dynamics which evolve in personalist systems are by nature self-perpetuating. Politicians are likely to engage in personal rule if the rules and regulations of the state are not well understood or appreciated and are poorly enforced, and if they know that others are aware of this and are unlikely to conform to the rules in their own conduct.[45] The prevalence of patrimonial politics is equally important. Because networks of loyalty and kinship are so central to their maintenance, patrimonial systems breed the dominance of personal ties over institutional means, often to the extent that political institutions become vehicles at the mercy of powerful individuals.[46]

Among personalist regimes, a few are headed by charismatic figures. Such leaders differ from others in both the nature of their regimes and in the underlying justifications with which they legitimise their rule. The masses share their hero's conviction that his reign is part of a historic mission. The charismatic leader is not only a political leader, he is also the bearer of a 'message' of some sort for his people.[47] He is not only a destroyer of the old order, but is the builder of a new one in its place.[48] His aim is not merely to usurp power, but rather to steward the body politic in a specific direction. He literally charts new, often traumatic, courses for the political drama, one based on his ideals and promises and zealously supported by countless followers. The messianic tendencies inherent in charismatic rule combine to endow the charismatic leader with increasingly mythical qualities. Especially in countries where the ramifications of intense social change are rampant, those who come close to fitting patterns of traditional myths themselves become popularly endowed with mythical qualities.[49] For groups excluded from the mainstream of society before the charismatic leader's appearance, the leader acquires the image of socially popular mythical legends. This ascription of legendary qualities to the charismatic figure, even if only subconscious and implicit, is reinforced by the leader's abilities to master obstacles that not long ago appeared to be insurmountable. This allusion may not necessarily be cultivated by the government or by the charismatic leader himself. The deep-seated nature of most myths, coupled with the immense popularity of the charismatic figure, result in his association in the public's mind with legendary and mythical figures. Just as 'Imam' Khomeini's crusade ran tellingly parallel to Shi'ite mythology, Mao's deification as a prophet, Mustafa Kemal's as 'the Father of Turks', and Nkrumah's as 'the Saviour, Redeemer, and Messiah', all had deep roots in the mythical traditions of their respective countries.[50]

It is no surprise that even autocratic leaders who do not have the slightest degree of charisma try hard to portray themselves as charismatic. In most Third World countries, massive pictures of the leader adorn billboards, city walls, government offices, and postage stamps, showing him in smiling poses and acknowledging his people's adoration. Charitable foundations, schools, hospitals, and sports stadiums are named after him, and routine efforts are made to forge emotional bonds between the masses and the person of the leader. But such artificial attempts seldom bear any fruit, often invoking negative reactions by those who see through the manipulations and are angered by them. Since they do not have the genuine, hero-like devotion of the masses, autocratic leaders instead often resort to ascribing grandiose characteristics of historic importance to their reign. Not unlike charismatic leaders, they embroil themselves in a 'mission complex', convincing themselves that they indeed have a historic mandate to fulfil. In every opportunity, in speeches, writings, and in press conferences, autocratic leaders elaborate on their grand visions. 'March toward Great Civilization' was the Iranian Shah's encapsulated political catch-phrase;[51] an 'epic struggle . . . that will give life and sustenance to our national vision of a New Society', Marcos never tired of propagating his rule.[52]Unlike charismatic leaders, however, their followers are far less convinced of the historic importance of the concocted mission, remaining sceptical and hesitant rather than heartedly involved.

Whether or not embroiling themselves in a mission complex, the primary goal of non-charismatic, autocratic leaders is mere political survival. Their agenda is not economic development or political democratisation but rather simple survival and longevity in the uncertain and hostile political arena. Governing takes place on the basis of mercenary incentives, with the autocratic leader personally controlling the civil service and the armed forces. Personal loyalty and fear are the mainstays of the government, wrapped in a patina of familiar political symbols and traditionally respected practices.[53] A series of patron–client relations is developed, through which autocratic leaders recruit local and regional clients and perpetuate their rule by giving them privileged access to resources.[54] It is also through such clientalist relations that personal control over the armed forces and the bureaucracy is ensured. Loyalty to the person of the leader, or at least to his clan or tribe, becomes the main criterion for the promotion of military officers and civil servants.[55] At the same time, considerable efforts are made to ensure that no one person or group of individuals gathers enough power and clout to be able to challenge the personalist leader. Intra–elite discord and factionalism are deliberately sown in order to minimise the possibility of an orchestrated assault on power by those not entirely endowed with it. Offices and institutions are created primarily to counter-balance the weight of other ones, and personal animosity between subordinates is perpetuated so that lieutenants could keep each other's powers in check.

In order to further solidify their rule, personalist leaders often devise an extensive network of auxiliary institutions through which they hope to augment their personal reach into the depths of their society. Personalised military and police forces, government ministries and bureaus, and official political parties are some of the more common organisational tools which autocratic leaders employ to strengthen their personalised reigns.[56] Similar to purely charismatic forms of government, entirely personalised polities are rare and often include strong amalgams of bureaucratic and military organisation. In such systems, the personality of the ruler permeates the various aspects of the body politic, serving as the primary binding force which holds the polity together and on whom the political system's survival depends. But to effectively enforce his rule and to keep his regime intact, the autocratic leader relies on a host of institutions and organisations specifically designed to maximise his political longevity. Tailor-made constitutions, self-serving ideologies, and artificial cults of personality have already been alluded to. Equally, considerable energy is put into turning the military and the bureaucracy into pillars of personal support and, in turn, vehicles through which the leader's personality cult is socially and politically sustained. Hence the personalist nature of political rule is increasingly transformed into militarily and bureaucratically institutionalised polities. Purely personalist regimes have thus become rare and infrequent, while bureaucratic-authoritarianisms inundate the Third World's political landscape.

Frequently, bureaucratic-authoritarian regimes disguise themselves as democracies driven by party and electoral politics, presidential systems, and de-politicised bureaucracies and security forces. In actual practice, however, such regimes are kept intact by a powerful combination of often direct military interference into politics, highly politicised bureaucracies, overwhelmingly powerful if not solely official political parties, and doctored elections in which the winners and losers are predetermined. The regime relies on a series of elements that are highly conducive to authoritarian politics. Its survival is dependent on the longevity of an autocratic leader with a penchant for political manipulation, a personally loyal military keeping the regime's opponents at bay, and an official political party designed to generate mobilised support for the regime but itself an inseparable part of the bureaucracy. Patrimonial and clientalist practices bond both the regime's higher echelons to its rank and file and to the larger society. The situation is little different in overtly military regimes which grow out of successful coups d'état, with a powerful officer or a junta replacing the civilian autocrat.

State-sponsored political parties often play pivotal roles in the functioning of authoritarian-bureaucracies. One-party systems emerge either as a result of structural transformations within personalised systems, through which autocrats hope to augment the institutional reach of their rule, or are products of successful liberation struggles in which a single party dominated the movement.[57] In either case, social and political bifurcations are essential to the maintenance of one-party systems.[58] In such regimes, actual political power often lies with a single party under whose auspices all political activities are supposed to take place. All political appointments are made from within the ranks of the party, the party's platform is a reflection of the government's policies, and, at least nominally, all of the various branches of the state, such as the legislature and the bureaucracy, adhere to the party's ideology. It is this ability to effectively monopolise various forms of political activity, and to turn dissenters into supporters, on which the political viability of one-party systems depend.[59]

State-sponsored parties serve four specific yet entwined functions. They include political institutionalisation, legitimisation, recruitment of officials, and the mobilisation of popular support. Frequently born out of personalised autocracies, state-sponsored parties institutionalise the powers of the ruling elite and facilitate their access to power. In countries where existing political and social institutions lack autonomy and strength, state-sponsored parties fill the vacuum by providing organisational cohesion and order to otherwise fragmented social and political settings. Except for the military, such parties are often the most organised and structured institutions, fusing the state to societies torn by parochial tendencies and disjointed political loyalties.[60] As a result, the party affords the ruling elite the opportunity to expand their institutional base by penetrating further into society and strengthening their hold on power. This is particularly the case in African countries, such as Zaire and Kenya, where the single-party is designed to curtail and eventually to replace tribal, clan, and other parochial sources of identity.[61] At the same time, the party aims to maintain the ruling incumbents' monopoly on power by creating an exclusive domain within which the political drama can be played out.[62] Thus participation in the party and adherence to its goals and doctrines become an integral part of the political process.

Related to the institutionalising functions of state-sponsored parties is their role as legitimising agents. This role is played at both a functional and an ideological level. Functionally, the party acts as a legitimising agent by providing institutional links between the state and society. At the same time, it gives cohesion and legitimacy to ideas espoused by political leaders. State parties offer a forum through which government officials and policy-makers doctrinally justify their continued hold on power as well as their policies and actions. Through devising a popular ideology, the party attempts to convince the public that it in fact has a mandate to rule. Invariably, this ideology is heavily embedded with nationalist symbols and ideas, even in communist states, where the regime's official doctrine is a variation of the Marxist theme. Through its organisation and ideology, the party also mobilises popular support for the regime and its policies. Moreover, the local branches of the party provide means for political socialisation at the local level, a function of immense significance given the absence of other similar, organised bodies. The state party forms a crucial and often unique nexus between the government on the one hand and the masses on the other. Through the party, doctrines and ideologies are propagated and popularised, policies and initiatives are formulated and laid out, and mass rallies are often arranged in support of the regime or individual leaders.

In addition to mass mobilisation, the official party is often the only mean through which the average citizen can become actively involved in the political process. Being an agent of institutionalisation and indoctrination, the state party becomes one of the most significant vehicles for entry to and advancement in the government machinery. In fact, the ability to recruit top political leaders from among the masses significantly enhances the popular legitimacy of the official party.[63] At a more popular level, participation in the activities of the official party is often the first and only form of political activity that most people living under such systems engage in. Thus, at least as far as the population is concerned, the importance of the party as an eye-opener to the world of politics is unparalleled. More significantly, the party's rank-and-file activists form a sizeable pool from which dedicated loyalists can be recruited into positions of leadership.

The structure of state-sponsored parties is often based on a rigid hierarchical arrangement that stretches in rank from the autocratic leader down to mid- and low-ranking civil servants. Theoretically, the state party's structure is frequently based on a form of 'democratic centralism'. According to this interpretation, the party is endowed with a highly centralised and isolated leadership cadre, while its aim is to appeal to wide segments of society. Since the party's primary function is to give popular legitimacy to the policies that have already been devised by the government, there is little room in it for a free debate of ideas and options. Thus the *democratic* aspect of 'democratic centralism' has little more than cosmetic value. Instead, what is emphasised is the centralised character of the party's structure. In countries governed by civilian dictators or by soldiers in mufti, usually the governing dictator is the real if not the nominal head of the state party. At the same time, membership in the party by cabinet ministers, legislators, bureaucrats, and by other political figures is often obligatory or at least an implicit rule. Apart from those in policy-making positions, however, few have a say in determining the party's platform and its policies.

Exclusionary regimes, whether purely personalist or based on some form of bureaucratic-authoritarianism, are inherently brittle and are susceptible to violent and sudden collapse. The maintenance of the political status quo depends primarily on the preservation of an exclusive elite enclave held together by a combination of coercion and patrimonial ties. Because of their very exclusion from the political process, politically excluded groups are disenchanted with the system and, given an opportunity, attempt to grab at political power. Moreover, the coercive and patrimonial bonds that hold the regime together are themselves susceptible to unravelling under strenuous conditions. Wars and economic setbacks can reduce a regime's coercive abilities, as can the inability to deliver promised goods cause internal dissension and elite squabbling. Thus despite their outward appearance, which often portrays them as deadly and invincible, such bureaucratic-authoritarian regimes are highly vulnerable to crises and otherwise insignificant shifts in the political arena.

Inclusionary populist regimes, in contrast, enjoy far greater solidity both in so far as their institutional viability is concerned and in relation to their popular legitimacy throughout society. Whereas bureaucratic-authoritarian regimes rely on the exclusion of the masses from politics, populist ones specifically aim to establish a mass-based political system. They rely on collective behaviour and on other forms of mass mobilisation as one of their primary supporting pillars. Emphasis is put on the symbolic dimensions of public affairs, manifested in the form of street marches, demonstrations, and collective outbursts of political jubilation and support. Although such ritualistic ceremonies are often 'little more than a cheap means to achieve political acquiescence', they are intrinsically valuable as they often bestow on people a sense of self-identity and self-concept.[64] For the masses who were once excluded from the political process, participation in events heavily impregnated with political symbolism results in a sense of enhanced popular involvement in national political life.[65] Although such regimes may be as dictatorial as traditional bureaucratic-authoritarianisms, their incorporation of the masses into the political process makes them appear as popular democracies. In this sense, populist regimes enjoy a degree of popular legitimacy unsurpassed by others. It is this heightened sense of regime legitimacy, brought on by the ostensibly democratising effects of mass mobilisation, which enables such regimes to motivate their population to make supreme sacrifices for the nation.[66]

Significantly, populist inclusionary regimes are almost invariably post-revolutionary polities that were brought on as a result of the collapse of bureaucratic-authoritarian systems. Mass mobilisation is achieved even before the establishment of new political institutions, and at a time when emotional and ideological bonds linking revolutionary leaders with the masses are strongest. Such links are greatly strengthened with the acquisition of power by the revolutionaries, reinforced by an increasing, mutual reliance by both sides on the other. The new leaders need their supporters more than ever before in order to augment their tenuous hold on power, while the masses rely on their leaders to deliver the promised goods for which they endured the traumas of revolution. What thus emerges out of revolutions is ideologically reconstructed national identities involving the sudden incorporation of formerly excluded popular groups into state-directed projects.[67] Such projects frequently include economic self-help programmes, intensive efforts aimed at inculcating a new culture and national identity, and, when congenial, international wars. Many post-revolutionary regimes have excelled at channelling popular participation into international wars. Because of the way that revolutionary leaders mobilise popular groups during their struggle for state power, the new regime can tackle mobilisation for war better than any other task, including the promotion of economic development. The realisation of this potential depends on threatening but not overwhelming geopolitical and international circumstances.[68]

Wars are, however, materially and humanly costly ventures and are as a result impermanent. Even the longest of the protracted wars in which post-revolutionary regimes engage, such as Iran's war with Iraq in the 1980s, eventually simmer down and turn into bombastic rhetoric. Outlasting wars as politically solidifying agents are ceaseless efforts aimed at redefining popular national identity and the citizens' perceptions of themselves and of their nation. In its ambitious quest to create 'a new man', the state micro-manages politics. It initiates various programmes and projects – through the media, the sponsorship of various acts of collective behaviour, and 'educational' efforts of varying subtlety – in order to enhance its own legitimacy by minimising the state-society gap and in the process creating a new political culture suited to its own purposes. As an observer of Cuba's post-revolutionary politics has noted, even the apparently spontaneous demonstrations of support for the Cuban regime are staged and carefully coordinated:

> What may appear to the untrained eye as an immense sea of anonymous faces of persons temporarily detached from their customary social relations to participate in the jurnadas of the revolutionary calendar is instead a publicly acknowledged, carefully

rehearsed, and studied choreographic exercise of groups who are firmly attached to existing institutions and occupy clearly specified and lasting niches.[69]

The conventionalisation of collective behaviour is a particularly rewarding practice for keeping the elite's ideology alive and maintaining elite–mass linkage. By encouraging mass participation, it separates the devout from nominal followers. Furthermore, it perpetuates the legitimacy of the regime by keeping the revolutionary spirit alive.[70]

Popular legitimacy, or more aptly mass devotion, greatly strengthens the solidity of the central government. An additional element that significantly enhances the powers of post-revolutionary states is their greater willingness to rely on coercion and brute force in order to maintain power. Reliance on coercion as a politically sustaining means is especially apparent in post-revolutionary states, where the new elites have won power only after a long and protracted struggle. Success in the violent pursuit and defence of power habituates leaders to the political use of violence. 'Elite who have secured state power and have maintained their position by violent means are disposed to respond violently to future challenges.'[71] Revolutions do indeed eat their own children, with the more powerful victors brutally suppressing former colleagues for the sake of solidifying their new powers. The bloody and savage purges that invariably follow every violent revolution, from the infamous purges of the Stalin era to those that followed the Chinese, the Cuban, and the Iranian revolutions, are more than mere historical coincidences. They demonstrate a preoccupation on the part of new elites to secure their powers first against counter-revolutionaries and then against would-be separatists. Having relied on violence to acquire their new powers, and in the process having risked a great deal, revolutionary elites seldom have any inhibitions about continuing to rely on violence in order to protect their new privileges.[72] As a result, emerging post-revolutionary states are often far more brutally coercive than the ones they replace, suppressing actual or perceived sources of opposition with considerably less restraint than their predecessors did. Such states are thus much stronger not only because of the popular support that they cultivate but also owing to the ease with which they employ coercion in order to stay in power.

Populist, bureaucratic–authoritarian, and personalist regimes have often been called 'praetorian'[73] or 'avant garde'.[74] These and other similar labels are meant to denote systems with generally low levels of political development and institutionalisation. The muted political evolution of such regimes is largely due to oligarchical, colonial, and neocolonial experiences, where popular political participation at the institutional level was nonexistent or at best severely curtailed.[75] Excluded from the political process, popular groups yearning for political participation confront each other against a backdrop of unevolved political institutions and an uncommon heritage of political principles and expectations. As a result, regimes that evolve within such contexts are characterised by an absence of 'effective political institutions capable of mediating, refining, and moderating groups political action'.

> In a praetorian system social forces confront each other nakedly; no political institutions, no corps of professional political leaders are recognized or accepted as the legitimate intermediaries to moderate group conflict. Equally important, no agreement exists among the groups as to the legitimate and the authoritative methods for resolving conflicts. In an instutionalised polity most actors agree on the procedures to be used for the resolution of political disputes, that is, for the allocation of office and the determination of policy . . . In a praetorian society, however, not only are the actors varied, but so are also the methods used to decide upon office and policy. Each group employs means which reflect its peculiar nature and capabilities. The wealthy bribe; students riot; workers strike; mobs demonstrate; and the military coup. In the absence of accepted procedures, all these forms of direct action are found on the political scene.[76]

Political power is not derived from constitutional sources or electoral legitimacy, but rather from extralegal and non-institutionalised means such as social prestige, patrimonial and clientalist loyalties, charisma, or brute force.

Since the decade of the 1980s, a tide of democratisation has swept across parts of the Third World. Particularly astounding has been the experience of Latin America, where military juntas and governing generals, once inseparable from the political arena, have been handing over the reins of power to democratically elected civilians in one country after another. Peru, Brazil, Argentina, and Chile, to name a few of the more notable examples, have all undergone dramatic transformations in their respective political systems, their colonels and generals having left presidential palaces and returned to their

barracks. South Korea has also taken significant steps toward in-
augurating a more democratic political system, although democratisation as a whole has been haltingly slow there. A few African
countries, such as Kenya and Cameroon, continue to toy with
various political experiments ranging from multi-party systems to *de
facto* life presidencies.

The break-up of military-authoritarian regimes, especially of the
type which inundated Latin America in the 1960s and the 1970s, is
in large measure a result of the failure of the economic policies which
they pursued. In the early days of their rule, such regimes saw
themselves as more than just caretaker governments, wanting to
bring about rapid industrialisation and espousing numerous development projects.[77] They staked much of their legitimacy on promises
of an impending 'economic miracle', in the process heavily borrow-
ing from international agencies and brutally suppressing domestic
opposition. Their efforts were greatly facilitated within the international climate of the time, especially by the approval of successive
administrations in Washington. From the Kennedy administration's
'Alliance for Progress' programme to the Nixon–Kissinger doctrine
of 'multi-polarity', Washington believed that only development-
oriented, conservative regimes were capable of countering the threat
of communist growth in the Third World.[78] Much American economic and diplomatic support was thus given to military-dominated,
pro-Western regimes throughout the Third World. Singapore and
South Korea in East Asia, Pakistan, Iran, Turkey, and Egypt in the
Middle East, Somalia, Zaire, and Nigeria in Africa, and practically
the whole of Latin America except Cuba received unprecedented
amounts of American military and economic aid.[79] But in the late
1970s and the 1980s, America's priorities gradually began to change
as its foreign policy readjusted itself to the realities of the post-
Vietnam era. The United States' changed diplomatic outlook that
followed the end of its costly war with Vietnam, most tellingly
represented by President Carter's concern with human rights, was
reinforced by massive budget deficits and the end of the Cold War in
the 1980s.[80] Military-dominated regimes in the Third World were
left largely on their own. Lacking what was once unconditional
military and economic support from abroad, and domestically ridden
with debt and unfulfilled economic miracles, such regimes began
collapsing one after another. Most gave up power peacefully, spon-
soring elections and handing governments over to civilian victors.

Only a few, like Somoza in Nicaragua, the Shah of Iran, and Marcos in the Philippines, were overthrown in mass-based revolutions.

From among those countries in which bureaucratic-authoritarian regimes broke up in the 1980s, only the ones in Latin America have been able to establish genuinely democratic polities. Iran's post-revolutionary experience can hardly be described as democratic, while those that have appeared in the Philippines, South Korea, Pakistan, and Turkey have led a highly precarious existence. Even the fledgling democracies of Latin America continue to be threatened by occasional signs of unease within the military establishment and by lingering economic dilemmas. In 1992, Peru's civilian president suspended his country's democratic constitution on economic and political grounds. Nevertheless, within the Third World, Latin America's experience with democratic systems since the 1980s has proven by far the most enduring. Several factors have underlain this relative strength. Latin America's long tradition of multiparty politics, dating back to the nineteenth century, is a definite factor,[81] as is the unabatedly high esteem of democratic principles throughout the continent.[82] Moreover, with the important exception of Peronist Argentina, Latin American political culture does not embody a continuous strand of personality cults. The cultural salience of *personalismo* has in recent years been generally muted at the hands of highly rationalised bureaucracies and non-governmental organisations.[83] Even the military regimes of the 1960s and the 1970s, except those of Fulgencio Batista and Anastasio Somoza, were headed by collective juntas rather than by personalist leaders.[84] Pressures for fundamental political changes by international lending agencies such as the World Bank and the International Monetary Fund were also instrumental in prompting most Latin American nations to undertake sincere efforts toward establishing democratic systems. All of these factors have combined to strengthen the viability of Latin America's democratic systems, fledgling as they still are.

CONCLUSION

Third World political systems and processes are marked by symptoms of skewed political development. Except in a few instances, political institutionalisation remains but a mirage and the nexus between state and society is tenuous at best. Governments function largely void of meaningful popular legitimacy, supported instead by coercive police forces and mushrooming bureaucracies. Extralegal and non-institutional means, from patrimonial and clientalist ties to personal charisma and ideology, underwrite the legitimacy of inherently brittle political systems rather than democratic, constitutional practices and principles. Populist regimes which thrive on mass mobilisation are equally authoritarian, yet their inclusion of previous outcasts into the body politic gives them a democratising sense and enhances their strength relative to other regime types. In the last decade, a trend toward representative democracy has appeared in selected parts of the Third World. While the transition to democratic rule involves dynamics that are unique to each individual case,[85] several similar economic and international developments have led to a flourishing of democratic systems in Latin America. Whether other countries in the Third World will follow suit remains to be seen.

Central to an understanding of the essence of Third World politics is an appreciation of the fluid nature of state organisations and institutions. The institutionalisation that has taken place in much of the Third World has been a product of the efforts of those already in power. Since political institutions by themselves have little or no autonomy and strength, incumbents and other holders of office have moulded and shaped them in accordance with their interests. Additionally, there are no established or popularly accepted 'rules of the game', political principles and doctrines often holding as much sway as the people who propagate them. Institutions are at the mercy of those in power, and the forcefulness of personalities overwhelm the strength and appeal of principles.

As a result of this lack of political common-ground, the path to power in much of the Third World lies outside the methods prescribed by constitutional or civic laws. Access to power lies not in institutionalised procedures but depends on the utilisation of personal attributes such as charisma and chivalry or, in frequent instances, the stewardship of the armed forces into rebellion. Only recently have there been cases of free and untampered elections in a few Third World countries, as the notable examples of Argentina, Brazil, and Pakistan demonstrate. Yet even in such recent democracies, the continuing likelihood of military coups threaten civilian administrations. In these and in other countries, only a combination of personal dedication and political willpower, a general shift in social attitudes concerning the viability of democratic institutions, and compelling domestic and international circumstances will guarantee the survival of non-authoritarian regimes. For the rest of the Third World, numerous variations of authoritarian regimes are entrenched and supported by deep-rooted political dynamics.

NOTES

1 Myron Weiner. 'Institution Building in South Asia', in R. Scalapino, S. Sato, and J. Wanandi, eds. *Asian Political Institutionalization*. (Berkeley, Calif.: Institute of East Asian Studies, 1986), pp. 305–6.
2 Lucian Pye. 'The Concept of Political Development', in Harvey Kebschull, ed. *Politics in Transitional Societies*. (New York: Appleton-Century-Crofts, 1973), p. 51. Pye gives the label of 'integration crisis' to this development.
3 Robert Scalapino 'Legitimacy and Institutionalization in Asian Socialist Societies', in R. Scalapino, S. Sato, and J. Wanandi, eds. *Asian Political Institutionalization*. p. 59.
4 Dan Horowitz. 'Dual Authority Polities'. *Comparative Politics*. vol. 14, no 3, (April 1982), p. 329. Horowitz calls these systems 'dual authority polities'.
5 Mehran Kamrava. *Revolution in Iran: Roots of Turmoil*. (London: Routledge, 1990), p. 50.
6 Jean-Yves Calvez. *Politics and Society in the Third World*. M.J. O'Connell, trans. (Maryknoll, NY: Orbis, 1973), p. 79.
7 Gloria Hernandez. 'Political Institution Building in the Philippines', in R. Scalapino, S. Sato, and J. Wanandi, eds. *Asian Political Institutionalization*. p. 268; in the same book see also, Han Sung-joo. 'Political Institutionalization in South Korea'. p. 120, and Chung Chin-wee. 'The Evolution of Political Institutions in North Korea'. pp. 22–3.
8 Chai-Anan Samundamanija. 'Political Institutionalization in Thailand: Continuity and Change', in R. Scalapino, S. Sato, and J. Wanandi, eds. *Asian Political Institutionalization*. p. 248
9 B. O. Nwabueze. *The Presidential Constitution of Nigeria*. (London: C. Hurst & Co., 1982), pp. 4–5.
10 See Shaul Bakhash. *The Reign of the Ayatollahs*. (London: I.B.Tauris, 1985), Chapter 4.
11 B. O. Nwabueze. *The Presidential Constitution of Nigeria*. p. 5.
12 Robert Jackson and Carl Rosberg. 'Personal Rule: Theory and Practice in Africa'. *Comparative Politics*. vol. 16, no 4, (July 1984), p. 438.
13 Jean-Yves Calvez. *Politics and Society in the Third World*. p. 79.
14 Robert Jackson and Carl Rosberg. 'Personal Rule: Theory and Practice in Africa'. p. 438.
15 J. Lloyd Mecham. 'Latin American Constitutions: Nominal or Real'. Harvey Kebschull, ed. *Politics in Transitional Societies*, p. 224.
16 Ibid. p. 225.
17 Charles Butterworth. 'State and Authority in Arabic Political Thought', in Ghassan Salame, ed. *The Foundation of the Arab State*. (London: Croom Helm, 1987), p. 91.

18 Paul Cammack, David Pool, and William Tardoff. *Third World Politics: A Comparative Introduction.* (London: Macmillan, 1988), p. 70.
19 S. N. Eisenstadt. 'Problems of Emerging Bureaucracies in Developing Areas and New States', in Harvey Kebschull, ed. *Politics in Transitional Societies.* pp. 290–1.
20 Fredrick Bent. 'A Comparative Analysis of Public Administration in Modern, Traditional, and Modernizing Societies', in Chandler Morse, ed. *Modernisation by Design: Social Change in the Twentieth Century.* (Ithaca, NY: Cornell University Press, 1969), p. 191.
21 Chung Eun Sung. 'Transition to Democracy in South Korea'. *Asia Profile.* vol. 17, no 1, (February 1989), p. 31.
22 For more on the role of the bureaucracy in Third World countries see below, Chapter 2.
23 This was the case in pre-revolutionary Iran, as well as in contemporary South Korea, where, despite massive bureaucratization, political instability and crises occur(ed) with frequency.
24 Robert Scalapino 'Legitimacy and Institutionalization in Asian Socialist Societies'. p. 59.
25 Lucian Pye. 'The Concept of Poltical Development'. p. 50.
26 Max Weber. *On Charisma and Institution Building.* (Chicago, Ill.: University of Chicago Press, 1968), p. 48.
27 Ibid. p. 54.
28 Ibid. p. 22.
29 For discussions of images of oneness with people see Lisa Anderson. *The State and Social Transformation in Tunisia and Libya, 1830–1980.* (Princeton, NJ: Princeton University Press, 1986), pp. 260–1 for Libya's Mummar Qaddafi; Moshe Ma'oz. *Syria Under Hafiz Al-Asad: New Domestic and Foreign Policies.* (Jerusalem: Hebrew University Press, 1975), pp. 6–10 for Asad, and Dankwart Rustow. 'Attaturk's Political Leadership', in R. Winder, ed. *Near Eastern Round Table 1967–8.* (New York: NYU Press, 1969), pp. 145–9 for Turkey's Ataturk.
30 James Bill and Robert Springborg. *Politics in the Middle East.* (Glenview, Ill.: Scott, Foresman/Little, Brown, 1990), p. 161.
31 Ibid. For a careful analysis of patrimonialism in the Middle East, see, ibid. Chapter 4.
32 Percy Hintzen. 'Bases of Elite Support for a Regime: Race, Ideology, and Clientalism as Bases for Leaders in Guyana and Trinidad'. *Comparative Political Studies* . vol. 16, no 3, (October 1983), p. 364.
33 Ibid. p. 365.
34 See below, Chapter 2.
35 For more on corporatism see Rod Hague and Martin Harrop. *Comparative Politics and Government: An Introduction.* (Atlantic Highlands, NJ: Humanities Press, 1987), pp. 134–7.
36 Rose Spalding. 'State Power and its Limits: State Power in Mexico'. *Comparative Political Studies.* vol. 14, no 2, (July 1981), p. 155.
37 Roger Scruton. *A Dictionary of Political Thought.* (London: Pan Books, 1983), p. 98.
38 Jeff Goodwin and Theda Skocpol. 'Explaining Revolutions in the Con-

temporary Third World'. *Politics and Society*. vol. 17, no 4, (December 1989), pp. 494–5.

39 Percy Hintzen. 'Bases of Elite Support for a Regime: Race, Ideology, and Clientalism as Bases for Leaders in Guyana and Trinidad'. p. 365.

40 Aldo Vacs. 'Authoritarian Breakdown and Redemocratization in Argentina', in J. Malloy and M. Seligson, eds. *Authoritarians and Democrats: Regime Transition in Latin America*. (Pittsburg: Pittsburg University Press, 1987), p. 17.

41 For a discussion of the 'second stratum' see Leonard Binder. *In a Moment of Enthusiasm: Political Power and the Second Stratum in Egypt*. (Chicago: University of Chicago Press, 1978).

42 A case in point is the recurrence of coup attempts by the military in Argentina after its political retreat in the mid 1980s.

43 E. B. Portis. 'Charismatic Leadership and Cultural Democracy'. *Review of Politics*. vol. 41, no 2, (Spring 1987), p. 242.

44 Richard Sandbrook. 'The State and Economic Stagnation in Tropical Africa'. *World Development*. vol, 14, no 3, (1986), p. 321.

45 Robert Jackson and Carl Rosberg. 'Personal Rule: Theory and Practice in Africa'. p. 437.

46 Jacqueline Braveboy-Wagner. *Interpreting the Third World: Politics, Economics, and Social Issues*. (New York: Praeger, 1986), p. 37.

47 E. B. Portis. 'Charismatic Leadership and Cultural Democracy'. p. 241.

48 Ann Ruth Willner and Dorothy Willner. 'The Rise and Role of Charismatic Leaders', in Harvey Kebschull, ed. *Politics in Transitional Societies*. p. 233.

49 Ibid. p. 231.

50 Bankole Timothy. *Kwame Nkrumah from Cradle to Grave*. (Dorchester: Gavin Press, 1981), p. 156.

51 Mohammad Reza Pahlavi. *Answer to History*. (New York: Stein & Day, 1980), pp. 175–7.

52 Ferdinand Marcos. *Five Years of the New Society*. (Manila: Marcos Foundation, 1978), p. 3. In North Korea, admittedly an unusually extreme example, Kim Ill Sung has created somewhat of a political religion revolving around 'self reliance' (chuch'e). See. Chung Chin-wee. 'The Evolution of Political Institutions in North Korea'. pp. 35–8.

53 Richard Sandbrook. 'The State and Economic Stagnation in Tropical Africa'. p. 323.

54 1bid. p. 324.

55 Tribal reference points are particularly instrumental in appontments and promotions in Africa (e.g. the Ishantis having more leverage under Flt Lt Rawlings in Ghana), while in the Middle East it is religious affiliations that are more important. Most high-ranking military officers in Iraq share Saddam Hussein's Sunni sect of Islam, while in Syria most are of the same Alawi background as is Asad.

56 Samuel Huntington. 'Social and Institutional Dynamics of One-Party Systems', in S. Huntington and C. Moore, eds. *Authoritarian Politics and Modern Society*. (London: Basic Books, 1970), p. 7.

57 Jacqueline Braveboy-Wagner. *Interpreting the Third World*. p. 31.

58 Samuel Huntington. 'Social and Institutional Dynamics of One-Party Systems'. p. 14.
59 Ibid. p. 44.
60 Ibid. p. 12.
61 Jean-Yves Calvez. *Politics and Society in the Third World*. p. 105.
62 Samuel Huntington. 'Social and Institutional Dynamics of One-Party Systems'. p. 12.
63 Clement Moore. 'The Single Party as a Source of Legitimacy', in S. Huntington and C. Moore. *Authoritarian Politics in Modern Society*. p. 51.
64 E. B. Portis. 'Charismatic Leadership and Cultural Democracy'. pp. 237–8.
65 Theda Skocpol. 'Social Revolutions and Mass Military Mobilization'. *World Politics*. vol. XL, no 2, (January 1988), p. 149.
66 Ibid. p. 150.
67 Ibid. p. 164.
68 Ibid. pp. 167–8.
69 B. E. Aguirre. 'The Conventionalization of Collective Behavior in Cuba'. *American Journal of Sociology*. vol. 90, no 3, (1984), p. 549.
70 Ibid. p. 563.
71 Ted Robert Gurr. 'War, Revolution, and the Growth of the Coercive State'. *Comparative Political Studies*. vol. 21, no 1, (April 1988), p. 49.
72 Ibid. p. 53.
73 Samuel Huntington. *Political Order in Changing Societies*. (New Haven, Conn.: Yale University Press, 1968), p. 196.
74 Yehezkel Dror. 'Public Policy-Making in Avant-Garde States', in Harvey Kebschul, ed. *Politics in Transitional Societies*. p. 278. As a characteristic of avant-garde states, Dror also includes a colonial heritage terminated after an intense manifestation of nationalism, the absence of the middle classes, and a small elite aspiring to achieve rapid social and economic transformations.
75 Samuel Huntington. *Political Order in Changing Societies*. pp. 199–200.
76 Ibid. p. 196.
77 Mitchell Seligson. 'Democratization in Latin America: The Current Cycle', in J. Malloy and M. Seligson, eds. *Authoritarians and Democrats: Regime Changes in Latin America*. Pittsburg: University of Pittsburg Press, 1987, pp. 4–5.
78 Thomas Paterson, J. G. Clifford, and Kenneth Hagan. *American Foreign Policy: A History*. (Lexington, Mass: D.C. Heath & Co., 1991), p. 529. President Kennedy's speech in 1960, quoted in ibid, is instructive of America's foreign policy direction at the time: 'I think there is a danger that history will make a judgement that these were the days when the tide began to run out for the United States. These were the times when the communist tide began to pour in'.
79 See especially, Robert Litwak. *Detente and the Nixon Doctrine: American Foreign Policy and the Pursuit of Stability*. (Cambridge: Cambridge University Press, 1984).
80 Thomas Paterson, J. G. Clifford, and Kenneth Hagan. *American Foreign Policy: A History*. p. 689.
81 Jean-Yves Calvez. *Politics and Society in the Third World*. pp. 76–7.

82 Aldo Vacs. 'Authoritarian Breakdown and Redemocratization in Argentina'. p. 17.
83 For an examination of the role and structure of NGOs see Leilah Landim. 'Non-governmental Organizations in Latin America'. *World Development*. vol. 15, Supplement. (1987), pp. 29–38.
84 Mitchell Seligson. 'Redemocratization in Latin America: The Current Cycle'. p. 5.
85 Chung Eun Sung. 'Transition to Democracy in South Korea'. p. 26.

Chapter 2

Industrial development

The dilemmas of political institutionalisation and longevity are by no means the only difficulties that Third World leaders must grapple with. The challenges posed by industrial development, or lack thereof, are equally cumbrous. The quest for industrial development and economic growth has been a consistent feature of Third World countries in recent decades, especially in the light of growing disparities between levels of development in the West as opposed to the Third World. The race toward industrialisation has been particularly intense since the 1960s, when, having come of age, Third World leaders became uncomfortably conscious of their industrial and technological backwardness vis-à-vis the West. A 'Decade of Development', as declared by the United Nations, was ushered in in the 1960s. The hope was to accompany the tide of political independence and self-rule sweeping over Africa and other parts of the Third World with the termination of Western economic domination and instead to initiate rapid, indigenous industrial development. These hopes and expectations were somewhat fulfilled in the 1970s, although often only after considerable economic readjustment, when increased global demands for raw materials and liberal lending practices by multinational credit agencies fuelled growth and expansion in numerous Third World countries. But the rapid pace of economic growth turned out to be short-lived. The boom of the 1970s was unceremoniously followed by the bust of the 1980s, a decade burdened with famine, destitution, political instability, and domestic and international wars. The economic downturn of the 1980s was in large measure a result of unreasonable hopes and expectations, misguided policies, unimaginative planning, and rampant corruption and mismanagement, all of which in one way or another plagued the Third World in the 1970s. As economic realities set in, Third World politicians began desperately searching for ways to restructure or to completely relinquish the enormous debt that they had accrued from Western creditors in previous years. Yet, more than a decade later, solutions to the debt problem continue to remain elusive and contentious. How Third World governments, particularly those in Latin America and in Africa, propose to deal with their international debt has come to be a lingering dilemma in the 1990s.

And still, after thirty years of debates, trials, and promises, the fundamental question that confronted Third World leaders at the dawn of independence remains unanswered. The dilemma of reaching economic development and industrial growth is as big an enigma now as it has ever been; indeed, it is more of a mystery now than ever before. This chapter does not answer this question, nor does it seek to demonstrate supposed superiorities inherent in one approach to industrial development as opposed to another. The task here is to examine the process of industrial development through charting the different courses which various Third World governments have taken. To do so, it is first necessary to examine the theoretical frameworks within which development policies are devised.

It is conventionally assumed that there are two dominant schools of thought prevailing in the study of Third World development: the modernisation and the dependency approaches.[1] Despite the connotations attached to it, branding the modernisation approach as a framework for the analysis of *industrial development* in the Third World is not entirely accurate. The study of development in the Third World has indeed taken place within these two broad and very different theoretical frameworks. It is, however, important to realise that those group of scholars who have come to be known as modernisationists focus primarily on *political modernisation* rather than on industrial and technological development. As reflected in their publications, such authors have been concerned primarily with the ramifications of *political development* on levels of industrial growth.[2] Consequently, modernisation theory remains largely a framework for the analysis of Third World politics rather than industry. Nevertheless, as a school of thought, modernisation theory has contributed to the understanding of Third World industrialisation, albeit in an indirect manner. Emphasis on the political process has not precluded discussions of industrial and technological development. In one form and extent or another, political stability is seen to be of paramount importance in achieving desired levels of industrial advancement. Within this vein, theories of modernisation assume the evolution of capitalist development along a linear path toward modernisation.[3] Modernisation is seen to occur within stages not very different from those that took place in the West centuries ago: feudal relations were changed into capitalist forms of production, leading to the subsequent growth and spread of industrial technology.[4]

Despite such digressions into the study of Third World industry, the primary emphasis of modernisation theory remains in the domain of politics. Most modernisationists identify lack of adequate political superstructure and capable leadership as the underlying causes of the Third World's industrial backwardness vis-à-vis the West. Notable modernisation theorists such as Rothstein, Weiner, Pool, and Huntington all argue, in one form or another, that elite maintenance is a necessary precondition for the achievement of industrial, social, and political progress. For his part, Huntington claims that it is the *degree* of government and not necessarily its form that is important in determining its ability to bring about progress.[5] It is necessary, Huntington and others argue, to devise policies not threatening to the elite and to others who are in decision-making positions, so that they could plan and oversee the country's modernisation with safety and confidence. Otherwise, insecurity at best impedes their ability and willpower and at worst compels them to immigrate from their country.[6]

The modernisation approach found much scholarly purchase in the 1950s and the 1960s. Before long, however, the conservative underpinnings of the approach, resulting from its emphasis on political stability and leadership, evoked sharp responses from a growing number of mostly native Third World scholars. A general re-evaluation of merits and viability of the modernisation approach was prompted largely by the abuse and excesses that were committed by Third World dictatorships in the name of industrial development and growth. An alternative theoretical framework was thus devised, focusing on the dependency of Third World governments on more powerful patrons. Instead of lack of political stability and capable leadership, proponents of dependency theory see global imperialism and neocolonialism as the main forces inimical to genuine industrial development in the Third World. Pioneered primarily by scholars of Latin American politics, dependency theory has over the years come to represent the radical approach to the study of Third World development.[7] It focuses on the dependent relationship that has evolved between Third World countries on the one hand and Western governments and multinational firms on the other.

Emphasis on the compartmentalisation of history into different periods, especially since the dawn of the colonial era, forms one of the main cornerstones of the dependency theory's approach.[8] Referring extensively to the colonial history of Latin America and Africa, and the current omnipresence of Western European and North American influence on the economy, culture, and the politics of these regions, the 'dependistas' maintain that the West has reached its present high levels of development largely through under-developing the Third World. The great divide, it is argued, began around 1800, when the development of industry in the West led to the exploitation and de-industrialisation of what is now known as the Third World.[9] This exploitation was made feasible through colonialism, resulting in an international division of labour whereby colonies and semi-colonies offered the cheap labour and raw materials that were needed for the development of industries in the West. Colonial Africa's relations with Europe were a prime example of this type of exploitative relationship. The industrial sector in Africa was primarily designed to supply cheap raw materials for Europe's industries and to furnish colonial settlers with luxury goods and consumer items.[10] The colonies were meant to be profitable enterprises, at least for shareholders and companies back in the colonial power, and to pay their way for military and administrative rule as much as possible. With the international market as the dominant force, what was produced in the colonies was determined not by the colonies' needs and capabilities but by economic competition in the world market.[11]

According to the dependency approach, the economic legacy of colonialism did not end with its political demise, which in most cases was merely a symbolic abdication of colonial privileges. The colonies were economically too profitable and their economies were structurally too dependent on colonial powers for dependent relationships between the two to be easily relinquished. Western governments and multinational firms devised various means and methods to maintain the economic dependence of former colonies despite their newly-achieved status as independent states. Since nationalist sentiments and political restrictions often made direct investments impossible, new methods, such as international loans and assistance programmes, were utilized to achieve the same old goals of capital exportation and exploitation.[12] In fact, various forms of international assistance programmes became the cornerstone of the evolving and expanding world economy beginning in the 1950s. International agencies and banks provided underdeveloped countries with loans for food, agriculture, experts, and technical equipment, almost all of which were imported from the developed countries. However, the intent of these loans was not only to facilitate the establishment of the necessary industrial infrastructures in the Third World (e.g. dams, roads, railways, communication systems, etc.), but, more important, to enable the Third World to increase its imports from the West.[13] The very nature of capitalism, dependency theorists argue, requires continued economic penetration of the Third World. With the rise of monopoly capital in the industrially advanced countries, it is necessary to expand markets in the Third World in order to mitigate problems arising from over-production at home.[14] One of the ways by which Third World countries are enabled to increase their imports from the West is through lucrative loans and grants. Some have even gone so far as to argue that

> agriculture and livestock credit to the poor is a scheme hatched out by the business and financial leaders of the industrial countries in their offices in New York, Washington, and Frankfurt for the sole purpose of giving themselves a good image and making it appear as if they were concerned about resolving the problems of the Third World. None of this can be taken seriously, and still much less in the beef cattle and meat industry where there is no room left for the peasant and much less for poor-credit-schemes.[15]

Even if the allocation of generous aid packages to Third World countries by the industrial West takes place with the genuine goals of development in mind, real economic growth cannot take place as long as the goods exported remain mostly raw materials. In fact, the degree to which countries specialise in the export of raw materials has a significantly negative impact on their economic growth.[16] Continued reliance on the export of raw materials by Third World countries, which is the cornerstone of the prevailing international trade system, leaves exporters vulnerable to fluctuations in the international market arising out of global supplies and demands.[17]

Proponents of the dependency approach further maintain that the unequal and dependent relationship between the centre (i.e. the West) and the periphery (the Third World) has in turn resulted in the formation of acute differences in the class structure of the peripheral societies themselves. Dependency is said to be not just a condition but a series of relationships among unequal classes of power, whether between nations or within nations.[18] The linkage between centre and periphery only benefits a small class of people in the underdeveloped countries, whose profits continue to mount despite declining terms of trade. Instead of promoting an international equalisation of income or technology, trade accentuates existing inequalities within the Third World.[19] 'Superexploitation' is the condition which most observers ascribe to those who comprise the less privileged stratum of the Third World's bifurcated, dependent societies.[20] In specific relationship to Latin America, where dependency theory finds its most widespread applicability, 'the centre of wealth and power' is seen as 'a grouping of big corporate-financial interests' who exist side-by-side with a mass of immiserated people at the bottom of the social ladder, called a 'surplus population' or 'marginalised classes'.[21]

As earlier mentioned, the dependency approach owes much of its origin to works by observers of Latin American politics and economy. Admittedly, certain aspects of dependency theory are remarkably accurate in describing the pattern of economic growth and development in Latin America over the past few decades. North American influence on Latin America's industry, infrastructure, economic projects, and even political life and cultural orientation is pervasive and in fact at times overwhelming. The unprecedented economic growth of the 1960s, the 'development decade', and that of the 1970s, which witnessed an incredible rise in the level of industrialisation throughout the continent, were aided and financed primarily by loans and grants from public and private institutions in the United States.[22] Beginning in the 1960s, in fact, the Kennedy administration launched a concerted effort to expedite American-sponsored social and economic development in Latin America under the auspices of the Alliance for Progress programme. Through such a programme, President Kennedy hoped to alleviate or to at least minimise in other Latin American countries causes for political upheavals of the kind that had taken place in Cuba.[23] Latin America's continued geo-political significance for American policy-makers, coupled with its enormous investment opportunities and vast consumer markets, abundant raw materials, and cheap labour, have all combined to result in a concentration of American investments and economic activities in virtually all Latin American countries. As a result, capitalist economies have flourished in Latin America largely with the aid of American investments, capital, imports, and credits and loans. In major Latin American cities, as well as in smaller towns and villages, American influence on such economic activities as the purchase of consumer items, industrial production, mining, transportation, and even city planning and architecture is paramount. Within this context of overwhelming concentration of North American-based economic activity in Latin American countries, the appearance of a dependent relationship between the 'centre' (the United States) and the 'periphery' (Latin America), to borrow dependency theory's jargon, is irrefutable. Over the past few decades, almost every single Latin American country, from Mexico in the north to Argentina in the south, has become highly dependent on investments, imports, loans, and grants from the United States. As the decade of the 1980s demonstrated, this dependence has reached gigantic proportions. When the United States sneezed, Latin American countries were stricken with pneumonia: the economic downturn that occurred in the USA in the 1980s was concurrent with catastrophic economic setbacks across Latin America. From 1980 to 1988, Argentina's rate of inflation averaged at 88.6 per cent, Brazil's stood at 188.7 per cent, Peru's at 119.1 per cent and Mexico's at 73.8 per cent, to cite a few examples. Meanwhile, average annual rate of growth for Gross National Product per capita from 1965 to 1988 was 0.0 per cent for Argentina, 2.3 per cent for Mexico, −0.5 per cent for El Salvador, 0.1 per cent for Peru, and −0.9 per cent for Venezuela.[24] Overall, the average rate of inflation for Latin America and the Caribbean stood at 117.4 per cent, with their per capita GNP growth at only 1.9 per cent.[25]

Dependency approach has brought great insight into the study of Latin American development, particularly in highlighting the role played by multinational firms and agencies, hitherto largely ignored. In its sharply pointed analysis of Third World economies, dependency approach has made clear that not only is the attainment of political independence alone not a panacea for solving problems of economic development, but it also does not necessarily end the *economic dependence* of peripheral states on stronger centres.[26] However, dependency theory's applicability to Latin America does not bestow it with universal validity, particularly in relation to countries and regions whose histories radically differ from the Latin American experience. The emphasis that proponents of dependency theory place on historical, economic, and political circumstances that are specific to Latin America, such as the exploitation of 'agromineral' societies, circumscribe dependency theory's applicability to other regions and geographic settings.[27] Extensive reliance on the dynamics of colonial exploitation, the reasons underlying colonial expansion, and the manners in which it was brought about make dependency theory almost uniquely applicable to only those countries with a colonial past. Dependency theory's specificity vis-à-vis Latin America is its very source of nemesis.[28] Those Third World countries whose history was spared the colonial experience, which are, admittedly, few, or whose colonial penetration did not fit the Latin American pattern and extent, are left largely outside the purview of the dependency approach. Dependistas, for their part, counter with the argument that those countries not subject to outright colonialism were later victims of neocolonialism, which was politically less risky but still equally lucrative. Thus a similar set of analytical principles apply to them in examining their struggle toward industrial development.

Besides its narrow specificity, another shortcoming of the dependency approach lies in its emphasis on greater international and economic dynamics at the expense of other relevant factors such as indigenous political cultures, policy initiatives, and available resources. Dependency theory concentrates almost entirely on the exploitative nature of the relationship between the centre and the periphery, between large banks and multinational firms and the developing countries, while brushing aside fundamental factors *within* the developing country that also affect its course of development and its industrial projects. Attributing a sense of omnipresence to a largely elusive 'global imperialism', proponents of dependency theory place the blame for the current economic shortcomings of Latin American countries squarely on the shoulders of American banks and the US government, ignoring domestic policy initiatives and circumstances indigenous to each Latin American country. The latent conspiratorial assumptions that underlie dependency approach – attributing present economic circumstances to master-plans contrived by multinational corporations, while overlooking factors such as human greed, corruption, and short-sighted policies – frequently cast a doctrinal gloss over factors with otherwise deep social, political, and historic roots. The tendency within the dependency school to place the blame for the miseries of the Third World on foreign sources, be they governments or private firms, explains in part the widespread popularity of the dependency approach among Third World intellectuals and even commoners. It is easier to blame someone distant for one's agonies than be willing to accept responsibility. Given the colonial history of much of the Third World, and the avaricious tactics frequently used by multinationals in winning Third World markets, it is not difficult to see why many in the developing countries readily agree with many of the dependency approach's premises.

PATTERNS OF DEVELOPMENT

The applicability of a particular theoretical framework to industrial development largely depends on specific strategies adopted by individual governments. Undoubtedly, policies designed to expedite economic progress and industrial development vary greatly from country to country. Nevertheless, development strategies can broadly be divided into the import-substitution strategy and that relying on exports. Before examining these two varying courses of attaining industrial development, it is necessary to analyse the broader political and economic contexts within which development strategies are adopted and formulas for economic and industrial growth are devised.

Third World governments use a variety of vehicles in order to achieve development objectives and carry out industrial policies. Such means include, among others, state agencies and public parastatals, multinational corporations, and, to a lesser extent, smaller workshops and privately owned enterprises. One of the most prevalent tactics used in seeking to expedite industrial development is nationalising key industries and bringing them under direct government control, a frequently used tactic in newly independent states in the 1960s and the 1970s. Leaders viewed nationalisation as the only effective mean to control their country's economy and expedite its industrial development.[29] To many in the Third World, nationalisation also symbolised control over their own destiny and economic future, an opportunity lost during decades of foreign economic domination. But the trend toward nationalisation was gradually halted, and in some cases reversed, when government-run industries proved wasteful, inefficient, and unable to effectively compete in international markets. Growing demands for readjustments and enhanced productivity by international creditors were also instrumental in bringing about a general re-evaluation of the merits of large-scale nationalisation. Beginning in the 1980s, strict government control over industries began giving way to joint ventures involving both government agencies and domestic as well as international investors. Although nationalised industries still dominate many Third World economies, a number of governments have initiated measures to attract foreign capital and have nationalised only those industries which they view with special significance.[30]

National strategies for industrial development are often encapsulated in comprehensive development plans. In pursuing the path to development, Third World countries are confronted with a number of dilemmas concerning social practices, demographic factors, economic needs versus capabilities, and the political feasibility of specific projects. The very purpose of achieving industrial development brings about a number of basic issues which force Third World policy-makers to make and implement significant policy decisions. These include choices of reliance on indigenous as opposed to exogenous sources of development, self-reliance versus interdependence, growth versus distribution, and centralised planning versus operations of the market.[31] These decisions determine the very structure of the economy and are thus of paramount importance to political leaders and policy-makers. It has become common practice among most Third World governments to present their development objectives as comprehensive packages in the form of seven- or, more commonly, five-year development plans. Still others devise catchy names with which they denote their development objectives, such as the late Shah of Iran's pursuit of the 'Great Civilization',[32] or, somewhat less ostentatiously, South Korea's 'New Community Movement'[33] and Tanzania's Ujamma.[34] These doctrinally impregnated programmes are intended to provide a national ideology under the auspices of which development plans can be conceived and launched.[35] The provision of such development plans is seen as necessary in achieving the complex tasks of development and overcoming seemingly insurmountable obstacles. Every aspect of development, from the doctrinal framework within which it is to occur to provisions considered for its implementation, is supposed to be formulated in development plans. Most significantly, development plans set clear objectives to be reached and identify the obstacles that need to be overcome.[36]

Political considerations weigh heavily in formulating development plans. To begin with, devising development plans gives Third World leaders and policy-makers control over crucial economic resources and, ultimately, over their national destiny. This partly explains the prevalence of development plans in most African states soon after independence in the 1960s. Some 60 per cent of Africa's newly independent states devised 'transitional schemes' or 'plans intérimaires' in order not only to re-adjust their economies to post-colonial conditions but, more important, to assert their unquestioned authority over the economic sphere.[37] Other international and domestic political factors also figure prominently in the provision of development plans. Clearly, leaders and policy-makers formulate

development plans in accordance with their own agendas and ideological persuasions, most of which are often highly pronounced and
rarely flexible. Political realities do, nevertheless, often influence the
contents and even the intended direction of development plans.
Some of these factors include the volume of aid received from
various development agencies, such as the US Agency for International Development (US AID), or conditions under which
international lending institutions such as the World Bank and the
International Monetary Fund (IMF) agree to grant loans. Frequently,
the World Bank and the IMF attach strict conditions to the loans that
they grant, often requiring the initiation of measures aimed at
curbing the ill-effects of economic mismanagement such as hyperinflation and rampant unemployment. Internal political considerations similarly limit the scope and contents of development
plans. Resource allocation is invariably influenced by political constraints arising out of dynamics such as clientalist relations between
the central government and various social classes, anticipated reactions by those most directly effected by the plan's various projects,
and practical limitations on the capabilities of the government.

The dilemmas of pursuing industrial growth through development plans or by other means do not stop at political considerations.
Ingrained patterns of social relations, demographic and geographic
factors, unrealistic hopes and expectations, difficulties associated
with execution and implementation, and economic limitations and
infrastructural inadequacies all in one way or another circumvent the
scope and viability of development plans. Often times, political
leaders and bureaucrats themselves do not have a full and complete
understanding of the complexities and consequences of modernisation. They thus often embark on modernisation programmes with
blurred images of the future or with conflicting goals, hoping to
either emulate foreign success stories or to regain an elusive and
long-lost historic glory.[38] In most Third World countries, especially
in places where political instability prompts leaders to make lofty
promises of rapid economic gains, unrealistic objectives render many
development plans inoperable rather early on, leading to their alteration through a series of unannounced amendments and modifi-
cations. As a result, the value of such plans as reliable guides to
economic and industrial growth diminish greatly before the end of
their term.[39]

Similarly, development plans need to take into account historically accepted and practised patterns of social relations and

organisations. A striking example of the effects of social organisation on development planning is the existence of caste relations in India, which greatly influences the feasibility, applicability, and implementation of development projects.[40] The prevalence of tribal loyalties and bonds exerts a similar influence on the development objectives of most African countries. Although tribalism as a viable social force in Africa has been steadily on the decline, it is still powerful enough to influence the planning and execution of various development projects. Geographic characteristics are also important, particularly in so far as access to navigable waters and major ports is concerned. Being land-locked is a major political and economic handicap for a number of Third World countries, forcing them not only to cultivate good-neighbourly relations with countries that have access to water but also diverting much of their efforts to developing costly aerial or land-based transportation networks.[41] There are thirteen land-locked countries in Africa (Botswana, Burkina Faso, Burundi, Central African Republic, Chad, Lesotho, Malawi, Mali, Niger, Rowanda, Uganda, Zambia, and Zimbabwe), five in Asia (Afghanistan, Bhutan, Laos, Mongolia, and Nepal), and two in Latin America (Bolivia and Paraguay).

Lastly, demography plays an overwhelmingly important role in the outlining of development plans and pursuit of industrial objectives. In smaller countries specifically, there are extremely high costs attached to social overheads and public services as well as to those manufacturing industries which involve economies of scale.[42] Such countries also suffer from a general lack of competition from within, a limited pool of natural resources, and low productivity and standards resulting from relative intellectual isolation.[43] The curtailed development potentials of countries with limited human and geographic resources is most evident in many Third World island nations and other countries with relatively small populations. Island countries such as Malta, Jamaica, Cuba, Haiti, and the Dominican Republic, as well as several smaller African states like Burkina Faso and Uganda, share similar predicaments of limited population and natural resources, thus being drastically limited in scope of the development objectives they can pursue. Only Hong Kong and Taiwan, whose industrial development was at least initially launched with massive infusions of Western capital, radically differ from other small Third World countries.

It is within these limitations and constraints that strategies for industrial growth are adopted and development plans formulated. As mentioned earlier, such development strategies fall into the two broad categories of industrialisation through heavy reliance on foreign imports, the so-called 'import-substitution' strategy, and export-oriented development. Import-substitution strategies for development gained increasing prevalence in the 1950s and the 1960s throughout Latin America, much of east Asia, and parts of the Middle East and Africa.[44] The primary assumption underlying this strategy envisions relying on technology developed in the more advanced countries in order to build up a domestic industrial infrastructure. Imported technology is thus used as substitute for domestic technology, which is presumed to be backward and inferior by comparison. It is hoped that this imported technology will stimulate growth and development in other local industries and, ultimately, itself become locally adapted and absorbed. The most telling evidence of import-substitution strategies in Third World countries is their ever-increasing number of foreign-owned and controlled assembly plants, assembling a wide range of products from household consumer goods to automobiles and industrial products.[45]

Despite its widespread popularity in the 1950s and the 1960s, the import-substitution strategy for development has largely failed to produce its intended results. By and large, import-substitution policies have accentuated unequal and dependent relationships between Third World governments and Western suppliers. Part of the problem is the failure to thoroughly follow through with import-substitution policies in a comprehensive manner and instead to merely emphasise reliance on the policy's 'import' aspect. On the surface, import-substitution policies have met with great success, especially for those Third World leaders and policy-makers whose preoccupation with their countries' international image supersedes their concern for substantive growth and development. The increasing numbers of assembled consumer and industrial goods such as refrigerators, colour television sets, automobiles, and even factories is seen as testimony to economic wealth and technological advancement. However, assembly plants are of little value if their underlying technology remains alien and unintegrated into the local economy. Throughout the Third World, the actual design, production, and engineering of locally assembled products often remain the exclusive domain of foreign companies. Growing economic nationalism and unease with the powers of multinational corporations have in recent years prompted Third World policy-makers to insist on increases in the local contents of import-substitution industries. Nevertheless, owing to inherent assumptions of dependence on foreign technology for industrial development, import-substitution strategies have led to considerable increases in both imports from abroad and in economic influence by multinational corporations.[46]

Whether out of political timidity in dealing with multinationals or lack of political will to fully implement intended policies, many Third World governments which follow import-substitution strategies have become subject to increasing influence by foreign companies. This influence is often concentrated in areas most vital to the host country's economy: in Mexico in the 1970s, multinational corporations owned and controlled 84 per cent of the rubber industry, 80 per cent of the tobacco industry, 79 per cent of the electrical machinery industry, 62 per cent of the non-electrical machinery industry, and 67 per cent of the chemical industry. Brazil was in a similar situation, with foreign companies owning 100 per cent of the automobile, 85 per cent of pharmaceutical, and 55 per cent of the machinery and equipment industries. In Argentina, meanwhile, multinational firms owned some 85 per cent of the car industry, 96 per cent of petroleum refining, 82 per cent of the non-electrical machinery, and 75 per cent of the rubber industry.[47] As these examples demonstrate, import-substitution strategies have the potential to substantially deepen the dependence of the host country on multinational firms and to perpetuate their continued local operations. Moreover, the monopoly which these companies often establish over the host country's market insulates industrial development from foreign competition, thus reducing the incentive for acquiring improved technology and keeping the level of domestic integration in manufacturing relatively low. As a result, technological capabilities in most countries using import-substitution policies have frozen at the level of initial imports and acquisition.[48] The frequency of late-model cars in streets do not necessarily attest to technological advancement but are, more likely, products of liberal import policies or foreign-owned assembly plants. The basic pattern of importing manufactured goods and exporting raw materials continues to persist in much of the Third World.[49]

Despite its seeming futility, there are examples, albeit only very few, of Third World countries that have used import-substitution policies with great success. South Korea is one of the most notable examples of a Third World country that has successfully transformed an import-substitution strategy into export-oriented development, as are, to a lesser extent, India and even Mexico and Brazil. For a growing number of Third World countries, export-oriented development has become the major venue through which industrial development is reached. Export-oriented strategies of development enable countries to develop internationally competitive industries and to overcome limitations imposed by small domestic markets. Since cheaper labour costs enable Third World exporters to sell their products at lower prices, often the markets targeted for penetration are those of other Third World countries, as exemplified by the export to other Third World states of armaments and light aircraft by Brazil and railway carriages and heavy industry by India. South Korea and formerly Yugoslavia even attempted to compete in the United States' automobile market, perhaps the world's largest. While South Korea's Hyundai Motors has met with relative success in the United States, Yugoslavia's attempt at marketing cars there proved largely unsuccessful and was short-lived.

A successful transition from import-substitution to an export-oriented strategy for development does not necessarily entail complete independence from multinational corporations or from foreign technology. In most instances, dependence on multinationals continues to be a lingering reality. In fact, only in relatively rare instances has the ability to export manufactured goods been developed entirely from within and free of reliance on foreign firms. Domestic companies have often not had the opportunity to develop adequate technology to produce a large variety of manufactured goods for export, a disadvantage accentuated by their limited knowledge of foreign marketing and distribution techniques.[50] Much of the technology and know-how needed for producing and manufacturing exportable industrial goods has, as a result, come from multinational corporations. This has in turn led to an increase in the influence of multinational corporations on the economies of countries in which they operate, to the point of making some of them highly dependent on their operations.

In order to expedite the process of development, a number of Third World countries have designated specific areas and regions where export-oriented industrial plants and factories are concentrated. Often called Export Processing Zones (EPZs), these areas are in essence industrial parks designed to accelerate industrialisation, generate employment, and further develop export capabilities. Through providing infrastructure and other production facilities, Export Processing Zones are intended to attract prospective investors, most of whom are multinational corporations whose products are largely earmarked for exports.[51] EPZs and other industrially designated areas have gained increasing prevalence in the Third World in recent years, with an estimated fifty-five countries having some form of Export Processing Zones in 1980.[52] Despite this widespread popularity, however, the effects of such zones on industrial development remain minimal and largely elusive. To begin with, these segregated areas function mostly as isolated enclaves in the economy that are only marginally linked with domestic suppliers and users, thus prohibiting significant technological spill-overs to local industry.[53] Moreover, the skills that are employed in such zones are mostly the same as the rudimentary ones needed for the assembly of pre-manufactured parts, such as tightening screws or welding rods together. As a result, very little meaningful technological transfer takes place. According to one estimate, over seventy per cent of the labourers in Export Processing Zones are comprised of low-skilled, female labourers whose jobs can be learned in about a week.[54]

The conceptual provision of development plans is one thing; their actual implementation is quite another. Throughout all different stages, from their initial doctrinal conception to their actual implementation, development plans are subject to a variety of forces and influences which in one way or another mute their effectiveness. Such obstacles are often as subtle as they are varied. Most fundamentally, development plans are for the most part experimental projects through which policy-makers and politicians try out their beliefs and political ideologies, not all of which are always necessarily compatible with the needs of their country. Geopolitical and strategic considerations, often taking the forms of regional rivalries or internal conflicts, are equally prominent in influencing development plans in ways that may be not only not conducive to industrial growth but may even prove detrimental. Heavy emphasis on military industries or on weapons procurements frequently warp development plans by diverting funds earmarked for industrial projects. Grand promises and expectations of miracles similarly render most development plans unrealistic and inoperable. Over-ambitious plans, often intended more for public consumption than for practical application, are frequently altered before even getting started and their goals are dramatically muted. Even when the watered-down versions of development plans eventually reach the implementation stage, they face massive obstacles arising from practical restraints and limitations.[55] Politicians and policy-makers, whether products of the domestic educational system or holders of foreign degrees, are often out of touch with the realities of everyday life in their own society, thus overlooking many of the finer details of implementing their plans at the local level. Policies devised in and directed from national capitals are not always thoroughly understood or welcomed by those whose lives they directly influence. In most other instances, the actual mechanisms needed for the local implementation of development plans – skilled manpower, local bureaucracy, and tools and machinery – are simply absent or are inoperable.

The success or failure of development plans to a large extent determine the degree to which a country has progressed toward industrialisation. More important, development plans provide blueprints according to which industrial objectives are determined and paths toward reaching them are charted. It is here that the relationship between industrial planning and the structure of economy is most directly consequential. The specific pattern of development directly influences the structure of economy. Adversely, development projects are formulated within existing doctrinal frameworks and available economic resources. The extent and nature of industrial development projects in turn determine the structure of the domestic economy in terms of the types of economic activities in which various social strata engage.

STRUCTURE OF ECONOMY

Throughout the Third World, the economic structures of the urban and rural areas differ radically. In the countryside, most economic activities occur within the field of agriculture, varying in form from artisanship and trading handicrafts to farm labour and various gradations of land and livestock ownership. In cities and other large metropolitan areas, the range of economic activities is far wider. Broadly, four primary sources of urban employment can be identified. They include the state, particularly its massive bureaucratic network, local subsidiaries of multinational corporations or domestic enterprises and industries, mid- to small-scale plants and workshops, stores, and the streets, in which most rural migrants attempt to earn their livelihood. It is these various sources of employment, and their prevalence and overall strength in economic life, that determine the shape and functioning of a country's economy. In a broader sense, factors influencing the structure of a country's economy are largely political, influenced by the ideological agendas which leaders seek to implement. In countries whose leaders adhere to socialist ideologies, for example, there are far greater numbers of bureaucrats and other state employees than there are in countries where the prevalence of market forces result in a flourishing of entrepreneurial classes. Similarly, some states impose severe restrictions on certain types of economic activities, be they street peddling or establishing large enterprises (in China, for example). None the less, there are certain economic ramifications of industrial development over which even the most restrictive governments cannot impose effective controls. As a result, the structures of economies are, in essence, products (in fact, directly symptomatic) of development policies and projects.

The different sources of employment found in Third World cities belong to either the formal or the informal sectors of the economy. The informal sector, also called the 'bazaar economy',[56] is comprised of that category of economically active population whose employment and economic activities are not linked to any types of formal organisations, public or private. Small traders and shop-owners, street vendors, construction workers, and any other segments of population whose economic activities fall outside the purview of formal organisations are part of the economy's informal sector. Because of its amorphous and fluid nature, the activities encompassed in the informal sector are mostly labour intensive and require little or no prior skills. On the other hand, the formal sector often requires formal schooling and technical or administrative know-how.[57] It revolves around organised forms of economic activity that involve set procedures, hierarchical authority structures, and rationalised methods for production and capital accumulation. Whether owned and controlled by the state or by private firms, components of the formal sector embody decidedly *corporate* structures and methods that are completely antithetical to the informal and unorganised nature of activities permeating the informal sector.[58] Notable participants in the formal economic sector include the state bureaucracy, which in the Third World is one of the predominant sources of income for the burgeoning middle classes, government-owned enterprises and parastatals (see p. 56), large-scale and capital intensive industries, and medium to small-scale private enterprises which employ more than five or six employees.

The dichotomy of the urban economy into the formal and the informal sectors can be further broken down to include the various types of economic activities found in Third World cities. These include those activities that are in one way or another linked to the state, to privately-owned, large-scale enterprises and industrial concerns, or to the indigenous urban economy. Throughout the Third

World, the state tends to be by far the largest single employer, often employing as much as 60 to 70 per cent of the urban labour force. The state is, in fact, the primary vehicle within which development policies are formulated and carried out. The assumption of numerous tasks, from the initial conception of development objectives to their supervision and actual implementation, has resulted in a proliferation of various ministries and departments, often with overlapping duties whose jurisdictions at times overlap.[59] What has thus emerged in most developing countries is a 'development bureaucracy', pragmatic and dedicated to promoting the goals of development, but at the same time unwilling to relinquish its immense political powers or to at least share it with others.[60]

With very few exceptions, the Third World's 'development bureaucracies' have turned into gigantic institutions slugging around aimlessly and riddled with inefficiency and corruption. The civil service in the Third World is by far one of the most beneficial venues for upward social mobility, job security, political and administrative power, and wealth and affluence.[61] To the average citizen, a position in the state bureaucracy means a steady and secure salary, which, although probably lower than that paid by the private sector, is almost never in jeopardy of termination. The growing importance of the civil service in the overall process of development, coupled with its sheer numerical size and social prestige, have largely made it immune to government policies that may have negative consequences for the bureaucracy. Rarely are there ever massive lay-offs of bureaucrats by governments, and in most Third World bureaucracies an implicit (and at times even official) system of job tenure prevails. Because of their control over important state resources and projects, governments are often cautious not to arouse the ire of civil servants by encroaching on their privileges.[62] In some countries, particularly those that have undergone extensive and early bureaucratisation, the powers of the state bureaucracy have grown to such an extent that large numbers of civil servants quietly pursue their own political agendas as opposed to those of the government. Bureaucratic enclaves emerge, unpenetrated by the executive and pursuing more or less independent agendas.[63] Thus Third World bureaucracies have given birth to what some have called a 'second stratum', public officials who work for the government but at the same time sympathise with those opposing its policies. Through their sensitive positions, members of the second stratum are able to slow down the government's response to the opposition or to lessen the intended effects of its policies.[64] The civil service is, at any rate, a powerful and significant political ally whose sympathy and support governments try hard to harness and maintain.

Yet the overwhelmingly patrimonial political systems of the Third World are hardly capable of fostering environments which are *not* inimical to administrative capacities.[65] Despite the organisational rigidities that are supposed to mark government agencies, most Third World bureaucracies are characterised by fluidity and lack of established procedures. In these bureaucracies a situation predominates in which interests are articulated only infrequently and policy inputs are often impossible to identify clearly.[66] Instead, there is considerable weight attached to personal connections and loyalties. Symptomatic of the broader patrimonial arrangements which govern political conduct, the cultivation of personal ties and loyalties is an important aspect of one's position in the civil service. As the established avenues of access to power are limited and are largely the monopoly of an oligarchy, extra-legal means such as personal contacts, and even bribery and corruption, are often employed in order to achieve desired objectives. When due procedures are seen as obtrusive impediments, log-rolling and bribery become commonplace. When an industrialist needs official permission to establish a particular factory or to import certain products, when a conscript soldier seeks to dodge military service, when a civil servant wishes to move up within the bureaucratic hierarchy, or in any other instances when cumbrous administrative procedures are involved, resort to bribery and corruption is common and indeed often fruitful.[67] But corruption is by no means the only plague besetting Third World bureaucracies. In many Third World countries, the state itself has become an instrument of accumulation. Through its ability to regulate economic and financial transactions, attract foreign and domestic capital, award contracts, and grant permits, the state in most Third World countries controls the economy's most significant resources. Thus for most individuals access to the economy is contingent upon access to the state.[68] At the same time, lack of ideological convictions or loyalty to the government, low salaries, and control over the allocation of lucrative contracts and grants make many civil servants amenable to bribes and gifts. It is not uncommon, therefore, to find Third World civil servants with life styles far more affluent than what their government salaries would allow.

Whereas the middle classes are concentrated in the state bureaucracy, the working classes predominate in the industrial sector. It is difficult and at times misleading to label the working classes as a single 'class' owing to its heterogeneity and vast internal differences. There are several categories of working class professions, ranging in nature from street vending to working in large industrial complexes. Broadly, three different economic strata within the working class can be distinguished. They include rural migrants and unskilled workers, known as the lumpenproletariat, semi-skilled labourers, and skilled industrial workers. As a sub-class, the lumpenproletariat is comprised of unskilled migrants from the countryside who work at whatever menial jobs they can find, whether as construction workers, coolies, domestic servants, trash collectors, and the like. Sometimes referred to as the 'protoproletariat', these economically marginalised labourers are 'engaged in individual or family enterprises and . . . are not regular salary or wage earners – a group neither proletariat nor peasant'.[69] Their economic activities fall into four general categories: distribution (such as the manual transportation or sale of goods as middlemen), the provision of services (car-minders, professional queuers, prostitutes, house-guards, shoe-shines, etc.), handicrafts (broom-makers, hat-weavers, food-makers, and the like), and, for the ones who are slightly better off, financial manipulation, such as money-lenders and rentiers.[70] Most lumpenproletariats work in the streets, often engaging in the sale of odds and ends like lottery and chance tickets, cassette tapes, candy and gum, knives and mechanical tools, or stolen goods and jewellery. Many sell ready-made products on behalf of merchants who allow them to keep a portion of the profits. There is a proliferation of these street traders in the poorer areas, although they are also found in most major intersections and busy inner-city streets.[71] Their jobs require little or no formal education but instead dexterity, quick-wittedness, bargaining skills, an honest face and an engaging personality, and on-the-job experience.[72] Male adults predominate in street occupations, although women and children are also numerically significant. Only prostitution is almost exclusively a female preserve, although more women engage in retail activities (e.g. sale of fruits) than men, who tend to perform manual labour. For their part, child workers are usually active in small trades, such as shining shoes or washing cars, activities which are the least remunerative, have lowest status, and require minimal access to capital.[73] On the whole, however, male adults who work in the streets generally do not consider themselves to be better-off than their younger or female competitors. Still, the fierce competition and labour-intensive nature of small-scale enterprises and street occupations keep both productivity and profitability at very low levels for both males and females, young or old.[74] For this economic underclass, upward mobility is all but an impossibility. The intensely competitive nature of their work, which for many is not just a job but essentially a struggle for survival, their individualistic mentality, and their seemingly perpetual poverty and economic dependence prevent most street workers from achieving levels of social and economic organisation that could enhance their economic status and well-being.[75]

Semi-skilled working-class labourers are mostly employed in large industrial complexes and factories. Despite their occupation in technologically sophisticated factories, however, these labourers possess few technical skills and their jobs are mostly limited to rudimentary functions. The industrial activities of most are limited to non-technical tasks such as tightening screws, pulling levers, or welding. These semi-skilled labourers are former members of the lumpenproletariat who have been able to secure jobs in the industrial sector. In size, semi-skilled labourers are less numerous than the lumpenproletariat but still out-number skilled labourers. Their upward mobility into the ranks of the skilled is circumscribed by a general lack of education and know-how, although there are those who gain sufficient skills to improve their social and economic standings. For their part, skilled workers are in a distinct minority, possessing by far greater depth of skills and knowledge than any other segments of the working class. They are concentrated in industries that require higher levels of technical specialisation, such as oil refineries, modern factories, and automobile assembly plants. Their small numbers and comparative technical specialisation turn skilled workers into a 'labour aristocracy', becoming a self-conscious and conservative stratum cognizant of their comparatively privileged position.[76] Although they are still sharply differentiated (and socially segregated) from engineers and technicians, who are considered to belong to the middle and upper classes, skilled workers know a great deal about the machinery with which they work. Lack of spare parts and regular maintenance services force these workers to become intimately familiar with the machines they and their crew work on, some even performing major repairs on sophisticated equipment with makeshift tools. However, precisely because it is part of a labour aristocracy, the skilled stratum of the working class tends to be less productive because of awareness of its privileged position vis-à-vis other workers. The very fact that these skilled labourers are part of an elite is itself a form of job security, alleviating their fear of being readily replaced by others. This lack of productivity is further reinforced by an absence of efficient and advanced management techniques in large Third World industrial complexes, where skilled workers tend to be concentrated.[77]

The working classes are not employed by any one particular sector of the economy, public or private. While most work for small-scale plants and factories which employ ten or less people, others work for major parastatals. Parastatals are public corporations set up by the state in order to run major industries, most notably oil, steel, mining, insurance, and even banking. Prevalent in almost all Third World countries, parastatals are essentially instruments through which governments intervene in various economic sectors, especially in key industries deemed to be of vital importance to national development.[78] More specifically, parastatals are mostly set up to control foreign trade on behalf of the state in the hope of strengthening its bargaining position in the international arena.[79] Along with local subsidiaries of multinational corporations, parastatals employ the majority of skilled and semi-skilled labourers who are not employed in the private sector. Working for larger industrial complexes usually entails greater job security and fringe benefits, most notably health insurance and paid vacations. None the less, scarcity of skilled labour also forces many smaller employers to provide attractive work conditions and competitive salaries.[80]

Frequently in Third World countries, the drive toward industrialisation forms the main thrust of national development policies. Politicians and policy-makers alike view lack of industrial development and its slow spread as the main impediment to economic and political parity between themselves and the West. Added to international concerns are domestic political pressures, with local populations constantly comparing themselves with the peoples of the West and feeling troubled by their glaring disadvantages. Development and modernisation plans are thus hurriedly implemented, often with little regard for local needs and conditions and with even less attention to their ensuing social and economic ramifications. Socially and culturally, rapid industrialisation dramatically accelerates social change by introducing change agents hitherto alien to indigenous conditions.[81] Economically, among other developments, industrialisation fragments the process of proletarianisation, leading to several gradations of distinctive and segregated strata of the working class. Even more important, industrialisation severely retards the growth of agriculture as a viable economic sector by diverting scarce resources into industrial projects and away from agricultural concerns. It is within the context of rapid industrial development, and largely as its auxiliary, that agricultural policies in the Third World are formulated and put into effect.

AGRICULTURE

While the drive toward technological modernisation and industrial development has steadily been gaining momentum and intensity in the Third World, increasingly less attention is being paid to agriculture. This trend has reached such proportions that many of the Third World countries which were once net exporters of agricultural products are now importing much of their agricultural needs. In the short span of only a few decades, the vast agricultural resources of most Third World countries have been severely depleted owing to neglect and abuse. Once a primary source of revenues and a thriving force in the national economy, the provision of agricultural goods and products has become one of the main causes of international indebtedness and internal strife in many Third World countries. The sharpest reversals have taken place in Africa and the Middle East, where chronic drought and deforestation have compounded the negative effects of institutional neglect and public policy. In Africa, the fields of human immiseration inundated with famine and hunger in the 1980s and the 1990s were productive farmlands only as far back as the 1960s.[82] In the Middle East, reversals in agriculture have also been sharp, although not comparable to Africa's devastating magnitude. The nations of the Fertile Crescent, from the southern shores of the Mediterranean to the valleys of the Tigris and the Euphrates, have become agriculturally all but barren, importing increasing quanities of food and agricultural products year after year.[83] Once net exporters of agriculture, the Egypt, Jordan, Syria, and Iran of the 1990s spend much of their revenues on buying foodstuffs from abroad.[84] A similar downward trend has also been taking place in the agro-mineral industries of most Latin American countries, albeit to a less accentuated degree. Only in east Asia, particularly in South Korea and to a lesser extent in the Philippines, Malaysia, and Indonesia, has agriculture retained a seminal role in the national economy. Still, in the region's many war-ravaged nations, notably Vietnam, Laos, and Kampuchia, agriculture (along with most other sectors of the economy) continues to decline in strength and vitality.

Several causes underlie this steady decline in the importance of agriculture in Third World national economies. They include factors that are indigenous to rural areas as well as those which arise out of national policies. Most notably, the restrictive social structure of most villages and rural communities, inadequate distribution mechanisms and transportation networks, and low wages, among others, obstruct the development of conditions conducive to a flourishing of agriculture and agriculture-based industries in the countryside. At the same time, strict and often uninformed government policies, heavy emphasis on industrial growth, and 'urban bias' also combine to hamper agricultural productivity and thus its contribution to the economy.

The social structure of farming communities and villages plays an equally important role in impeding the progress of agriculture and in reducing its importance in the overall national economy. This impediment is manifested in several ways, beginning with the farmers' own mentality and views. Most farmers have more confidence in traditional technology than in modern methods, preferring old methods over new ones. Farmers are not necessarily averse to new ideas, most readily accepting hygiene, wage work, radios, television sets, and other products of modernisation. They are not, however, equally enthusiastic about ideas on new farming methods and practices since their old ways are low-risk, low-cost, and are validated by generations of practice.[85] This reservation is turned into resentment especially when the new ideas are introduced through government initiatives or by urban-based bureaucrats. Government programmes and policies are often forcibly enforced and leave farmers with little option but to obey official rules. Farmers tend to be self-reliant and resentful of outside intervention, especially if the interferer happens to be the central government, whose intentions are almost always viewed with distrust and scepticism. Confiscation and nationalisation of land under nationalist banners or various ideological guises have made most farmers suspicious of their government's intentions and initiatives, even in instances where such initiatives are launched with sincere objectives in mind. Moreover, traditional methods of farming enjoy general social validity within the village community. 'When it is traditional to choose particular seeds, plant varieties, cultivation practices, and cropping systems, the choice means that a local social apparatus exists to support individual decisions.'[86] Ploughing a field by a tractor may be faster and more expedient, but in most villages provisions for renting cows and traditional ploughing equipment are far more easily accessible than there are for renting tractors, not to mention repairing them if the need arises.

Differentiations in social strata and wealth within farming communities also reduce productivity and further impede the development of agriculture as a viable economic sector. Broadly, farmers can be divided into the two categories of landowners and labourers, most of the latter working for the former. Within themselves, landowners are further subdivided according to the amount of land they own, with the majority possessing small to medium-size parcels and a small minority with relatively large land-holding. There are, additionally, other landed proprietors who are often absentee and live in nearby cities. Nevertheless, the social composition of Third World villages is for the most part made up of landless farm labourers, small scale land-holders, and a few, comparatively wealthy, farmers with more land than others. A vast majority of villagers consider life outside of the village to be much better, certainly more glamorous. Farmers tend to have a low opinion of their own social standing, thinking (often not without justification) that they occupy the bottom of the social ladder and that all non-farmers are better off regardless of their occupation and source of livelihood.[87] Migrants to cities are seen as deserters, and government agents sent to rural areas to improve local conditions are viewed as unwelcome strangers seeking to give unnecessary and intrusive advice. Most literacy programmes designed by central governments for village inhabitants are, meanwhile, elitist and arrogant, equating illiteracy with ignorance and thus reinforcing the farmers' feelings of self-pity and inferiority.[88] Lethargic and lacking self-confidence and the drive to succeed – which are, by way, not inherent characteristics but rather products of the social and economic context – most farmers view government initiatives designed to increase agricultural productivity as futile and pointless, and, more important, as further ploys to wrest control of their meagre resources. As long as they can produce enough to feed themselves and their families, most farmers prefer to be left alone.

Farm labourers and most small-scale farmers earn very little and are often forced to augment their income by means other than farming. Thus the resources and the manpower that could be devoted to agricultural production are instead diverted to alternative economic activities such as wage migration, small-scale trade, and artisanship.[89] Migration, both cyclical and permanent, has become a lasting feature of the village economy, draining villages of one of their most important resources, the young.[90] Large landed proprietors, meanwhile, do little to improve local village conditions or the economic well-being of the less fortunate. Apart from providing work for landless peasants as farm labourers or at the most as sharecroppers (tenant farmers), wealthier farmers are generally reluctant to reinvest their income into the village economy. They are, however, more receptive to government-initiated plans and projects as they often stand to gain most from such improvements. Yet because of this very reason, they are often reluctant to take part in development efforts that would benefit the entire village, preferring instead to participate in projects whose benefits they alone can reap.[91] But even widespread local participation in rural development projects does not guarantee success in improving agricultural output, largely because most projects of this kind are in reality crude means for establishing peasant loyalty to those in power.[92] Only in countries with detailed official policies for the development of rural areas, where extensive local participation has been permitted and self-help programmes launched, as in South Korea, have government-sponsored plans met with any meaningful success.[93]

Other impediments to the growth and development of the agricultural sector arise out of the very manner in which Third World industrialisation has evolved over the past few decades. One of the major dilemmas facing Third World agriculture is that of distribution.[94] Emphasis on key industries has led to a frequent neglect of regional and rural roads, as well as other components, needed for the development of a viable transportation system that would link the country's more remote areas to its main economic centres. The result has been the isolation of most rural communities and agriculture-producing areas from major cities and commercial zones, thus preventing or significantly reducing the efficiency of transporting and marketing agricultural products in the national market. Consequently, most Third World governments find it less expensive and troublesome to import their agricultural needs from abroad than to establish the infrastructures needed for the transportation and marketing of domestic agricultural products. Underlying this reluctance to invest in rural areas or to at least improve their links with urban centres is a general tendency to favour urban over rural development. Urban bias, prevalent throughout the Third World, continues to be a major source of rural under-development and the resultant neglect and decline of agriculture.[95]

A growing number of Third World countries have in recent years attempted to initiate measures aimed at reversing their dependence on the import of agricultural products from major international exporters such as Australia, New Zealand, Brazil, and the United States. This has particularly been the case in countries where popular political and economic nationalism have made leaders uneasily aware of their growing dependence on other countries for foodstuffs. Concurrent with and complementing this emphasis on the development of the domestic agricultural sector has been a general re-orientation of most development projects away from official propaganda tools and into more realistic formulas for rural growth. Relying more on military-bureaucratic apparatuses rather than on specific interest groups for their political survival, most Third World governments are also becoming increasingly more willing to remove the obstacles that landed proprietors often create in order to block rural projects which they see as threatening to their interests. Despite these improvements, agriculture continues to be the dark horse of Third World development, continuing to be accorded low priority within the overall schemes of national development.

CONCLUSION

The tangible consequences of industrial development rage on with unimpeded force and dramatic results. Among the many metamorphoses that Third World nations undergo by virtue of being *developing* states, those resulting from technological modernisation and development are by far most noticeable if not necessarily politically and socially most consequential. Yet to this day the theoretical debate over the nature and manner of industrial development continues. Few subjects have perplexed scholars and political leaders of the Third World as much as the ways and means of achieving industrial development. Controversy and debate over the nature of development, its requisites and ramifications, and its actual application and practical possibilities continue to rage in college textbooks and lecture halls as well as in cabinet meetings and policy-making sessions. Scholarly treatments of the subject remain ambivalent and inconclusive, revealing more about their authors' doctrinal orientations than about the merits of one approach over another. Proponents of the dependency and modernisation approaches remain as far apart in mutual understanding and respect as they have ever been.

Within this context of theoretical ambivalence, a few observations are in order. To begin with, as vociferously proclaimed by the dependistas, industrial development is indeed an inherently exploitative process, one in which the natural resources, labour, and interests of Third World countries are exploited by the parties concerned, especially multinational corporations. But the mere identification of multinational firms as uncaring giants bent on the exploitation of the Third World is a gross over-simplification of much larger and deeper dynamics. It is a position adopted more by people with inflexible ideological perspectives than with keen analytical insight. Intellectual elements within the Third World, especially among the middle classes, are also often eager to place the blame for the difficulties that plague their societies squarely on the shoulders of foreign enemies and their local proxies than on other factors. Not surprisingly, Third World intellectuals are more fond of writing florid expositions on imperialism than engaging in searching examinations of their own social and political roles and on fundamental deficiencies in their societies.[96] Nevertheless, absolving multinational giants from exploiting the Third World is an equally inaccurate over-simplification. The placement of billboards glorifying the taste and the elevated social status arising from drinking Pepsi or Coca-Cola in the remote villages of Uganda, Peru, Mali, and countless other Third World countries, where most basic necessities of life are considered as luxuries, is tantamount to nothing less than the exploitation of people's fantasies and dreams. It is true that these billboards would not have found their way into such remote corners had it not been for the permission of local and national office-holders. But not all Third World countries can stand up to giants like the Coca-Cola corporation in the same manner as India did.[97] Most Third World politicians, having ascended to their exalted positions through systemic corruption and the patronage of others, possess few bargaining chips when it comes to dealing with multinationals. Even then, there is much room for criticising the practices adopted by multinationals in expanding their global markets. Making money through exploiting the poor may not be illegal, but it certainly clouds the distinction between what is and what is not ethical.

Another observation that merits further elaboration is the relationship between industrial development and political conservatism. The question of whether industrial development encourages political conservatism, or vice versa, has long been a central issue in the study of Third World politics. Many modernisationists have in fact argued that in order to effectively carry out industrialisation programmes, a centrally organised and powerful authority structure is needed, one whose centralised powers would enable it to overcome the many obstacles faced in implementing modernisation projects.[98] This line of argumentation was pioneered by Samuel Huntington and a group of like-minded colleagues in the 1960s and the 1970s and found much purchase among Third World political aspirants and leaders.[99] It was little accident that those two decades witnessed a proliferation of dictatorships bent on the rapid modernisation of their countries. Brazil, Argentina, Iran, and South Korea, and to a lesser extent the Philippines, Pakistan, Iraq, Syria, Egypt, Libya, plus the many one-party states that sprang up in Africa, were all governed by modernising dictators who, in various ways, wished to modernise all aspects of their societies except its politics. For the most part, the longevity of these regimes was tied to the success of their economic programmes and industrial policies, especially in Latin America and Africa, where economically instigated palace coups were a common occurrence. Economic success still continues to be the main *raison d'être* for many Third World governments who justify the curtailment of civil liberties on grounds of expediting industrial development and modernisation.

Despite the significant contributions of scholars such as Huntington and Pye to the understanding of Third World modernisation, a consistent connection between strong and even authoritarian regimes and industrial development is yet to be established. For the many examples of modernising dictatorships that achieved industrial growth in a short period there are as many dictatorships which merely terrorise their populations and whose industrialisation policies are limited to blindly inviting foreign investments. Specifically, Latin America and Africa were and still are replete with examples of these despotic regimes, content merely to survive rather than to evolve.[100] Haiti's Duvalier, Paraguay's Strossner, Zaire's Mobutu, Ethiopia's Mengistu, and the countless other general-cum-presidents whose avarice for power was limited only by length of their tenure in office did little for the industrial development of their respective countries. In the long run, economic development is key to political stability. But it does not follow that in the short run political stability and conservatism are keys to industrial development. This is particularly true if what is stabilised is 'the political power of a narrow elite which puts its own interests above those of the country's poor majority.'[101] A similar conclusion can be reached regarding the role and significance of the military in economic growth and industrial development. Military expenditure and size neither necessarily help nor hurt economic growth in the Third

World to any significant degree.[102] A positive or negative overall relationship between the two can be detected only by focusing on a specific time period, adopting certain specifications, or limiting the sample of countries studied.[103]

The late 1980s and the 1990s have ushered in an era in which dictatorships are collapsing in rapid succession and being replaced by more democratic regimes, as exemplified by the events in Argentina, Brazil, South Korea, and, more dramatically, in eastern Europe. There are also indications, albeit faint ones, of 'winds of change' blowing across the African continent. There is little evidence to suggest that the democratisation of such regimes will impede their economic and industrial progress or lead to a reversal of their previous achievements. In fact, the economic fortunes of eastern European nations may improve following the abandonment of large-scale, centralised planning. India has indeed managed to carry out massive modernisation plans while maintaining a multi-party form of government. Greater input from the public and changes in decision-making mechanisms and processes will, nevertheless, affect the nature of development plans and the manner in which they are implemented. For instance, growing environmental concerns on the part of an electorate eager to exercise its new voting privileges may curtail the scope of the development policies that Third World leaders once devised without much concern for the ecology. Whether such concerns will bring a halt to large-scale modernisation remains to be seen and largely depends on a willingness to adopt alternative industrialisation strategies and techniques. What is clear is that one-party or military rule can no longer be justified solely on grounds of expediting industrial development.

The direction of Third World industrial development has changed over the past decades, with emphasis on heavy industries gradually giving way to lighter and technologically more advanced ones. In the 1950s, 1960s, and 1970s, hydroelectrical power plants, steel mills, enormous mining operations, and assembly plants were built with unprecedented frequency and formed the very industrial infrastructure of many Third World countries. In the 1980s and 1990s, instead, there are more factories and plants whose products are geared toward expanding markets for household consumer goods such as television sets, refrigerators, stereos, water heaters, and the like.[104] Foreign-owned and controlled assembly plants still predominate in the industrial infrastructure of most Third World countries, but a growing number of these countries have made

significant strides toward adopting and absorbing imported technology. There has also been a concurrent re-orientation of emphasis
toward more advanced industries, particularly in fields such as com-
puter science and nuclear energy. There are few Third World
countries today that do not have active programmes for the development of alternative energy sources, most, for political reasons, preferring nuclear energy over solar power.

Changes in the orientation of industrial projects and development
plans reflect inevitable progress in industry and the subsequent needs
of people. Yet industrialisation is by no means the only arena in
which fundamental changes in the Third World are occurring. There
are equally far-reaching changes taking place in the Third World's
urban landscape and in the social and political attitudes of its population, developments which themselves are in one way or another
directly related to the process of industrialisation. Apart from its
economic and technological ramifications, industrialisation's two
most significant contributions include unprecedented urbanisation
and demographic changes on the one hand and alterations in the
social composition of urban inhabitants and in their attitudes and
cultural orientations on the other. Particularly in the Third World,
there are strong and interconnected consequences arising from
industrialisation, urbanisation, social change, and popular cultural
orientations. Only through a comprehensive study of all of these
developments can a thorough picture of the social and political
make-up of the Third World be attained. These developments are
examined in the following chapters.

NOTES

1 Kevin Clements. *From Left to Right in Development Theory: An Analysis of
the Political Implications of Different Models of Development.* (Singapore: The
Institute of Southeast Asian Studies, 1980), p. 6.
2 Most of these scholars, it should be noted, are political scientists by
training and not economists (e.g. Samuel Huntington, David Apter,
Lucian Pye, etc.).
3 Ronald Chilcote. 'Introduction: Dependency or Mode of Production?
Theoretical Issues', in Ronald Chilcote and Dale Johnson, eds. *Theories
of Development: Mode of Production or Dependency?* (London: Sage, 1983),
p. 9.
4 Kevin Clements. *From Left to Right in Development Theory.* p. 6.
5 Richard Higgot. *Political Development Theory: The Contemporary Debate.*
(London: Croom Helm, 1983), p. 32.
6 Ibid. p. 34.

7 Rosemary Galli. 'Colombia: Rural Development as Social and Economic Control', in Rosemary Galli, ed. *The Political Economy of Rural Development: Peasants, International Capital, and the State.* (Albany, NY: SUNY Press, 1981), p. 15.

8 Kevin Clements. *From Left to Right in Development Theory.* p. 6.

9 Andre Gunder Frank. 'Crisis and Transformation of Dependency in the World-System', in Ronald Chilcote and Dale Johnson, eds. *Theories of Development: Mode of Production or Dependency?* p. 186.

10 Jens Erik Torp. *Industrial Planning and Development in Mozambique.* (Uppsala: The Scandinavian Institute of African Studies, 1979), p. 14.

11 Katherin Marton. *Multinationals, Technology, and Industrialization: Implications and Impact in Third World Countries.* (Lexington, Va: Lexington Books, 1986), p. 26.

12 Carlos Johnson. 'Ideologies in Theories of Imperialism and Dependency', in Ronald Chilcote and Dale Johnson, eds. *Theories of Development: Mode of Production or Dependency?* p. 85.

13 Rosemary Galli. 'Rural Development and the Contradictions of Capitalist Development', in Rosemary Galli, ed. *The Political Economy of Rural Development: Peasants, International Capital, and the State.* p. 214.

14 Ronald Chilcote. 'Introduction: Dependency or Mode of Production? Theoretical Issues'. p. 11.

15 Ernest Feder. 'The World Bank-FIRA Scheme in Action in Temporal, Veracruz', in Rosemary Galli, ed. *The Political Economy of Rural Development: Peasants, International Capital, and the State.* p. 173.

16 Randall Stokes and David Jaffee. 'Another Look at the Export of Raw Materials and Economic Growth'. *American Sociological Review.* vol. 47, no 3, (June 1982), p. 148.

17 Jonathon Chileshe. *Third World Countries and Development Options: Zambia.* (New Delhi; Vikas, 1986), p. 148.

18 Dale Johnson. 'Class Analysis and Dependency', in Ronald Chilcote and Dale Johnson, eds. *Theories of Development: Mode of Production or Dependency?* p. 232.

19 Rosemary Galli. 'Rural Development and the Contradictions of Capitalist Development'. pp. 215–6.

20 Henry Veltmeyer. 'Surplus Labor and Class Formation on the Latin American Periphery', in Ronald Chilcote and Dale Johnson, eds. *Theories of Development: Mode of Production or Dependency?* pp. 204–5.

21 Dale Johnson. 'Class Analysis and Dependency'. pp. 244–5.

22 Rosemary Galli. 'Rural Development and the Contradictions of Capitalist Development'. p. 214.

23 See above, Chapter 1.

24 All data is collected from The World Bank. *World Development Report 1990.* (Oxford: Oxford University Press, 1990), pp. 178–9.

25 Ibid.

26 Jonathon Chileshe. *Third World Countries and Development Options.* p. 145.

27 Richard Higgot. *Political Development Theory.* p. 57.

28 For a critique of the dependency approach see, Carlos Johnson. 'Ideologies in Theories of Imperialism and Dependency'. esp. p. 90.

29 Samuel Mushi. 'Community Development in Tanzania', in Ronald Dore and Zoe Mars, eds. *Community Development*. (London: Croom Helm, 1981), pp. 145–6.
30 Erik Jens Torp. *Industrial Planning and Development in Mozambique*. p. 17.
31 S. C. Dube. *Modernization and Development: The Search for Alternative Paradigms*. (Tokyo: United Nations University, 1988), pp. 6–7.
32 Mohammad Reza Pahlavi. *Answer to History*. (New York: Stein & Day, 1980), pp. 175–7.
33 Vincent Brandt and Man-gap Lee. 'Community Development in the Republic of Korea', in Ronald Dore and Zoe Mars, eds. *Community Development*. pp. 60–1.
34 Bruno Musti de Gennaro. 'Ujamaa: The Aggrandizement of the State', in Rosemary Galli, ed. *The Political Economy of Rural Development: Peasants, International Capital, and the State*. p. 152.
35 Vincent Brandt and Man-gap Lee. 'Community Development in the Republic of Korea'. p. 67.
36 Jonathon Chileshe. *Third World Countries and Development Options*. p. 174.
37 Ibid. p. 53.
38 S. C. Dube. *Modernization and Development*. p. 23.
39 Jonathon Chileshe. *Third World Countries and Development Options*. p. 77.
40 V. R. Gaikwad. 'Community Development in India', in Ronald Dore and Zoe Mars, eds. *Community Development*. pp. 275–88.
41 Jonathon Chileshe. *Third World Countries and Development Options*. p. 41.
42 Donald Keesing. 'Small Population as a Political Handicap to National Development', in Harvey Kebschull, ed. *Politics in Transitional Societies*. (New York: Appleton–Century–Crofts, 1973), pp. 319–20.
43 Ibid. p. 320.
44 Alan Gilbert and Josef Gugler. *Cities, Poverty, and Development: Urbanization in the Third World*. (Oxford: Oxford University Press, 1982), p. 44.
45 Katherin Marton. *Multinationals, Technology, and Industrialization*. pp. 20–1.
46 Ibid. p. 22.
47 Ibid. pp. 23–4.
48 Ibid. p. 37.
49 Jonathon Chileshe. *Third World Countries and Development Options*. pp. 5–6.
50 Katherin Marton. *Multinationals, Technology, and Industrialization*. p. 38.
51 Ibid. pp. 41–2.
52 Ibid. p. 43.
53 Ibid. p. 44.
54 Ibid. p. 43.
55 See, for example, Bruno Musti de Gennaro 'Ujamaa: The Aggrandizement of the State'. p. 153.
56 Bryan Roberts. *Cities of Peasants: The Political Economy of Urbanization in the Third World*. (London: Sage, 1978), p. 110.
57 Joan Nelson. *Access to Power: Politics and the Urban Poor in Developing Nations*. (Princeton, NJ: Princeton University Press, 1979), pp. 25–6.

58 Bryan Roberts. *Cities of Peasants*. p. 110.
59 S. C. Dube. *Modernization and Development*. p. 97.
60 Manning Nash. *Unfinished Agenda: The Dynamics of Modernization in Developing Nations*. (Boulder, Colo.: Westview, 1984), p. 45.
61 Richard Higgot. *Political Development Theory*. p. 35.
62 Dharam Ghai and Cynthia Hewitt de Alcantara. 'The Crisis of the 1980s in Sub-Saharan Africa, Latin America and the Caribbean: Economic Impact, Social Change and Political Implications.' *Development and Change*. vol. 12, (1990), p. 421.
63 Rose Spalding. 'State Power and its Limits: Corporatism in Mexico'. *Comparative Political Studies*. vol. 14, no 2, (July 1981), p. 155.
64 See above, Chapter 1.
65 Richard Sandbrook. 'The State and Economic Stagnation in Tropical Africa'. *World Development*. vol. 14, no 3, (1986), p. 325.
66 Richard Higgot. *Political Development Theory*. p. 37.
67 Concerning the endemic spread of corruption in Third World bureaucracies, Spalding writes: 'Unrestrained corruption can pervade the civil service, statutory boards, and public corporations; what begins as occasional acts of public misconduct, such as occurs in all bureaucracies, spreads like a cancer. The result is a pathological condition of "systemic corruption" – an administration in which "wrong-doing has become the norm", whereas the "notion of public responsibility has become the exception, not the rule"'. Richard Sandbrook. 'The State and Economic Stagnation in Tropical Africa'. p. 326.
68 Sara Berry. 'Work, Migration, and Class in Western Nigeria: A Reinterpretation', in Fredrick Cooper, ed. *The Struggle for the City: Migrant Labor, Capital, and the State in Urban Africa*. (London: Sage, 1988), p. 255.
69 T. G. McGee. 'The Persistence of the Proto-Proletariat: Occupational Structures and Planning of the Future of Third World Cities', in Janet Abu-Lughod and Richard Hay, eds. *Third World Urbanization*. (Chicago: Maaroufa Press, 1977), p. 258.
70 Ibid. pp. 267–8.
71 Bryan Roberts. *Cities of Peasants*. p. 121.
72 Ray Bromley. 'Working in the Streets: Survival Strategy, Necessity, or Unavoidable Evil?', in Joseph Gugler, ed. *The Urbanization of the Third World*. (Oxford: Oxford University Press, 1988), p. 164.
73 Ibid. p. 177.
74 Bryan Roberts. *Cities of Peasants*. p. 130.
75 Ray Bromley. 'Working in the Streets: Survival Strategy, Necessity, or Unavoidable Evil?' p. 169.
76 Val Moghadam. 'Industrial Development, Culture, and Working Class Politics: A Case Study of Tabriz Industrial Workers in the Iranian Revolution'. *International Sociology*. vol. 2, no 2, (June 1987), p. 165.
77 Ibid. p. 164.
78 Katherin Marton. *Multinational, Technology, and Industrialization*. p. 25.
79 Jonathon Chileshe. *Third World Countries and Development Options*. pp. 125–7.
80 Sara Berry. 'Work, Migration, and Class in Western Nigeria: A Reinterpretation'. p. 261.

81 See below, Chapter 4.
82 Paul Cammack, David Pool, and William Tordoff. *Third World Politics: A Comparative Introduction.* (Baltimore, Md: Johns Hopkins University Press, 1988), p. 252.
83 See, for example, import and export statistics for Middle Eastern countries in *The Europa Yearbook 1989*, 30th edn (London: Europa Publications, 1989), volumes 1 and 2.
84 Ibid.
85 Wayne Rohrer. 'Developing Third World Farming: Conflict Between Modern Imparatives and Traditional Ways'. *Economic Development and Cultural Change.* vol. 34, no 2, (January 1986), p. 303.
86 Ibid.
87 Ibid. p. 309.
88 Ibid. p. 308.
89 Ibid. p. 93.
90 See below, Chapter 3.
91 Vincent Brandt and Man-gap Lee. 'Community Development in the Republic of Korea'. p. 92.
92 Rosemary Galli. 'Colombia: Rural Development as Social and Economic Control'. p. 40.
93 Vincent Brandt and Man-gap Lee. 'Community Development in the Republic of Korea'. pp. 62–9.
94 S. C. Dube. *Modernization and Development.* p. 8.
95 See below, Chapter 3.
96 Mehran Kamrava. 'Intellectuals and Democracy in the Third World'. *Journal of Social, Economic, and Political Studies.* vol. 14, no 2, (Summer 1989), pp. 230–1.
97 In order to permit the marketing and distribution of its soft drink in India, the Indian government demanded that the Coca-Cola Co. inform it of the beverage's formula, which the company maintains is secret and known by only a handful of officials. A stalemate ensued, and the Indian government refused permission for Coca-Cola's marketing in India. Instead, an Indian firm began marketing its own version of the soft drink, named Kampa Cola.
98 Yossef Cohen. 'The Impact of Bureaucratic-Authoritarian Rule on Economic Growth'. *Comparative Political Studies.* vol. 18, no 1, (April 1985), p. 133.
99 See, especially, series of chapters in Lucian Pye *et al. Crises and Sequences in Political Development.* (Princeton, NJ: Princeton University Press, 1971).
100 Richard Sandbrook. 'The State and Economic Stagnation in Tropical Africa'. p. 327.
101 Elizabeth Hartman and James Boyce. 'Needles Hunger: Poverty and Power in Rural Bangladesh', in Rosemary Galli, ed. *The Political Economy of Rural Development: Peasants, International Capital, and the State.* p. 206.
102 For more on the relationship between economic development and military rule see Yossef Cohen. 'The Impact of Military-Authoritarian Rule on Economic Growth'.

103 Basudeb Biswas and Rati Ram. 'Military Expenditure and Economic Growth in Less Developed Countries: An Augmented Model and Further Evidence'. *Economic Development and Cultural Change.* vol. 34, no 2, (January 1986), p. 362.
104 Warwick Armstrong and T. G. McGee. *Theatres of Accumulation: Studies in Asian and Latin American Urbanization.* (London: Methuen, 1985), p. 47.

Chapter 3

Urbanisation

One of the most immediate and dramatic consequences of industrial development in the Third World is rampant and unchecked urbanisation. In the decades following the Second World War, urbanisation has proceeded in the Third World at a dizzying pace. Even in countries where significant portions of the population still live in rural areas, sprawling metropolitan centres with large concentrations of urban dwellers, cramped houses and narrow streets, and even high-rise buildings have appeared. Development, in its broadest sense, has entailed not only economic and industrial changes but rapid urbanisation and the growth of cities as well. In fact, the preference of Third World governments and industrial concerns alike to establish factories and plants near existing large urban areas has resulted in the development of a complementary and mutually reinforcing relationship between the two processes of industrialisation and urbanisation. On the one hand, industrialisation serves as a main locus in augmenting the economic and political powers as well as population and geographic size of existing urban centres. Concurrently, cities have facilitated access to and provided the infrastructure, the skilled and the abundant labour, and almost all of the other ingredients that are necessary for industrial growth and development. It is within this context, one which considers industrialisation and urbanisation as intertwined and complementary processes, that both phenomena need to be examined. Industrialisation and its various economic, political, and cultural ramifications for Third World countries were discussed in the previous chapter. Here an examination will be made of the causes, processes, and consequences of urbanisation in the Third World. However, before examining these developments in detail some general observations regarding the nature and characteristics of urbanisation in the Third World are in order.

Urbanisation is commonly understood as a rise in the proportion of people living in urban as opposed to rural areas. More specifically, it refers to the 'transition from a dispersed pattern of human settlement to one concentrated around cities and towns'.[1] In addition to changes in patterns of residence, the change from rural to urban surroundings carries with it definite, though at times gradual and latent, alterations in the values and the behaviour of those involved. Urbanisation involves considerably more than a mere transfer of residence from rural to urban areas. It sets into motion a set of social and cultural processes which fundamentally influence the course and direction of social change and the political culture of the country involved.[2] Rural migrants to the cities, having left their rural surroundings for urban areas in search of better jobs and higher living standards, become subjects of an intense social and cultural turmoil set off by urbanisation and, sooner or later, willingly or through force of time, even the more recent arrivals develop an 'urbanised' culture of their own which resembles neither the values they adhered to in the countryside nor those commonly held by the urban mainstream.

In addition to providing great impetus for social and cultural change, urbanisation has the potential of serving as means for the accumulation of capital, and by inference economic and political power, not only for rural and urban residents but also for the state, local investors, and multinational firms. Some observers have even gone so far as to refer to cities as 'theatres of accumulation', arguing that metropolitan centres provide both the institutional framework and the *modus operandi* for local oligopoly capital, transnationals, and modernising states.[3] Cities, they argue, are not only 'theatres of accumulation' but are also

> centres from which are diffused the culture and values of westernization. They act simultaneously as centres of operation for modern commerce, finance, and industrial activity, and providers of appropriate environment for capital's expansion and deepening. Cities are the arena in which foreign and local capital markets, advertise and sell the philosophy of modernisation, efficiency and growth through imitative lifestyles and consumerism, and, in so doing, undermine non-capitalist production systems and values. In this sense, diffusion is a further means to enhance and to promote the end of capital accumulation.[4]

Throughout the Third World, urban-based industrialisation has become the dominant economic force, gradually supplanting and replacing rurally based, agro-mining economy.[5] Yet viewing urbanisation as merely a process whereby citizens and the state amass wealth, as implied in the above quotation, is not entirely accurate. Undeniably, compared with rural areas, Third World cities do provide favourable investment conditions through which investors and the state can reap substantial profits, aided by the abundance of cheap labour and by a prevalence of 'urban bias' (discussed below) among Third World policy-makers. Nevertheless, there are other developments with equal or greater significance which also result from urbanisation.

A further characteristic of Third World urbanisation is its lack of uniformity within a given country and between different countries and regions. Despite its seemingly frantic pace throughout the Third World, urbanisation remains a largely fragmentary and sporadic process, affecting some cities and altering their geography and demographic make-up fundamentally while only remotely influencing other, often smaller, cities and towns. The extent to which an existing city, a country, or an entire region undergoes urbanisation is dependent upon a variety of factors, ranging from historic traditions to current government policies, economic capabilities, and environmental and demographic considerations. Generally, Latin America as a whole has comprised some of the most urbanised regions of the Third World, with the three countries of the Southern Cone – Chile, Uruguay, and Argentina – ranking among the most urbanised in the world.[6] Contrarily, Sub-Saharan Africa encompasses a number of very sparsely urbanised countries, contrasting sharply with some of the more heavily urbanised countries in the north, notably Morocco, Algeria, Tunisia, Libya, and Egypt.[7]

Such striking contrasts in the levels of urbanisation between Latin America and Africa arise partly from the former's almost uniform colonial experience under Spanish rule as opposed to Africa's partition among several competing colonial powers. Population density levels, access to ports and navigable rivers, and the availability of arable land are also important contributing factors, the abundance of which in Latin America greatly facilitated the establishment and growth there of numerous urban communities. Much of North Africa is endowed with similar geographic features, resulting in its relatively higher rates of urbanisation in comparison with the rest of the continent. In Asia, meanwhile, high concentrations of population density in the easternmost countries has resulted in much higher levels of urbanisation there than has occurred in the Middle East, which is marked by vast expanses of desert and a harsh climate.

Even more striking, and ultimately more important for the study of Third World urbanisation, are vast disparities in levels of urbanisation within almost all Third World countries themselves. Internal regional urban imbalances will be discussed in greater detail in the following sections. Suffice it to say here that the uneven and largely uncontrolled manner in which urbanisation has occurred in much of the Third World has greatly inflated the population, size, and resources of one or at the most two primary cities at the expense of all other cities. Mexico City's population of 18.7 million, 22 per cent of Mexico's total population, Seoul's 9.4 million, 22.3 per cent of South Korea's total population, and Cairo's 6.3 million inhabitants, which comprise 12 per cent of Egypt's total population,[8] are some of the more dramatic examples of the overwhelming urbanisation of one city compared with the others. There are countless other examples of Third World countries where only sparse urbanisation has taken place outside the immediate periphery of the largest city, which is usually the national capital. Third World countries as diverse and distinctive as Afghanistan and Zimbabwe share, among other things, the one salient feature of uneven and skewed urbanisation.

Lack of adequate resources and appropriate infrastructural capacities is another chronic feature of most Third World cities. Throughout the Third World, rapid urbanisation often takes place without the necessary structural transformations that are needed to accommodate large populations.[9] Urbanisation places a high financial burden on Third World governments, which need to meet the rapidly rising demands for urban services such as the provision of water and electricity (in much of the Third World, telephone and gas services are considered luxuries), the building and maintenance of schools and hospitals, the provision of sewage systems and garbage collection, public transport and libraries, and the like. Naturally, public expenditures are higher in larger cities than in intermediate-size or smaller towns.[10] Given the pubic's preference for investing in private enterprises rather than in matters relating to public consumption, investment in necessary urban services is left almost exclusively to the government.[11] It is thus up to Third World governments to provide the necessary urban services, often in the face of uncontrollable population growth rate and the scarcity or complete unavailability of the financial and economic resources that such projects require. The difficulties involved are further compounded by the costs associated with industrialisation, since commercial and industrial users place a much greater demand on public services (especially on utilities) than do urban residents. The increasing demands for and strains on the urban infrastructure is in large part directly related to commercial and industrial activities carried out in urban areas.[12] Thus the more rapid and intense the process of industrialisation, the more burdensome and costly is urbanisation likely to be for Third World governments.

Within this context of rising costs associated with urbanisation, the allocation of resources to urban services and to local administrative networks in the Third World has steadily declined in recent years. In terms of numbers, far fewer employees are assigned local government jobs as opposed to jobs in the national government. While on the average some 57 per cent of the gainfully employed population in the West work for the local government, in the Third World the figure is only 15 per cent.[13] Within the Third World, Asia has the highest pecentage of people working in local administration, 37 per cent, as opposed to 21 per cent in Latin America and only 6 per cent in Africa.[14] The few local administrators who do exist often lack sufficient technical and administrative skills, are not given access to enough funds, and are often forced to work with run-down and left-over equipment.[15] Their work, meanwhile, is dominated by the national political system, most being political appointees rather than elected politicians or experienced policy-makers.[16]

Two reasons underlie this seeming neglect of urban local administration throughout the Third World. To begin with, state-building is in much of the Third World still an on-going process and in many instances continues to be in its embryonic stages. Thus a considerably greater portion of available resources and manpower is directed toward the building of a stronger state and national government. That is why in Africa, for example, where most countries are only now entering their fourth decade of self-rule, the percentage of people working for the national government is overwhelmingly higher than those in local administration. Secondly, there is much greater social prestige attached to jobs in the national government, where wealth, economic mobility, and political power are concentrated, than to positions in local administration. Throughout the Third World, those working for the national government are viewed as having a much more important task at hand than those administering local affairs, even if the former duties are highly menial and without much significance. The belief in the greater importance of positions in the national government is due largely to the public's perception of the government as the builder of a strong, viable state. This perception of the importance of positions in the national government is further strengthened by the government's frequent praises of civil servants working in the various cabinet ministries and by other forms of propaganda. What has resulted have been highly inflated national bureaucracies co-existing alongside under-staffed, ill-equipped, and neglected local administrations. Fattened bureaucracies, coupled with and reinforced by the incessant propaganda of central governments in praise of civil servants and other state employees, are part of larger processes of political development, industrialisation, and, subsequently, urban growth.

URBAN GROWTH

By far the most glaring feature of urbanisation in the Third World has been the incredible rate with which it has proceeded in recent decades. Within a period of two or three decades, sprawling urban centres have appeared in almost all Third World countries, with almost every country having at least one city with several million inhabitants. In the 1970s, there were approximately thirty million more people in the cities of industrialised countries than in the cities of the Third World. By 1985, the size of Third World cities outnumbered those of industrialised countries by some three-hundred million. By the year 2000, there will be twice as many urban residents in the Third World as in Japan and other industrialsed nations.[17]This frantic pace of urban growth in the Third World is primarily caused by two factors, each with its own special significance: natural increases in population, and urban-bound migration from rural areas.[18]Some scholars have attributed population growth to what they have labelled as 'vital revolution', a process whereby 'societies with high birth and death rates move to a situation of low birth and death rates', and to 'mobility revolution', which refers to 'the transformation of societies with low migration rates as they advance to a condition of high migration rates'.[19] Others have argued that the rapid rate of population growth in the Third World is part of a cyclical process not different from that which Europe underwent in the eighteenth and nineteenth centuries, in which a three-stage transition occurs: from high birth and high death rates to high birth and low death rates and, eventually, to low birth and low death rates. The Third World, it is argued, is currently in the second phase of the transition, embodying high rates of fertility and low mortality.[20] Regardless of the terminology used, it is clear that migration and natural population increase are the two highly important factors in bringing about urban growth. Typically, 40 to 50 per cent of urban population growth each year in major Third World metropolitan centres is due to in-migration from the rural areas.[21] According to other estimates, rural–urban migration on average accounts for two-fifths of the urban growth in the Third World.[22] Some observers have argued that the exceptionally rapid rate of population growth in the Third World is due more to natural population increases than to rural–urban migration.[23] Others claim, however, that natural increases within the city become an increasingly important contributor to urban growth as a country urbanises simply because of the sheer size of the urban population as opposed to people in rural areas.[24] This line of argument is, nevertheless, challenged by those who claim that rural exodus is more than compensated for by natural population increases and that rural population continues to grow in absolute numbers despite migration. Although urban centres grew unabatedly, still only about one-fourth of the Third World's population live in urban areas.[25]

To a large extent, high rates of urban growth in the Third World are due to substantially decreased rates of infant mortality resulting from medical advances in recent decades. At the same time, medical technology imported from the West has also resulted in rises in the life expectancy of Third World residents, with Latin America having benefited the most – average life expectancy there being 63 years – followed by southeast Asia – 53 years. Due to chronic famine, wars, and civil strife, Africa's life expectancy remains at only 45 years, the lowest in the Third World.[26] Nevertheless, as a result of concurrent overall rises in life expectancy rates and declines in levels of infant mortality, the populations of Third World countries have in recent decades grown at incredibly high rates (Table 3.1). Improvements in health education, prenatal care, immunisation, sanitation, housing, nutrition, and the availability of medical technology have all combined to significantly lessen the rates of infant mortality in Third World countries. At the same time, however, the effects of social change and improved education have not been sufficiently far-reaching to alter popular cultural values associated with high fertility.[27] In most societies, for example, male offspring assure not

only the longevity of the family name but also the continued economic security of the extended family since they are more likely to
engage in economically productive activities than are female offspring. As a result, reproduction is encouraged until there are at least
one or two male offspring. But even in societies where masculinity
is not a major factor in social status and economic activity, economic
factors are still of overwhelming importance in determining the size
of the family. In some societies wealth often flows from the children
to the parents owing to their productive contribution to the household economy, as in traditional agrarian societies or in newly indus-
trialising ones where younger people are more apt to be absorbed
into the industrial economy. In such places, it only makes economic sense to sustain high levels of fertility. A fertility transition
occurs when the flow of wealth from parents to children becomes of
greater importance. Thus as social and economic structures change,
and with them the role and division of labour within the household
economy is modified, levels of fertility can be expected to decline.[28]
Moreover, the gradual entry of women into the industrial labour
force, where jobs tend to be more stable and structured as opposed
to the informal sector, will also result in declining fertility rates. It is
thus not surprising to find the highest rates of fertility in regions
whose economies lag considerably behind in industrial development,
with the highest rates of population growth being found in Africa,
Asia, and South America respectively (Table 3.2).

In addition to rising rates of fertility and life expectancy and
declining levels of mortality, urban growth in the Third World owes
much to the increasing numbers of rural migrants flocking to the
cities in recent decades. If not necessarily the most determining cause
of urban growth in the Third World, rural–urban migration is
certainly its most conspicuous manifestation. In virtually all Third
World countries, a large and ever-expanding pool of recent migrants
from villages can be found in most major metropolitan centres.
Recent arrivals from the countryside have become an inseparable
feature of the Third World urban landscape. The unimpeded pace
with which rural hopefuls jam into the cities is brought about by a
number of compelling economic as well as social factors. In all cases,
there are a number of 'push' as well as 'pull' factors which compel
rural inhabitants to venture off into the cities in search of better lives
and greater heights of material and cultural enrichment. From the
migrants' perspective, escaping family friction and supervision,
romanticising about city life and rapid social mobility, and prospects

Table 3.1 Population growth rates for selected Third World countries (in percentages per year)

Africa

Algeria	3.1	Cameroon	3.4
Comoros	3.7	Cote d'Ivoire	3.6
Djibouti	4.2	Ghana	3.3
Kenya	4.0	Liberia	3.1
Malawi	3.1	Rwanda	3.3
Swaziland	3.4	Togo	3.0
Uganda	3.3	Tanzania	3.2

South America

Bolivia	2.6	Ecuador	2.9
French Guiana	3.5	Paraguay	3.2
Venezuela	2.8	Honduras	3.4

Asia

Burma	4.6	Iran	3.0
Iraq	3.6	Jordan	3.7
Kuwait	4.5	Nepal	3.4
Pakistan	3.0	Qatar	6.6
Saudi Arabia	4.1	Syria	3.3
UAE	5.8		

Source: *United Nations Demographic Yearbook*, 1986.

Table 3.2 Average population growth rates by continents (in percentages per year)

Africa	3.1
North America	1.6
South America	2.2
Asia	2.6
Europe	0.6

Source: *United Nations Demographic Yearbook*, 1986.

for better employment and higher living standards are all compelling motives to leave rural surroundings for the city. While economic calculations are of great significance in coming to a decision regarding migration, it is often non-economic factors that serve as the 'last straw' which bring the eventual departure about.[29] Broken romances, jealousy over the migration of others, a desire to become an urbanite, and a curiosity to explore the universe that lies beyond the village bounds can all add strength to the economic justifications of migrating to the city.

There are a number of specific factors which contribute to domestic migration in particular political and geographic settings. In Africa, for example, much of the domestic migration in recent years has been due to devastations caused by drought, famine, civil war, and the negative trend in the terms of trade for exporters of primary goods.[30] In countries where civil wars have settled into chronic and bloody stalemates, both in Africa and elsewhere, many rural residents have found refuge in the relative safety of the cities, where rebel activities are not likely to be as intense as they are in the countryside.[31] Similar displacements have taken place in South and Central America, where the rapid deforestation of the Amazon basin has disturbed the land and income supply of rural residents and thus accelerated their migration to nearby cities. These developments do not appear uniformly across the Third World. Nevertheless, three broad sets of factors can be distinguished which cause massive internal migration in almost all Third World countries. These developments, each varying in strength and significance according to prevailing economic and cultural trends, include the consistent adoption of policies by Third World governments which favour urban as opposed to rural development, the so-called 'urban-bias' of Third World policy-makers; the unprecedented growth and development of industrialisation in Third World cities and the ensuing abundance of employment opportunities there at the neglect of rural areas; and, the allure of city life and hopes of assimilation into the urban mainstream.

The most salient feature of Third World policy-making has been its unremitting bend in favour of urban-based industrial and economic development, often completely neglecting the economy, demography, and the social and cultural make-up of rural areas. Available resources are unproportionately allocated to urban areas, and, besides a few isolated examples such as China's Cultural Revolution and more recently Tanzania's Ujamaa movement, governments have made little or no effort to redress the gross inequalities that exist between cities and villages. 'Urban bias', most observers of Third World urbanisation would agree, is a problem endemic to nearly all developing countries, regardless of the ideological propagandas that emanate from their capitals.

The most important class conflict in the poor countries of the world today is not between labour and capital. Nor is it between foreign and national interests. It is between the rural classes and the urban classes. The rural sector contains most of the poverty, and most of the low cost sources of potential advance; but the urban sector contains most of the articulateness, organization, and power. So the urban classes have been able to 'win' most of the rounds of the struggle with the countryside; but in so doing they have made the development process needlessly slow and unfair. Scarce land, which might grow millets and bean sprouts for hungry villagers, instead produces a trickle of costly calories for meat and milk, which few except the urban rich (who have ample protein anyway) can afford. Scarce investment, instead of going to water pumps to grow rice, is wasted on urban motorways. Scarce human skills design and administer, not clean village wells and agricultural extension services, but world boxing championships in show-piece stadia. Resource allocations, within the city and village as well as between them, reflect urban priorities rather than equity or efficiency. The damage has been increased by misguided ideological imports, liberal and Marxian, and by the town's success in buying off part of the rural elite, thus transferring most of the costs of the process to the rural poor.[32]

In addition to infrastructural inadequacies, Third Word rural areas suffer from an unproportional concentration of skilled and trained professionals. In many instances, the percentage of medical doctors, teachers, and engineers residing in cities is incomparably greater than that of rural areas. Most professionals, who would not have attained their exalted positions had it not been for the urban-based educational system, are reluctant to give up the comforts and luxuries of city life for the relative discomforts of villages, unless they are sent there by the government for short periods as part of their tour of duty. Even the educational system in existence in most Third World villages, devised in and directed from urban centres, does not train youngsters to become better farmers, cattle ranchers, or to learn other pertinent subjects. Instead, political indoctrination and national integration receive greater emphasis in the education of village students. They are taught lessons about the national capital and its monuments, about the lives and careers of incumbent political leaders, and are made to memorize the national anthem and appropriate political slogans. The little substantive training that does take place prepares bright villagers for urban jobs.[33]

Related to and in fact a derivative of urban bias is the greater concentration of employment opportunities in the cities. Throughout the Third World, industrial complexes are located in the vicinity of major metropolitian areas (see below). Urbanisation and industrialisation have gone hand in hand throughout the Third World, reinforcing and encouraging one another. Since people have a tendency to move to regions where there are greater employment possibilites, trends in population distribution and growth are determined by the location of job opportunities and thus by prevailing patterns of industrialisation.[34] Within this context, a perpetuating cycle of urbanisation, industrialisation, and migration develops, each reinforcing and accentuating the other. Industrial, economic, and demographic centralisation thus ensues, with cities emerging as centres of industrial power and economic mobility. Local and regional identities and economic commitments, even in the remotest areas, are strained as a result of such centralising forces, leading in turn to greater migration away from the countryside.[35] As a result, it is not necessarily the poorest areas that have the highest rate of out-migration, but those areas that are located relatively close to economically thriving centres.[36] Within the context of hopes to maximise economic gains through better employment, migration is seen not so much as a risk as being based on an aversion to risk, with the small farmer family attempting to diversify its income portfolio through placing its best-suited member in the ever-expanding urban economy.[37]

The social and cultural dimensions of migration are equally significant. Cities form not only centres of industrial and economic wealth but also arenas in which social and cultural values are articulated and dispersed. These values are in turn inculcated among the country's population, both urban as well as rural, through the powerful medium of the electronic media. Throughout the Third World, radio and television programming reflect not merely urban values but in reality values which point toward and indeed often owe their genesis to the West.[38] Few if any programmes explore rural life, much less praise its values, and the few rural-oriented programmes that do exist are designed for purely entertainment purposes rather than the examination of rural issues and concerns. From the start, these programmes were intended for urban audiences rather than rural ones. Often in such shows, rural life is patronisingly depicted as simple, pure, and healthy, its very real ordeals and dilemmas brushed aside by nostalgic representations. Despite widespread illiteracy and under-education both in cities and rural areas, glossy magazines and newspapers also similarly propagate the allure of the city, most of which are riddled with sensationalist journalism and act more as conveyors of new social and cultural fetishes than as reliable sources of news and information. The culture of the city reigns supreme, constantly finding its way through raised antennae and into remote villages and towns. Cities appear to those looking at them from the outside – and even to inside viewers – as arenas within which all economic and social progress are formulated and realised. The larger the city, and thus the more intense its apparent role as progenitor of social and technological advancement, the greater is its attraction to those who are only too eager to abandon their stagnant lives and squalid rural surroundings. The state's official ideology, meanwhile, its continuous praise of science and technology and its promises of impending industrial miracles only accentuate the desire to become urbanised.

Rural–urban migration embodies a number of further features involving the manner of the move itself, its duration, and the ratio of those who migrate by gender, education, and other characterstics. Each of these features can have significant demographic and economic ramifications. The manner in which migration takes place, either direct or in stages, can either proliferate the population size of one primary city or those of several smaller ones. Migration can be conducted either directly, in the form of a direct relocation from the village to the city, or in stages, when the migrant moves from farm to village, from village to town, and from town to city. Owing largely to the costs involved, both material and emotional, the typical migrant manages only one or two stages in his lifetime.[39] That is why smaller cities in the Third World act primarily as rural agricultural service centres and maintain predominantly rural characteristics.[40] Forms of entertainment and other manifestations of culture in these cities revolve around rural idioms, especially as expressed through popular plays and music. The local economy is also geared toward servicing the needs of farmers and rural artisans, who often pass through such cities on their way to market their products in larger cities. Stage migration is, consequently, an important factor in absorbing some of the emotional, social, and economic perils associated with migration and prepares the migrant for some of the more challenging difficulties which await in the larger city. [41]

A second feature of migration is the length of its duration and its permanence versus temporary character. Generally, migration is either seasonal and temporary, or is permanent and involves gradual, complete assimilation and settlement into the city. Within the context of this dichotomy, three principal patterns stand out: temporary migration of men separated from their families; family migration to urban areas followed by return migration to the community of origin; and the permanent establishment of an urban family household.[42] Temporary migration usually peaks during the winter months, when most farmers and agricultural labourers are made redundant until the next crop season. Even when agricultural production is uninterrupted by seasonal changes or by natural calamities, very few subsistence farmers can hope to survive entirely from the products of their land or from domestic animals. Thus wage migration has become a permanent part of the village economy, with younger villagers dividing their labour between the informal urban sector and the rural agricultural sector.[43] Such short-term migrants are themselves divided into 'target' and 'cyclic' migrants. Target migrants return to their original rural surroundings and line of work when they reach their specific goals in the city, which almost invariably involve the accumulation of money. Cyclic migrants, meanwhile, combine rural and urban opportunities into a single, integrated field of opportunity and have a lifetime pattern of moving between the urban and the rural environments.[44]

Another feature of migration is the differences in the rates of migration across the sexes, levels of education, and age. One of the most noticeable characteristics of migration is its division along gender lines. In Asia and Africa, male migrants outnumber female migrants, while in Latin America the trend tends to be the opposite.[45] This development is due largely to the widespread prevalence of consumerist and comfort-oriented attitudes among Latin America's middle and upper classes in the face of rampant poverty and indigence of the lower classes.[46] There is thus great demand for domestic help in the cities, a field in which women have traditionally had a corner. In Asia and in most of Africa, on the other hand, the generally positive economic conditions of the 1970s, fuelled largely by the 'oil boom', created numerous job opportunities for manual labourers, especially in the growing construction industry. A pattern has thus gradually emerged throughout the Third World, with women comprising most of the migrants in Latin America and men predominating in Asia and Africa.

Irrespective of gender, the overwhelming majority of immigrants everywhere in the Third World tend to be unmarried young adults.

Even if married, they usually have very little at stake in their village community, lacking resources or control over sources of power such as land, livestock or seeds.[47] Within young adults, the propensity to migrate rises with the level of education.[48] Higher levels of education endow migrants with better skills and higher chances of securing positions in the formal sector, even if only at the clerical level. Moreover, better education eases some of the perils of migration, an advantage not afforded to the less educated and poorer members of the community.[49] In general, female migrants are less educated than male migrants, because existing village social structures tend to give higher priority to the education of male children.[50] This in turn reinforces the greater preponderance of male migrants in comparison to females.

The decision to migrate is rarely reached in solitude and with ease. It frequently involves a period of soul-searching and emotional trauma, although the younger city-dreamers are often only too eager to abandon their villages. The intensity and nature of aspirations, information about alternative possibilities, contacts, availability of financial resources, and a sense of capacity to cope with a strange environment all influence the decision of whether or not to migrate.[51] Close relatives are often consulted and their advice is sought, even if only as a gesture of courtesy when a definitive decision has already been made. The advice of those who have already passed through the uncertain road of migration weighs heaviest in the decision to migrate, as they provide valuable information about an unfamiliar and seemingly hostile environment. When the villager does eventually migrate, these 'old-timers' often provide food, shelter, connections, and a general sense of security. Migration, it is important to realise, takes place within a certain cultural milieu of relationships and expectations that support the move.[52]

Even when migration assumes a permanent character and few thoughts of returning to the village are entertained, most migrants retain strong bonds with their place of birth. The basic security of village life, epitomized by relatively inexpensive housing, access to land, and opportunities to trade, coupled with emotional and personal ties, combine to retain the attraction of the village and its affairs to those who have migrated.[53] Migrants remain particularly interested in economic developments occurring in their villages, especially concerning matters such as control over, or at least access to, land and water.[54] The economic bonds between migrants and their native community are also reinforced through the remittances which migrants frequently send back to their families. Remittances are either in the form of cash or in basic household goods such as heaters, radios, television sets, and other similar durable items which most villagers consider to be luxuries.[55] Such remittances are part of a self-enforcing, cooperative, contractual arrangement, or rather more an implicit understanding, between the migrant and those family members who stayed behind, and are designed to maximise both sides' mutual benefits.[56] 'Remittances', some observers have noted,

> may be seen as one component of a longer-term understanding between a migrant and his or her family, an understanding that may involve many aspects including education of migrant, migration itself, coinsurance, and inheritance. The family group as a whole can potentially gain from such arrangements, though the distribution of gains between the migrant and home may be a matter for bargaining, and each may be the net beneficiary at different phases. Indeed, it is precisely this sequencing of gains that help to render an understanding self-enforcing in addition to any feelings of mutual altruism.[57]

Over time, the frequency of remittances decreases as the migrant's length of residence in the city increases.[58] However, the village community and kinsfolk never lose their original place in the migrant's heart altogether.

SQUATTER SETTLEMENTS

Once the migrant arrives in the city, he or she typically ends up residing in one of the shantytowns that are located in the periphery of the city. Such shantytowns, also called 'transitional urban settlements',[59] can generally be divided into three different economic levels. The most prevalent are low-income bridgeheads, populated by recent arrivals with few marketable skills and comprised of dilapidated homes and shacks. In these settlements, access to the basic necessities of life is all-important. Also prevalent are the so-called slums of hope, in which income becomes available for items other than basic necessities such as food and housing. Radio and television sets are the most sought-after items which frequently find their way into such slums. While comprised of residents who are not as poverty-striken as some other migrants, these settlements are, nevertheless, also made up of huts that are a far cry from conventional housing. Lastly, a few squatters are able to move out of slum settlements altogether and become part of a group of middle-income status-seekers. Mostly made up of migrants whose venture into the city has reaped them relatively substantial economic fruits, these former squatters have a choice of location and are able to upgrade the quality of their housing.[60]

Despite the possible social and economic mobility of some rural migrants, most spend their residence in the city in one shantytown or another. In each country or region, these squatter settlements are often popularly given condescending names denoting their inferior social and economic status. In Latin America, they are commonly referred to as 'barrios', 'barriadas', 'favelas', 'ranchos', 'colonias', 'proletarias', or 'callampas'; in North Africa, especially in Algeria, they are known as 'bidonville' or 'gourbiville'; in India they are called 'bustees'; 'Kampongs' in Malay; 'barung-barongs' in the Philippines; 'gecekondu' districts in Turkey; and 'halab-abads' in Iran.[61] Despite their different names, however, squatter settlements share a number of strikingly common characteristics. Regardless of where it takes place, squatting is essentially a struggle for survival by a group of displaced villagers. It is an effort to survive and to succeed in an environment that is radically different from the familiar surroundings of the village community. Although each region and country has its own unique culture and values, the process of becoming part of the urban society by those previously excluded from it bears remarkable similarities across the board. Squatter settlements are established, conduct their internal dynamics, and respond to external pressures in a more or less uniform fashion throughout the Third World.

Squatting is an openly defiant act, with squatters taking over almost any urban land which is left undeveloped and whose owners, whether public or private, do not reside nearby. In a sense, the absence of official or private efforts to curtail squatting helps perpetuate the further establishment of such settlements. Over time, the success of land takeovers in turn encourages more squatting by other migrants in search of places of residence.[62] It is, nevertheless, erroneous to assume that squatters like squatting or prefer such settlements to conventional housing. Squatting does, no doubt, involve an element of opportunism.[63] However, there can be no denial in the fact that rapid urban growth in the face of inelastic land supplies pushes up the cost of urban housing beyond the means of recent arrivals from the countryside.[64] Housing famine and urban landlessness compel migrants to reside wherever a place with a semblance of residential dwelling can be found. Seldom are migrants fortunate enough to find accommodation in the centre of the city or in houses that were once occupied by former elites and aristocrats.[65] They are thus forced to occupy land that is left barren, setting up in it shacks made up of whatever materials they can find. Squatter shacks are typically made out of cardboards, tinfoils and other types of scrap metal, and any other usable materials that can be found. In older and more settled establishments, such as those found in Latin America, brick and mud huts can also be found. The land available for squatting is almost always located on the periphery of the city, where squatters can also get some reprieve from harassment by the authorities. The original establishment of squatter settlements on the city's periphery is often based on prior social relationships among the invaders, such as being members of the same ethnic or tribal minority or from the same general geographic area. Subsequent settlements also depend on having some type of common bond with the existing squatters, particularly in the form of shared ethnic or linguistic background.[66]

Within the squatter community itself, there are economic differences and subdivision. Such differences are often based on the types of dwelling that squatters reside in, and the degree of control and ownership which they exercise over their place of residence. Generally, the squatters' economic powers and status within the settlement grow with the length of their residence. Whereas younger migrants and recent arrivals tend to be more impoverished, those with greater experience in the urban arena and a longer history of residence in the settlement are more likely to be economically better off. While many never gain complete ownership over the land where they reside, they often become its *de facto* owner by default, to the point of renting it to others or converting it into stores and shops. Many, however, are not as fortunate and are forced to engage in all types of demeaning activities, from prostitution to sifting through garbage, in order to eke out a living.

Based on their ownership of and/or residence in various types of settlements, ten broad categories of squatters can be distinguished. They include:

1 the owner squatter, who owns his quarters and has set it up on any vacant land he can find. This type of squatter is the most common variety in the Third World;

2 the squatter tenant, usually a recent migrant and very poor, who rents from the owner squatter;

3 the squatter landlord, renting out huts at exorbitant profit;

4 the squatter holdover, a former tenant who has ceased paying rent but is not evicted by the landlord out of fear;

5 the speculator squatter, for whom squatting is a profitable venture, hoping eventually to acquire the land he has squatted on;

6 the store squatter or occupational squatter, who establishes a small lockup store on the land he does not own, mostly selling small items and some foodstuff;

7 the semi-squatter, who built his hut on private land and has since come to terms with the land's owner;

8 the corporate squatter, often formed out of a collectivity of squatters to protect it from outside intruders, public and private;

9 the floating squatter, who lives on a boat or a junk which is floated into the city's harbour. The float may be rented to other squatters, as in Hong Kong, and often serves as both a family home and as a workshop;

10 the cemetery squatter, made-up of poor and recent arrivals who reside in cemeteries (usually over graves that are covered by a tomb) or on the grounds of temples and other places of worship. This type of squatting is common especially in Islamic countries such as Egypt and Pakistan.[67]

One of the significant characteristics that these different types of settlement have in common is their role as agents of socialisation. This role is fulfilled in two ways. To begin with, squatter settlements often form the first lenses through which migrants see the city. Since squatter settlements are usually the first and often the primary base from which migrants undergo the process of urbanisation, they play an extremely important role in shaping the migrant's perception of and participation in the urban culture. Within this context, shanty-towns and squatters give a sense of preparedness and a measure of security to their residents through endowing them with some social and cultural understanding, however distorted and minimal, of the inner workings of urban life. They are, in essence, 'breeding-grounds for a new form of social organisation which is adaptive to the socio-economic requisites of survival in the city'.[68] Moreover, socialisation is achieved in squatter settlements through the development of internal organisations and associations within the squatter community itself. Neighbourhood communities assume greater importance among lower income levels than among those with higher income, largely because the former have little resources or time for engaging in outside activities such as travelling or going to the theatre. Leisurely activities are thus confined mostly to the neighbourhood, a confinement arising more out of necessity than choice. The associations that spring up in squatter settlements are almost always highly informal and frequently temporary, and are often centred around such activities as sports (often football), cock-fights and card-playing, group picnics, or venturing off into the city or spending time in the local coffeehouse. Such informal networks of social organisation facilitate adjustment to the urban environment through providing solidarity and support, emotionally as well as socially.[69] Often lonely and alienated from the surrounding urban culture, migrants often find their squatter settlement to be one of the few arenas from which they do not feel socially and culturally detached. Shantytowns are filled with those who are in pursuit of similar dreams and have mostly endured the same difficulties as others have. This provides a reassuring environment in which migrants are surrounded by people who at least understand and share each other's predicaments.

Within squatter settlements, kinship is by far the most important factor in determining a migrant's social and economic status and his general welfare. When migrants reach the city, they usually move in with a relative or fellow villager who possesses some knowledge of the city. The role of this connection is crucial, for it determines the migrant's place of stay, the type and degree of assistance he receives, his first job or line of work, and thus his economic status. Each migrant in turn helps several of his kinsfolk and friends settle into shantytowns by providing them with residence, tips about city life and securing a job, moral support, and other forms of assistance. Subsequent moves within the city tend to be made with reference to pre-existing groups of relatives and friends elsewhere.[70] In contrast, migrants who come to the city without any connections or prior relatives usually end up in even more dire economic circumstances, having to compete with other migrants for scarce jobs and places of residence.[71] Once a stranger in his neighbourhood and from others in his shantytown, a migrant may end up leading the life of a stranger throughout his stay in the city.[72]

Although they are left out of statistical studies, squatter dwellings are a major part of urban households and, naturally, are not without value.[73] In Latin America in the 1970s, squatters housed 10 to 20 per

cent of the urban population.[74] Given their size, both in terms of
population and the geographic area that they cover, squatters can
potentially be centres of intense economic activity. Within larger
settlements, residents can generate income by serving as shopkeepers,
craftsmen, preachers, and even dentists and physicians.[75] Even more
significant is the marketing of squatter dwellings. Squatter housing
markets tend to behave as economically rational entities which
valuate dwelling units similar to conventional markets.[76] Like other
strata of society, the poor are rational and engage in tradeoffs which
improve their living standards.[77] Although their choices are limited,
they nevertheless do try to improve their economic lot through the
meagre economic means that are available. This they may accomplish
by subletting or even selling their dwellings at exorbitant prices.[78]
During the first few months after arrival, as a result, much of a new
migrant's salary is spent on paying rent.[79] Those squatters who in
various ways – by either money, coercion, or sharpness of mind – lay
claim to their place of residence, meanwhile display remarkable
vigour and ingenuity in improving their living conditions and their
dwellings, thus increasing the monetary value of their shacks.[80]

Despite their role as agents of socialisation and as arenas in which
migrants feel a greater emotional and cultural affinity with their
surroundings, squatter settlements are far from being uniform and
undivided entities. They are often comprised of migrants from
different regions, each with distinct ethnic backgrounds and dialects.
Often times the only characteristic that residents of squatter settlements share is their common struggle to survive in the urban
environment and not shared places of birth or dialect. Internally,
shantytowns can be sharply divided along ethnic, linguistic, caste,
economic, and to a lesser extent religious lines.[81] Among these
differences, ethnic cleavages stand out, although there are other
social and economic gradations among the poor that exist but are felt
mostly only among themselves.[82] Differences arising from one's caste
can also be highly important means of differentiation among the poor
and residents of squatter settlements. However, caste and the social
and cultural significances attached to it are largely important in the
Indian subcontinent only and cannot be considered as a major force
in other parts of the Third World. Religious differences are also
important, particularly in instances when a religious minority group
happens to be an ethnic minority as well, such as the Sunni Kurds in
Iran, the Karen in Burma, and the Druze in Lebanon. Lastly, economic differences among members of the same squatter community

often also serve as means of causing internal divisions within the establishment. Such economically based differences originate not necessarily from the extent of the resources which migrants bring into the city but from the different types of jobs in which they engage after having found a place of residence. The majority of squatters are compelled by the force of circumstances to accept whatever menial jobs that come their way, be it sweeping streets, working as coolies, or becoming domestic servants to the middle and upper classes. Some, however, find their way into the lumpen-proletariat and even on to the middle classes.[83]

By far the most important sources of differentiation among residents of squatter settlements are differences in ethnic background and, consequently, differences in accent and dialect. With the bonds and loyalties of nationhood still fragile in much of the Third World and subject to periodic bursts of regional separatism, ethnicity continues to be a volatile and powerful force in many Third World countries. Within the context of migration and squatting, ethnicity's importance is greatly accentuated as it becomes not only a source of identity and belonging but also a means of support and security. The poorer and less educated a person, the more dependent he is likely to become on his co-ethnics for security and progress, as his alternative channels of non-ethnic assistance are limited.[84] When kinsfolk and relatives are not available, migrants and squatters rely on their co-ethnics for assistance and aid. Ethnically based cliques and segregationist tendencies within squatter settlements are thus not rare, tempered only by the struggles of surviving from one day to the next.

REGIONAL IMBALANCES

Another equally important characteristic of urbanisation throughout the Third World is its acute rate of unevenness within individual countries. In almost all Third World countries, there are regions with intense concentrations of urbanisation that are located not far from areas with extremely low urban density. Urbanisation within the same country is a highly uneven process, engulfing some regions to the point of saturation while barely touching others. Between urban centres of the same country, there frequently are glaring unevennesses in the pattern in which industry, economic power, and populations are concentrated. Larger cities encompass in them concentrations of social and political infrastructure – in the form of paved roads, housing, better and more modern facilities, government bureaus, better equipped libraries and hospitals, etc. – while smaller cities receive only token attention and are often left to develop as auxiliaries to larger metropolitan centres. Regional imbalances have, consequently, become one of the most striking features of Third World urbanisation.

Based on their population and geographic size, cities in the Third World can be divided into three types. The most noticeable are large metropolitan centres with highly dense concentrations of housing, roads, population, and office buildings. Examples of such sprawling giants, often called 'primary' cities, are most national capitals in small countries – such as Taipei in Taiwan, Seoul in South Korea, and Lima in Peru – or are regional capitals in large countries, as are Rio de Janeiro and Sao Paulo in Brazil, and Calcutta, Bombay, and Madras in India. 'Secondary' cities, in contrast, are smaller, with populations ranging between 100,000 to 2.5 million. Lastly, there are small cities and towns which are actually rural–urban interface centres, with populations downward of 100,000 depending on the particular characteristics of the country concerned.[85]

Primary cities can be found in Third World countries that are highly urbanised and have achieved considerable advances in industrialisation (e.g. South Korea, Argentina, and Taiwan), as well as in countries where high rates of urbanisation coexist with large-scale poverty (e.g. Egypt, El Salvador, Lebanon, Panama, Peru, and Chile). Also, in countries that have remained predominantly rural, existing and relatively small enclaves of urban population tend to be concentrated into one primary city.[86] Afghanistan is one such country, where the majority of the population is still comprised of tribes living in the country's central, mountainous plateau. The urbanised population, meanwhile, is concentrated almost entirely in Kabul, the national capital, as well as in some of the country's much smaller secondary cities. Similarly, most of the African countries located on or near the Sahara desert, especially Libya, Chad, Niger, and Sudan, have one large primary city in the face of mostly rural and tribal populations. Population concentration is by far the most glaring characteristic of primary cities, which are often home to an incredibly large percentage of the national population (Table 3.3). Yet unproportional concentrations of population are only one of the many features that set primary cities apart. Practically everywhere in the Third World, primary cities predominate in the politics, economy, and cultural life of the country. Industries, services, capital and resources, and political power are all concentrated in such cities, which are often considerably larger in size and population than the next largest city.[87] Whether national or regional capitals, primary cities exert an overbearing influence over the life of the entire country and have significant impacts on nearby secondary and smaller cities. In larger countries where there are a number of different primary cities, the national capital, which is frequently the largest in size and population, often invariably surpasses the wealth, power, and the concentration of industry found in other primary cities.

Table 3.3 Percentage of population in primary cities compared with national population in selected countries

	Population in primary city (in millions)	National population (in millions)	%
Algiers	1.7	23.85	7.2
Baghdad	4.6	17.1	27.0
Cairo	6.2	50.7	12.2
Dar es Salaam	1.4	23.2	6.0
Mexico City	10.35	84.3	12.3
Nairobi	1.3	22.8	5.7
Seoul	9.6	42.5	22.6
Tehran	8.7	53.9	16.1

Source: John Paxon, ed. *The Statemen's Yearbook, 1990–1991*. 127th edn. New York: St Martin's Press, 1990.

The seemingly unrestrained growth of primary cities can principally be attributed to three interrelated developments. To begin with, primary cities receive special attention from governments since they often symbolise national identity, industrial development, and worldly stature. For both the people and politicians alike, massive and overgrown cities evoke images of national strength and pride, a sense of 'coming of age'. For political leaders, such cities assume special importance since not only are they often the seat of government but, more important, are testimony to the development and military and economic prowess of the country. To turn one of these cities into a nerve-centre of internal and international trade is often seen as one of the first steps toward building a modern nation-state. A conscious policy is thus promulgated through which one or a few of the country's largest cities are portrayed as symbolic of the nation's pride. This is done not only through concentrating industrial, economic, and political power in these primary cities, but also through erecting national monuments and edifices, often in honour of past heroes or present leaders, through which the country's political leadership hopes to signal its present tenure in power and supposed contribution to history. The building of the *Shahyad* (King's Memorial) Square in Tehran by the late Shah of Iran, the gigantic People's Palace in Bucharest by Nicolae Ceausescu, the *Malagan* Palace by Ferdinand Marcos in Manila, and the huge statue of Kim Il Sung in the centre of Pyonyang are all representative of efforts by Third World leaders not merely to salute themselves but to enhance their nation's prestige and pride both among the domestic population and abroad.

The growth of primary cities is also facilitated by the existence of infrastructures which make further industrial and economic development there feasible. Primary cities are more likely to have better resources such as roads, buildings, utilities, and other forms of government services. The higher availability of skilled manpower and better educational facilities in larger cities further accentuates the concentration of factories, workshops, and businesses there in comparison with smaller, secondary cities and towns.[88] Similar considerations also figure prominently in the decisions of multinational firms seeking to invest in Third World countries, as these firms often prefer to situate their local operations near national capitals instead of in more remote areas. Apart from political considerations, Third World governments for the most part welcome a concentration of economic and industrial activities in primary cities as an astute means of achieving national development. It is often assumed that the benefits of investments which are concentrated in large metropolitan centres will eventually trickle down to other parts of the country and reduce urban–rural and inter-regional disparities. The development of the centre is thought to result in the concurrent development of the periphery.[89] This assumption has proved to be erroneous, however, as the growth of large metropolitan centres often produces 'backwash effects' which drain rural hinterlands of their capital, labour, and raw material.[90] At times, the growth of large cities may eventually lead to the growth of smaller ones, especially in cases where the largest city seems to have reached its growth saturation, as has for example Seoul, South Korea. However, such a trickling down is unlikely to occur unless the largest city has reached the limits of its growth in terms of demography, geographic space, and the capacity of the government to provide public services and utilities. Even when such a point is reached and the ensuing limitations have become insurmountable, they are hardly realised by the general public or are admitted to by the government.

A final reason for the overwhelming growth of primary cities as opposed to secondary and smaller cities is their higher rate of in-migration from rural areas. Secondary cities have generally played a weak role in absorbing population increases in the Third World or in creating a more balanced spatial distribution of population.[91] At the same time, cities with higher levels of income and more diverse and secure employment tend to have higher in-migration and lower out-migration rates than do other cities.[92] Since there are considerably higher prospects for securing long-term employment in the industrial sector, located as they mostly are in or near the largest city, more migrants choose primary cities as their eventual destination. For them, secondary cities serve only as temporary stopping-off points in which they may earn some money toward their journey on to the largest city.[93] Added to the actual economic advantages of employment in primary cities is the general perception, by both rural as well as urban populations, that living conditions are generally better in larger metropolitan areas than in smaller cities.[94] This perception, as earlier mentioned, is deliberately cultivated by the government through architectural campaigns and other forms of propaganda directed toward acheiving specific political ends.

Secondary cities are next in size and are often considerably smaller in geographic area, population, and significance than the national capital or other primary cities. Secondary cities lack much of the political status, social and cultural sophistication, and the economic vitality and diversity of primary cities, although the quality of social services there is still much better than in smaller towns and in villages.[95] Public services do exist in secondary cities and are on the increase, at times owing to local initiative and finance, though their growth is not as fast as in the largest cities. In contrast to primary cities, the economic base of secondary cities is dominated not by big industry and huge manufacturing plants but by the informal tertiary sector and by small-scale industries. This does not mean that secondary cities are not capable of having and supporting large-scale manufacturing establishments, and some often do. For the most part, however, secondary cities grow without the benefit of large-scale manufacturing establishments.[96] Bureaucrats, office workers, and other civil servants form a considerable portion of the employed classes in secondary cities. However, the proportion of such white-collar employees in secondary cities is much lower compared with those found in primary cities. Instead, jobs in services and in small-scale industries, mostly in family-owned and operated stores and workshops, and in the informal tertiary sector, such as various types of street vending and temporary employment, form the major types of economic activities in which residents of secondary cities engage. Stores selling small consumer goods such as bicycles, clothes, watches, automobile parts, herbs, and rugs, as well as shops specialising in fixing flat tyres, taking photographs, and carpentry are where the majority of employment opportunities in secondary cities lie. Such a predominance of small-scale industry appears to be a mixed blessing: on the one hand, it does not generate enough income or employment for those outside the families that own and operate them and its rate of profits returned is not great. On the other hand, small-scale industry provides low-cost goods and services for those with low income and acts as a potential source for further investments. [97]

Examining the various types of economic activities that predominate in secondary cities is important in understanding the demographic and sociological make-up of their residents. Secondary cities are mostly comprised of long-term residents who have migrated there from nearby villages in their youth and have decided to reside there permanently. Most secondary city residents are, therefore, only first or second generation urbanites and have relatives and kin in surrounding towns and villages. There is also a sizeable portion of migrants en route to primary cities who temporarily stay and work in secondary cities in order to augment their available resources before going on. Since secondary cities often form the geographic link between outlying villages and small towns and the primary cities, they serve as important transportation and communication links.[98] This factor makes them a favourite stopping-off area for migrants, many of whom find temporary employment in the vicinity of the city's bus terminal, where there is usually a flurry of informal economic activity, or in the local bazaar or marketplace, where low-skilled jobs in the tertiary sector abound. Generally, the paucity of opportunities for upward economic mobility in secondary cities reduces their retention rate of migrants and increases their rate of poverty and underemployment.[99]

While Third World governments allocate considerable resources and investments for establishing, maintaining, and modernising social and economic infrastructures and public services in primary cities, secondary and smaller cities often suffer from official negli- gence and structural disrepair. Government-run services such as the public transportation system, utilities, schools, and the medical clinics and hospitals that are located in secondary cities tend to suffer from lower quality and standards than those found in primary cities. In addition to the sparsity of direct government investments, second- ary cities are also less likely to become regional bases for inter- national or even domestic trade considering the reluctance of most multinational firms to base their local operations there. Nevertheless, there are a few secondary cities in the Third World which receive special government attention either owing to their potential for tourism or because of their historic or political significance. This special attention is often crystallised in the form of well-kept public services and impressive resort complexes that are geared more for foreign tourists than domestic visitors. Coastal towns with a favour- able climate are often among such secondary cities to which Third World governments pay special attention, especially in Latin America and the Caribbean, as are those cities that are outgrowths of ancient and historic places or events. The popularity of these cities with both foreign and to a lesser extent domestic tourists often prompts governments to allocate more resources to them than they otherwise would. Similar favoured treatment is also often given to smaller cities that happen to be birthplaces of prominent politicians and national leaders.

Last in terms of urban population, economic and industrial strength, and political and administrative significance are small cities and towns. These small cities are often geographically located in between outlying villages and the regional secondary and primary cities, serving mostly as agricultural service and distribution centres. Such cities often grow out of existing rural centres or newly estab- lished industrial growth poles that are frequently centred around a single plant, such as an oil refinery, a silo, a salt mine, or a sugar cane factory. With the growth of population and industrial infrastructures over time, these old villages or new towns gradually come to assume something of an urban character. In reality, however, most small cities and towns are overgrown villages that have paved roads and the other public amenities from which most rural areas have yet to benefit. Economically, the employment base of small cities is slightly different from that of secondary cities since most of the economically active population in small towns are in the employ of a single large plant or factory around which the economic life of the community revolves. Similar to secondary cities, however, small cities and towns have numerous family-owned and operated shops and stores. Nevertheless, great variations in wealth and status among the inhabitants of these cities are often difficult to detect.

CONCLUSION

As the above examination demonstrates, urbanisation embodies with it a number of fundamental structural difficulties with which most Third World governments are unable to deal adequately. These problems include the seemingly endless stream of rural migrants to major metropolitan areas, their subsequent residence in sprawling squatter settlements located in the periphery of cities, and their contribution to uneven rates of population growth and varying degrees of urbanisation within the same country. For the most part, Third World governments have been unable to halt or at least to slow down the rate at which these developments have been taking place. In most of the Third World, the unimpeded persistence and growth of such difficulties arise from the government's preoccupation in bringing about rapid industrial development, often with little regard for the ensuing ramifications. Embroiled in a race to lessen their industrial and technological inferiority vis-à-vis the West, Third World governments frequently ignore or pay insufficient attention to the less desirable side-effects that arise from development. Even in countries where the negative consequences of hurried industrial development and rampant urbanisation have been detected, there is often a conspicuous lack of political will and conviction to deal with them in a decisive manner.

The unimpeded flow of rural migrants to the cities is clearly one such ramification of Third World urbanisation which for a variety of reasons has not been curtailed. Migration of rural inhabitants, and with it their subsequent residence in subhuman conditions in squatters and ghettos, is a significant problem which, if left unabated, can and in fact has resulted in widespread social and political disruptions. More important, the misery which migrants unwittingly undergo during and after their migration to the cities – the depravation and degradation which they had never experienced before – can under no circumstances be justified in the name of progress and development. Third World cities can hardly support their indigenous populations, and they are completely incapable of supporting the ever-expanding pool of migrants. Migration is, undoubtedly, an extremely serious and volatile problem, one which Third World governments desperately need to tackle but are hopelessly ill-prepared for.

Four broad policy measures can be adopted to curtail rural–urban migration: direct control over population mobility by the central government; controlling rates of urban income vis-à-vis rural income; rural development policies; and the promotion of rural education.[100] Each of these policy initiatives requires strong commitment and the allocation of considerable resources by the government, requirements that few Third World governments are willing to meet even if they had the resources to do so. For example, establishing direct and effective control over the entire population and monitoring their movement from rural areas to the cities requires an enormous bureaucratic machinery. Nevertheless, two governments, China and North Korea, have long established severe restrictions on population mobility and have met with notable successes. For example, the population of the North Korean capital, Pyongyang, has remained constant at approximately 1,500,000 for almost ten years, and in Shanghai the actual size of the city's population decreased from 7.2 million in 1957 to about 5.7 million in 1972–73.[101] In North Korea and China, control over the mobility of the population is established by an overwhelming bureaucracy that controls almost all aspects of the people's life. Temporary visits to major Chinese cities by those living in rural areas are allowed but long-term residence is illegal and require registration with the appropriate authorities. Avoiding such registration is all but impossible.[102]

Despite the workability of such drastic measures to stop rural migration in China and North Korea, such policies remain highly costly and are too controversial to be practised by less authoritarian governments. They are also far less easy to enforce in countries that lack the overall totalitarian doctrinal beliefs and political mechanisms of the Chinese and North Korean governments. Much more practical and considerably less costly is the attempt to bring greater parity in the rates of income and the general levels of economic well-being that exist in rural and urban centres. As discussed earlier, the principal reasons underlying rural–urban migration are economic. Increasing rural income levels by themselves will not help and is in fact likely to increase migration since more villagers will be able to afford to migrate. Instead, what is needed are adequate measures that would hamper the growth of urban income while maintaining the purchasing power of the public. Narrowing the income gap between the urban and rural areas through stabilizing urban incomes is one of the most effective ways of reducing the flow of migrants.[103] At the same time, increasing the productivity levels of rural areas through the promulgation of rurally oriented development programmes, thus increasing the general wealth of rural residents, narrows the income differentials of rural versus urban areas and reduces the rate of internal migration.[104] Concurrent with the promotion of rural development is the need to place greater emphasis on rural education, not merely in the actual number of rural teachers and schools but, more important, in the quality of teaching. Instead of preparing bright young villagers for jobs that can be found only in the cities, rural schools need to reorient their focus in the direction of indigenous rural conditions and other relevant matters. Inculcating nationalist values through the educational system and the selective teaching of subjects is practised by almost all governments. However, doing so at the expense of teaching young villagers how to become better farmers, as is so often done in the Third World, only depletes rural areas of their most promising inhabitants.

NOTES

1 Andrei Rogers. 'Sources of Urban Population Growth and Urbanization, 1950–2000: A Demographic Accounting'. *Economic Development and Cultural Change*. vol. 30, no 3, (April 1982), p 486. Also see Jacques Ledent. 'Rural–Urban Migration, Urbanization, and Economic Development'. *Economic Development and Cultural Change*. vol. 30, no 3, (April 1982), p. 509.

2 See below, Chapters 4 and 5.

3 Warwick Armstrong and T. G. McGee. *Theatres of Accumulation: Studies in Asian and Latin American Urbanization*. (London: Methuen, 1985), p. 41.

4 Ibid. pp. 41–2.

5 Bryan Roberts. *Cities of Peasants: The Political Economy of Third World Urbanization*. (London: Sage, 1978), p 61.

6 Richard Hay. 'Patterns of Urbanization and Socio-economic Development in the Third World: An Overview', in Janet Abu-Lughod and Richard Hay, eds. *Third World Urbanization*. (Chicago: Maaroufa, 1977), p. 81.

7 Ibid. p. 79.

8 John Paxon, ed. *The Statesmen's Yearbook, 1990–1991*. 127th edn. (New York: St Martin's, 1990), pp. 446, 782, 864.

9 Charles Becker and Andrew Morrison. 'The Determinant of Urban Population Growth in Sub-Saharan Africa'. *Economic Development and Cultural Change*. vol. 36, no 2, (January 1988), p. 259.

10 Johannes Linn. 'The Costs of Democracy in the Developing Countries'. *Economic Development and Cultural Change.* vol. 30, no 3, (April 1982), p. 628.

11 Bryan Roberts. *Cities of Peasants.* p. 138.

12 Johannes Linn. 'The Costs of Democracy in the Developing Countries'. p. 630.

13 Richard Stern. 'The Administration of Urban Services', in Richard Stern and Rodney White, eds. *African Cities in Crisis: Managing Rapid Urban Growth.* (Boulder, Colo: Westview, 1989), p. 22.

14 Ibid.

15 John Herbert. *Urban Development in the Third World: Policy Guidelines.* (New York, NY: Praeger, 1979), p. 10.

16 Ibid. p. 9.

17 Ozzie Simmons. *Perspectives on Development and Population Growth in the Third World.* (London: Plenum, 1988), p. 47.

18 T. G. McGee. *The Urbanization Process in the Third World: Explorations in Search of a Theory.* (London: G. Bell & Sons, 1971), p. 16.

19 Andrei Rogers and Jeffrey Williams. 'Migration, Urbanization, and Third World Development: An Overview'. *Economic Development and Cultural Change.* vol. 30, no 3, (April 1982), p. 464.

20 Allen Findlay and Anne Findlay. *Population and Development in the Third World.* (London: Methuen, 1987), p. 30. For a detailed critique of the demographic 'transition' theory, see Ozzie Simmons. *Perspectives on Development and Population Growth in the Third World.* pp. 92–100.

21 John Herbert. *Urban Development in the Third World.* p. 7.

22 Josef Gugler. 'Overurbanization Reconsidered', in Josef Gugler, ed. *The Urbanization of the Third World.* (Oxford: Oxford University Press, 1988), p. 74.

23 Samuel Preston. 'Urban Growth in the Developing Countries: A Demographic Reappraisal', in Josef Gugler, ed. *The Urbanization of the Third World.* p. 14.

24 Bryan Roberts. *Cities of Peasants.* p. 105.

25 Andrei Rogers and Jeffrey Williams. 'Migration, Urbanization, and Third World Development: An Overview'. p. 25.

26 Allen Findlay and Anne Findlay. *Population and Development in the Third World.* p. 16.

27 Ibid. pp. 26–7.

28 Ibid. p. 32.

29 Joan Nelson. *Access to Power: Politics and the Urban Poor in Developing Nations.* (Princeton, NJ: Princeton University Press, 1979), pp. 50–1.

30 Rodney White. 'The Influence of Environmental and Economic Factors on the Urban Crisis', in Rodney White and Richard Stern, eds. *African Cities in Crisis: Managing Rapid Urban Growth.* p. 11.

31 Mass resettlements and other demographic dislocations are particularly commonplace in countries where guerrilla warfare and protracted civil wars have been waged for many years, such as in Afghanistan, Peru, El Salvador, and Mozambique.

32 Michael Lipton. 'Why Poor People Stay Poor: Urban Bias in World Development', in Josef Gugler, ed. *The Urbanization of the Third World.* p. 40.

33 Ibid. p. 43.
34 Johannes Linn. ' The Costs of Democracy in the Developing Countries'.
    p. 632.
35 Bryan Roberts. *Cities of Peasants.* p. 89.
36 Ibid. p. 99.
37 Oded Stark and David Lavhari. 'On Migration and Risk in the LDCs'.
    Economic Development and Cultural Change. vol. 31, no 1, (October 1982),
    p. 192.
38 See Chapter 4.
39 Bryan Roberts. *Cities of Peasants.* p. 101.
40 Dennis Rondinelli. *Secondary Cities in Developing Countries: Policies For
    Diffusing Urbanization.* (London: Sage, 1983), pp. 63–4.
41 Ibid. p. 163.
42 Alan Gilbert and Josef Gugler. *Cities, Poverty, and Development: Urban-
    ization in the Third World.* (Oxford: Oxford University Press, 1982),
    p. 60.
43 Bryan Roberts. *Cities of Peasants.* p. 93.
44 Joan Nelson. *Access to Power.* p. 53.
45 Ibid. p. 60.
46 Warwick Armstrong and T. G. McGee. *Theatres of Accumulation.* p. 47.
47 Alan Gilbert and Josef Gugler. *Cities, Poverty, and Development.* p. 59.
48 Gary Fields. 'Place to Place Migration in Colombia'. *Economic Develop-
    ment and Cultural Change.* vol. 30, no 3, (April 1982), p. 557.
49 Bryan Roberts. *Cities of Peasants.* pp. 96–7.
50 Joan Nelson. *Access to Power.* p. 81.
51 Ibid. p. 61.
52 Julian Laite. 'The Migrant Response in Central Peru', in Josef Gugler,
    ed. *The Urbanization of the Third World.* p. 64.
53 Bryan Roberts. *Cities of Peasants.* p. 104.
54 Julian Laite. 'The Migrant Response in Central Peru', in Josef Gugler,
    ed. *The Urbanization of the Third World.* p. 67.
55 Samuel Preston. 'Urban Growth in the Developing Countries: A Demo-
    graphic Reappraisal', in Josef Gugler, ed. *The Urbanization of the Third
    World.* p. 27.
56 Oded Stark and Robert Lucas. 'Migration, Remittances and the Family'.
    Economic Development and Cultural Change. vol. 36, no 3, (April 1988),
    pp. 465–6.
57 Ibid. p. 478.
58 Dennis Rondinelli. *Secondary Cities in Developing Countries.* p. 162.
59 Brian Berry. *Comparative Urbanization: Divergent Paths in the Twentieth
    Century.* (New York: St Martin's, 1981), p. 88.
60 Ibid.
61 Ibid. p. 83.
62 Charles Abrams. 'Squatting and Squatters', in Janet Abu-Lughod and
    Richard Hay, eds. *Third World Urbanization.* p. 293.
63 Ibid. p. 294.
64 Allen Kelley and Jeffrey Williamson. 'The Limits to Urban Growth:
    Suggestions for Macromodeling Third World Economies'. *Economic
    Development and Cultural Change.* vol. 30, no 3, (April 1982), p. 598.

65 Bryan Roberts. *Cities of Peasants*. p. 149.
66 Ibid. pp. 146–7.
67 Charles Abrams. 'Squatting and Squatters', in Janet Abu–Lughod and Richard Hay, eds. *Third World Urbanizaion*. pp. 297–8.
68 Larissa Lomnitz. 'The Social and Economic Organization of a Mexican Shantytown', in Josef Gugler, ed. *The Urbanization of the Third World*. p. 242.
69 Wayne A. Cornelius. 'The Political Sociology of Cityward Migration in Latin America: Toward Empirical Theory', in Janet Abu–Lughod and Richard Hay, eds. *Third World Urbanization*. p. 223.
70 Larissa Lomnitz. 'The Social and Economic Organization of a Mexican Shantytown', in Josef Gugler, ed. *The Urbanization of the Third World*. p. 245.
71 Alan Gilbert and Josef Gugler. *Cities, Poverty, and Development*. p. 58.
72 Ibid. p. 123.
73 Emmanuel Jimenez. 'The Value of Squatter Dwellings in Developing Countries'. *Economic Development and Cultural Change*. vol. 30, no 4, (July 1982), p. 751.
74 Bryan Roberts. *Cities of Peasants*. p. 137.
75 Ibid. p. 151.
76 Emmanuel Jimenez. 'The Value of Squatter Dwellings in Developing Countries'. p. 752.
77 Alan Gilbert and Josef Gugler. *Cities, Poverty and Development*. p. 87.
78 Charles Abrams. 'Squatting and Squatters', in Janet Abu–Lughod and Richard Hay, eds. *Third World Urbanization*. p. 296.
79 Andrei Rogers and Jeffrey Williams. 'Migration, Urbanization, and Third World Development: An Overview'. p. 474.
80 Brian Berry. *Comparative Urbanization*. p. 88.
81 Alan Gilbert and Josef Gugler. *Cities, Poverty, and Development*. p. 142.
82 Joan Nelson. *Access to Power*. p. 141.
83 Anthony Leeds. 'Housing-Settlement Types, Arrangements for Living, Proletarianization, and the Social Structure of the City', in Janet Abu–Lughod and Richard Hay, eds. *Third World Urbanization*. p. 333.
84 Joan Nelson. *Access to Power*. p. 217.
85 Dennis Rondinelli. *Secondary Cities in Developing Countries*. p. 48.
86 Ibid. pp. 28–9.
87 Ibid. p. 19.
88 Ibid. p. 93.
89 Ibid. p. 178.
90 Ibid. p. 16.
91 Ibid. pp. 59–60.
92 Gary Fields. 'Place to Place Migration in Colombia'. p. 557.
93 Dennis Rondinelli. *Secondary Cities in Developing Countries*. p. 159.
94 Ibid. p. 39.
95 Ibid. p. 78.
96 Ibid. p. 147.
97 Ibid. pp. 151–3.
98 Ibid. p. 153.
99 Ibid. p. 39.

100 Richard Sabot. 'Migration and Urban Surplus Labor: Policy Options', in
     Josef Gugler, ed. *The Urbanization of the Third World*. p. 96.
101 Martin King Whyte. 'Social Control and Rehabilitation in Urban
     China', in Josef Gugler, ed. *The Urbanization of the Third World*. p. 265.
102 p. 266.
103 Richard Sabot. 'Migration and Urban Surplus Labor: Policy Options'.
     p. 98.
104 Ibid. p. 103.

Chapter 4

Social change

The structural changes that occur in the Third World have paramount effects on the daily lives of people. The establishment of factories, the building of roads and new housing units, the fiscal and economic policies adopted by the government, the large-scale movement of rural inhabitants toward urban areas – all signify the *structural* changes taking place throughout the developing world. Concurrent with and in fact reinforcing such changes are somewhat less discernible yet equally significant alterations in people's attitudes, views, and general cultural orientation. It is within the context of a changing environment – politically, economically, as well as industrially – that what is generally known as 'social change' occurs. Thus a complete understanding of Third World politics and society is impossible without examining the process of social change. The study assumes added importance in the context of the Third World, where political systems, industrial infrastructures, and social and cultural value systems have proved to be highly elastic and impermanent. It is this very elasticity of norms and values that leads not only to social crises and intra-societal imbalances but also to political instability, upheavals, and even revolutions. The manner and processes through which social change is brought about are also highly important, as are the ramifications of social change on the various social classes and on other emerging social and economic groups.

Changes in social conduct and cultural outlook on the one hand, and in industrial and economic infrastructures of a society on the other, often develop simultaneously and as a result of one another, one frequently reinforcing the other. There has long been an intense academic debate over the primacy and greater political relevance of social and cultural changes as opposed to industrial and economic ones and vice-versa. The ultimate determinance of the significance of one approach over another frequently depends on the doctrinal lenses through which the subject is studied. However, particularly in so far as the study of political and sociological characteristics are concerned, minimising the importance of either socio-cultural or industrial-economic developments, whether independently or at the expense of one another, is at best academically short-sighted. Social change is fostered by complex and interrelated dynamics that arise out of both industrial and economic forces as well as social and cultural factors. Within this framework, an examination of processes and ramifications of social change in the Third World assumes great importance.

Simply put, social change refers to the 'alteration of a social system over time'.[1] It entails changes in the social and cultural underpinnings of a society.[2] More specifically, social change results in changes in attitudes, views, and the social and cultural outlooks of those whom it affects. As I have noted elsewhere, 'one of the effects of social change is the lack of persistence of norms (i.e. the expected pattern of behaviour)'.

> There are many conflicting varieties of accepted, or rather competing, modes of social behaviour in a society undergoing social change and it becomes impossible to detect a single and identifiably consistent set of norms. There is, therefore, conflict not only between the differing social values that prevail in society but also between norms. Rural immigrants, industrial labourers, wage-earners, the salaried middle class, and even the wealthy elite are all confronted with the enigmatic problem of how to behave properly in the presence of others with equal or superior social standing. The accepted and expected patterns of conduct and behaviour undergo such rapid changes, and new social groupings and segments develop at such rapid rates that the society as a whole cannot retain an interrelated set of norms. Each social group acquires its own set of norms, along with its attached values, and thus there often develops a vast gap between the value system of one group as opposed to those of another.[3]

Yet social change is not confined to mere behavioural and attitudinal changes. Cultural confusion, for lack of a better word, is only one side effect of social change. Social change leads to tensions and strains,[4] painfully reminding social actors of their constant need to change and to adapt to new and radically different circumstances. Changes brought on by industrial development require new thinking, a new outlook on life. And yet old attitudes and values are not the only items compromised by the advent of social change. Social relations change, be they those that bind together kinship networks or, for example, relations between employers and employees. New social groups are sprung into existence, each unique in their characteristics and social and economic positions. Previously non-existent social groups, who owe their very genesis to industrial development and modernisation, come into being, having distinct cultural orientations and value systems. Mobility increases, not only geographically but, more importantly, socially and economically.

The example of a new road linking a remote village to a neighbouring town well illustrates the process of social change as induced by industrial growth. The possibility of travel, especially to a place where there are greater and more diverse employment opportunities, disrupts prevailing social relationships and attitudes, many of which would not have changed otherwise. The need to travel and thus to spend less time in the village community disrupts, among other things, the traditional relationships between members of extended families that still continue to prevail in most Third World villages. Other aspects of the affected villagers' life also change, such as their perception of the surrounding environment, attitudes toward riding the bus or resentment toward strangers, and many other less tangible social and cultural differences that are brought on by a desire for social and economic mobility. How the villager was made aware of the possibility of social and economic advancement in the first place is itself a matter of crucial importance, discussed in later pages. Once exposed and subjected to alternative value systems and modes of behaviour, whether by free will or by the force of circumstances, the villager is confronted with a changing social and cultural environment, becoming a participant in the process of social change. He is faced with choices he never had to make before, must behave and think differently from what he is used to, and is forced to live in a constantly changing environment. His very actions, meanwhile, further reinforce and add to the strength and intensity of the process of social change. He is at the same time a product and a proponent of social change.

An analysis of social change cannot be complete without taking into account a number of central attributes, such as the magnitude of change, its direction, time span, rate, and the amount, if any, of the violence involved.[5] While hardly quantifiable, an appreciation of these attributes is crucial to understanding the very nature of the social changes taking place and the context within which they occur. Throughout the Third World, with the important exception of post-revolutionary states, the general direction in which social change has taken place is alternately referred to by most scholars as toward 'formalism', 'modernisation', 'structural complexity', or, rather crudely, 'Westernism'.[6] Social change brings about important shifts in the prevailing choices and the behaviour of social actors. Such changes involve a general erosion of particularistic exclusiveness (e.g. races or castes), with achievements and merits replacing the importance of ascriptive criteria.[7] The society as a whole becomes more adaptive, being able not only to generate continuous change but also to absorb changes from outside its own institutions. 'Modernization, from a sociological view', it has been argued, 'consists of a process of proliferation in which the basic elements of all social systems, the roles and institutions, are rapidly increasing.'[8] Moreover, there occurs a general increase in the formalisation of institutional arrangements because:

> traditional practices can no longer be depended upon to provide guides to action. Other means of administration must be utilized. This is accompanied by increasing formalization, which involves the continual encompassing of larger areas within the framework of formal organizations, social units whose base rests on a written charter and similar instrumentalities.[9]

The advent of formal organisations and procedures reduces the central role played by clientage and patrimonial practices. Patrimonial societies, which are extremely common throughout the Third World, are based on 'a highly flexible and paternalistic public order in which the spoils of office are used by the ruling groups to reward friends, co-opt potential and actual opponents, to satisfy local and regional allies, and generally to incorporate newly-emerging groups into the system'.[10] Such practices still predominate in the social, political, and economic lives of most Third World countries, in some more than in others, but they have been subject to strains of late owing to the valuational changes brought on by social change.

Some observers have equated the advent of social change with Westernism, believing that a general abandonment of older, more traditional values and modes of behaviour automatically means their replacement with those prevalent in the West.[11] This assumption is correct in some but not in all aspects. The general growth of formal organisations and practices in the Third World is indeed parallel to a similar process that occurred in most Western societies some time ago, where affluence and opportunity replaced the need to rely on personal relationships and informal networks to accomplish desired goals.[12] Thus the move from informality toward formality, interpreted narrowly, is synonymous with Westernisation. It also happens to be the case that most of the mechanisms through which social change is diffused, whether they are trips abroad, television and radio sets, or official government policies (see below), are often geared toward the promotion of values that are generally associated with the West. The weakening of kinship bonds as a result of the breakup of extended families and their conversion into nuclear ones, the abandonment of traditional attire in favour of uniforms or a certain dress code, the primacy to symbols associated with the modern state (like the national anthem) over other forms of folklore, and the emergence of allegiances and loyalties to secular bureaucratic and political figures instead of local, tribal, or ethnic patrons, all are examples of the more subtle undercurrents lessening the incredible social and cultural gaps between the Third World and the Western countries. Often the Westernising effects of social change are not nearly as subtle: the popular adoption of Western-style music, fashion, housing, even speech and literature. Whether blatant or less obvious, the Westernising effects of social change are immense and undeniable.

Yet to automatically equate social change with Westernisation is inaccurate, for while social change *may* result in Westernisation, it doesn't necessarily follow that it does. While most Third World governments promote Western social and cultural values, others, although relatively few, try to direct their societies' social change in the opposite direction by promoting culturally indigenous, at times anti-Western values. In the broadest sense, social change involves the transformation of values. What specific direction that transformation points toward varies from case to case. Generally, the trend is toward Westernisation, resulting in the promulgation of Western social and cultural values and the erosion of indigenous, traditional ones. However, in selected circumstances, where the state has highly pronounced social agendas, social change may occur in a manner whereby Western values are weakened and are replaced by others, at times traditional and at times highly radical but in any case anti-Western. That authoritarian government structures are often needed to nurture the evolution of politically motivated norms and values attests to the pervasive nature of social change. Post-revolutionary governments in the former Soviet Union, China, and Iran, and the

insular government of Saudi Arabia, all offer examples of political
structures which, either under the pretext of guarding against 'bourgeois' influences or those of 'the infidels', have with varying degrees
of success tried to engineer social change in order to attain specific,
anti-Western, popular cultural outlooks.

The spread of social change in its various manifestations, be it
formalism of an institutional or a social nature (i.e. formalism in
relationships among social actors) or social and cultural Westernisation, is by no means a uniform process, effecting certain social
strata or ethnic groups more than others. Some groups are more
eager than others to abandon the old and embrace the new.
Similarly, some values are less resilient to change than others. Certain
values and attitudes, such as kinship bonds, are highly tenacious and
largely resist the onslaught of change while others are eagerly aban-
doned and replaced.[13] The underlying causes for the acceptability of
certain new values among some social groups are discussed later in
this chapter. What is important is to realise that during the process of
social change all values do not necessarily change equally among
those affected. It is within this context that an understanding of the
magnitude of social change is important. In fact, because of the very
lack of uniformity inherent in the process of social change, there are
often great variations within the prevailing norms and values of the
same culture. A practice considered taboo by some segments of
society may be a daily routine for others within the same society
(such as the wearing of the head-cover by some and cosmetics by
other women in large Arab metropolitans), or a set of values widely
accepted in one part of the country may be frowned on in other
parts. Selective application of social change, coupled with the deliberate promotion of certain values aimed at target audiences, both of
which are commonly practised by Third World governments, intensify intra-society cultural differences. Dissynchronised social systems
are, as a result, a prominent feature of Third World societies.[14]

Ensuing social and political conflicts and instability are inevitable.
Social change is an inherently destabilising process, creating imbalances not only within the values of a society but also sharp and
deeply entrenched conflicts between those who hold such differing
values. The process of social change gives rise to new social strata
whose position in the social structure may be anomalous and who
may, therefore, express considerable dissatisfaction even though their
statures relative to other strata are rising.[15] The more intense the
process of social change, the more acute are the differences between

the varying social groups likely to be, whether between the working and the middle classes or between particular social segments and those in power. Intra-society conflicts between various social classes often crystalise themselves in the form of segregated neighbourhoods, tribal or inter-ethnic rivalries, and the ascription of culturally inferior standards to the inhabitants of certain cities or regions. The overall result is an intensification of social cleavages and cultural differentiations.

The disruptive effects of social change do not stop at the social and cultural plains and reach into the political sphere as well. Social change has the potential of disturbing the political process in two ways. It can nurture beliefs and values that are contradictory to those of the political establishment, or result in the creation of new groups exerting participatory demands on the system. Social change often results in the promotion of values that undermine the legitimacy of existing political systems, particularly in cases where the state does not actively promote a set of rigid socio-cultural guidelines. Values such as democratic rights and greater political mobility are not necessarily those that political systems in the Third World tend to champion, but are in fact widely circulated and popularly upheld by populations that have experienced social change and diffusion with Western cultures. Again and again, revolutions have occurred because the values of the political establishment and those adhered to by the society at large have been at variance.[16] Moreover, the growth of formal practices and the gradual shift toward a participant society exposes the power system to new forms of competition for which it is not prepared. Groups that had hitherto been in the sidelines begin moving toward the centre and participating in the struggle for political control.[17] The weakly articulated institutional apparatuses are incapable of absorbing the influx of aspiring political participants or to fulfil their demands.[18] Political conflict ensues, either in the form of regime changes or, in extreme cases, in the form of revolutions.

INSTRUMENTS OF SOCIAL CHANGE

Social change arises from the singular development or the combined interplay of four distinct sociological phenomena: modernisation, diffusion, indigenously initiated alterations within the social system, and, lastly, through what some scholars have called 'culture lag'. Brief mention was made of the effects that technological modernisation and industrial development have on entrenched values and norms. Closely linked with modernisation is a phenomenon of 'culture lag', caused by differential rates of change among the various parts of modern culture.[19] The lag in the rate of change in the 'material culture' as opposed to 'adaptive culture' (i.e. customs, beliefs, laws, etc.) leads to 'cultural maladjustments' and to social change.[20] A much more drastic way in which social change is brought about, particularly in the context of the Third World, is through diffusion with other cultures, a linkage often created via the electronic media and also, though to a lesser extent, by travel and literature. Indigenously induced social change may be political or sociological in nature, though political dynamics often play a more prominent role in causing social change. Yet sociological developments are at times equally important in fostering social change. Social change can occur when a society becomes unable to cope adequately with the various forces that are engendered in it, therefore rendering structural and systemic changes inevitable. Both Karl Marx and Talcott Parsons, for example, saw factors indigenous to the social system as the main cause of social change; while Marx focused on the 'contradictions' between the forces and the modes of production, Parsons examined the 'differentiations' and the 'variations' of a society's 'subsystems'.[21] Government policy initiatives are also commonly used to instil certain values among the population and to alleviate or to at least discredit certain others. The inculcation of specific values by the government becomes even more intense in post-revolutionary states, where new ruling elites seek even harder to find socially and culturally justifiable values for their political doctrine and social agendas. A similar overall cultural shift occurs during wars of national liberation, when previously cherished cultural symbols are discarded, at times even ridiculed, and are replaced by new ones.

Industrialisation contributes to social change by necessitating alterations in values, personal habits, kinship bonds and other forms of relationship, and in creating new social classes with new characteristics and patterns of life. More specifically, industrialisation results in the creation of a new occupational structure and new ways of manning it, leads to the appearance of migratory movements and a new ecological arrangement of people, and calls forth the creation of systems of organising and controlling people in their manifold industrial relationships. New groups of people are formed, as are new collective interests around which their lives are organised. Monetary and contractual agreements assume considerably greater significance than before, and new patterns of income and consumption begin governing people's lives.[22] The ensuing social changes, particularly in the context of the Third World where an industrial heritage has been noticeably absent, are of unparalleled proportions. In the urban environment of the Third World specifically, the overwhelming majority of the social classes owe their very existence to either the process of industrialisation itself or to its ramifications. Migrants and seasonal workers, industrial labourers, plant managers, and factory owners and so-called industrialists all come into being precisely because of the appearance and growth of industrialisation. Other groups, such as bureaucrats and civil servants, bankers and financiers, and import–export merchants and other middlemen are also formed as a result of industrial development. Each of these groups has its own values and related work ethics, its own patterns of income and consumption, and its own social and economic interests and pursuits.

The role of industrialisation as an agent of social change can be well illustrated by the example of migrant workers. The establishment of a new factory on the outskirts of a large metropolitan area invariably often results in the diversion of resources away from the rural areas and the agricultural sector and into the urban areas which contain the bulk of the industrial infrastructure.[23] The resulting rural depression and urban growth disrupt class formations both in the rural and urban areas. Farmers and peasants find agricultural activities less profitable and jobs in the industrial sectors become increasingly more appealing. Migrants are formed, soon comprising a class of their own with distinct pursuits and characteristics. Failure to become fully absorbed into the industrial labour force compels most migrants to seek odd jobs and vocations, many of which would probably never have existed had it not been for industrialisation and its ramifications: handy-men, car minders and window cleaners, drivers, etc. Those who are successful in joining the industrial labour force soon find some of their deeply entrenched values compromised by their new circumstances. Their extended family is no longer the central part of their life and economic livelihood as it once was, being replaced now by fellow workers, employers, managers, and the like. Religious principles and rituals are often ignored for the sake of social relationships and economic necessities. And one's priorities and desires are radically shifted, shaped by evolving circumstances and changing needs.

Industrial development has similar affects on other social classes, notably on the middle classes and the economic elite. They too find their social and cultural values changed owing to the onslaught of industrialisation, their priorities shifted, and their social and economic relationships altered. Since Third World industrialisation has come to be an inherently urban phenomenon, its most acute contributions to social change affect those groups that are in one way or another linked with the urban environment. Industrialisation brings about social change in the rural areas by effecting a reorganisation of social and economic relationships: the peasant becomes a member of a different social class, be it migrant labour, the proletariat, or the civil service, groups that are more closely in touch with the city than the village. While values prevailing in rural areas are changed as a result of industrially induced social change, their alteration is not as accentuated and immediate consequences are not as apparent as they are in metropolitan centres.

Of the groups in the Third World whose social positions are affected by social change, women stand out. This observation is important, for it deals not with socio-economic or ethnic stratifications but rather with differences in gender roles and the varying social positions traditionally ascribed to the different sexes. The introduction of women into the labour force is one of the most important contributions of industrialisation to social change. Similar to the male population, women's introduction into the labour force has been either a direct result of industrialisation or due to its numerous ramifications. In most Third World countries, some 80 to 90 per cent of the assembly industry's labour force is made up of women, reaching as high as 85 per cent in the electronics industry.[24] Positions created to facilitate the administrative aspects of industrialisation similarly involve the heavy participation of women, especially in lower ranking positions such as clerical jobs which do not require much technical knowledge and authority. Again, traditional values such as the importance of motherhood, the inadmissibility of women earning money, and other primordial core symbols are eroded as the general social and economic positions of women is somewhat ameliorated through industrialisation. Yet there is considerable debate on whether participation in the industrial process actually improves the status of women or merely changes the facade of their exploitation. Throughout the Third World, women's entrance into the labour force has been circumscribed and limited to participation at the lowest social and economic echelons. While women comprise the vast majority of assembly workers, typists, clerks, and other non-technical, non-authoritative personnel, managerial jobs requiring diplomas or special degrees are almost exclusively the domain of men. Women are propelled into the marginal economy, with their upward social mobility limited and their productive roles increasingly dependent on men.[25] Moreover, the large numbers of women in industrial plants, especially on assembly lines, does not necessarily attest to their emancipation from exploitation. Trans-national companies, for one, are alleged to prefer female labourers because they are more patient and tend to be less demanding.[26] Whether positive or negative, the profound effects of industrial-isation on the status of Third World women cannot be denied and has dramatically altered the social and economic composition of the Third World's urban landscape.

Closely related to industrialisation's effects on social change is a phenomenon known as culture lag. Culture lag refers to a differential rate of change among the various components of culture. Similar to industrialisation, social change is brought about through culture lag because changes in one aspect of society necessitate parallel adjust-ments in other aspects. 'The various parts of modern culture', pro-ponents of the culture lag theory argue, 'are not changing at the same rate, some parts are changing much more rapidly than others.'[27] Changes in one part of culture, industrial relations for example, require readjustments and changes in other cultural components, such as education. Such a differential rate of change eventually leads to changes in social values, relationships, and other manifestations of social change. On a purely theoretical level, it is difficult to dis-tinguish the varying ways in which industrialisation and culture lag result in social change. Both approaches are based on essentially the same premise and envisage similar results. An argument could be made that while industrialisation brings about changes to social norms because of *technological* advances, culture lag does so via changes in *material culture*. Such a distinction depends, however, on how *material culture* is defined (e.g. cultural forms associated with material objects, such as driving for example), but is still a blurred one none the less.

The effects of industrialisation and culture lag on changes in the social make up and the cultural orientation of Third World societies are enormous. They are, however, by far surpassed in magnitude by the dramatic consequences that diffusion with other cultures has had

on Third World societies.[28] Few cultural items emerge independently from within a society. Rather, they are borrowed from other
cultures or are heavily influenced by them. The passage of traits
native to one culture into another, to which they have hitherto been
alien, causes changes in social systems. Some of the mechanisms
through which diffusion usually leads to social change include ethnic
movements, military conquests, missionaries, commerce, revolutions, and gradual infiltration.[29] With the overwhelming role played
by the electronic media today, especially within Third World
societies, the cross-cultural diffusion of values and norms is made
even more commonplace.[30] Due to the special social and cultural
characteristics of Third World societies, several other practices and
developments also lead to diffusion with other cultures. Chief among
them are education, travel, and perceptions and images.

The importance of diffusion on social change in the Third World
can hardly be overstated. In early modernisers, modernisation was
mostly piecemeal and by innovation. In late modernising societies, in
contrast, modern institutions and practices are diffused at once and
literally intact.[31] Third World diffusion is marked by a one-way flow
of cultural influence from the West and into Third World societies.
The cultural diffusion that occurs in the Third World is a decidedly
one-faceted phenomenon: it accentuates the prevalence of Western
cultural traits in Third World societies. The underlying causes for
this one-way flow of influence are largely derived from the economic power behind Western cultural values. Western values are
either directly imposed through colonial or neo-colonial arrangements, or are inculcated and intensely propagated by indigenous
elites. Such values are often adopted by certain social classes and in
turn popularised throughout the population. The growth and spread
of Western industries in the developing countries further adds
impetus to the growing acceptance of Western norms and values.
The existing economic, political, and sociological factors progressively allow new values to penetrate individuals and masses.
Some have labelled this phenomenon 'sociological propaganda' since
it propagates new values.[32] It is argued, that:

> Such propaganda is essentially diffuse. It is rarely conveyed by
> catchwords or expressed intentions. Instead it is based on a general
> climate, an atmosphere that influences people imperceptibly
> without having the appearance of propaganda; it gets to man
> through his customs, through his unconscious habits. It creates

new habits in him; it is a sort of persuasion from within. As a
result, man adopts new criteria of judgement and choice, adopts
them spontaneously, as if he had chosen them himself. But all
these criteria are in conformity with the environment and are
essentially of a collective nature. Sociological propaganda produces a progressive adaptation to a certain order of things, a
certain concept of human relations, which unconsciously molds
individuals and makes them conform to society.[33]

This propagation and acceptability of Western values is in turn facilitated by a general sense of cultural inferiority vis-à-vis the West prevalent throughout the Third World.[34] In almost every Third World
country, it is commonly believed that prevailing social values (as well as
political despotism) are the main reasons for the technological gap with
the West.[35] As deeply entrenched as they are, such general feelings of
insecurity about social values increases the likelihood of their replacement with other, seemingly more beneficial values.

In the context of the Third World, some of the mechanisms
through which diffusion with Western cultural traits takes place have
proved especially potent. They include the media – particularly the
electronic media and other visual medians such as cinemas, television, and video tapes – travel, education, and missionary activities.
Within these, the role of the media as a tool for cultural diffusion is
most significant. This importance is due primarily to the crucial role
of the media in the Third World, not only as one of the main
mouthpieces of the government's official ideology and propaganda
but also as the disseminators of information relevant to the overall
process of development.[36] In many Third World countries, much of
the process of political institutionalisation is entrusted to the media.
In fact, the use of television as a specifically political tool has been
one of the main rationales for its appearance and operation in much
of the Third World. In Iran, television was introduced in order to
allow for the broadcast of the late Shah's coronation in 1967; in
Uganda to broadcast the meetings of the Organisation of African
Unity; and in Senegal in order to cover the 1972 Olympic games in
Munich.[37] Since the initial, hurried embrace of the electronic media
for propaganda purposes, the use of the media as a tool for the
promotion of alternative values gradually assumed a more subtle
character. Once the 'internal enemy' has been subdued and political
competition eliminated, regimes delegate their propaganda and ideo-

logical functions to the printed and the electronic media, guided by a commercial rationality.[38] Nevertheless, education, especially at the university level, and in some instances the activities of religious missionaries, is as important as are the electronic media in promoting foreign, often Western, values.

In much of the Third World, television programming is based on either the French, the British, or the American models. In most Latin American countries, the American model prevails, where commercial financing is mixed with libertarian ethics and socially responsible programmes. The British model, which like the British Broadcasting Corporation is comprised of a public service company and is supported by licence fees, can be found in most of Britain's former African colonies and in India. In most other Third World countries, an extreme version of the French example exists, where pervasive state control and financing is supported by marginal financial contributions from private industry in the form of commercial advertisements. While these models have not been particularly suited to the indigenous social and cultural conditions, their adoption is hard to resist because of the pervasiveness of the colonial heritage and the lack of original models to follow.[39]

Largely because of the adoption of Western models, with the important exception of post-revolutionary states, television in much of the Third World serves as a major tool for the promotion of Western values and culture. Western variety shows, documentaries, nature programmes, and soap operas and television series, especially those produced in the United States, inundate Third World televisions and are shown during days and times when the audience is at a maximum.[40] Feature movies produced in Italy, France, and the United States are also extremely popular, especially among young people, and form one of the most popular mediums of entertainment. In recent years, videocassette recorders have both deepened the breadth of Western cultural penetration in the Third World and have facilitated its growth in remote regions and distant villages.[41] VCRs have gained particular popularity in Asia, Africa, and in the Middle East, where strict government controls over television programming have accentuated the appeal of alternative programmes. In Latin America, in contrast, where commercial television stations operate with little interference from the government, VCRs do not have the gripping popularity which they do in other parts of the Third World.[42] The prevalence of VCRs in the Third World is, nevertheless, especially important since it undermines the government's monopoly on entertainment (and thus its ability to wage propaganda) by providing alternatives.[43]

As far as social change is concerned, the effects of Western movies on Third world societies is even greater than it may appear, because the audience is exposed to value-assumptions that are often implied rather than expressed.[44] People learn how to live and work through the demonstration effect that Western movies and shows have.[45] To achieve the (often fictional) style of life that is portrayed in Western movies, which Third World viewers readily associate with the luxury and affluence of life in the West, becomes a goal in itself. The ideals of the movies are taken for realities, and blurred images of Western life are fantasised and sought after. Clichés are formed, not all of which are conducive to one's self-esteem and pride. To the more impressionable groups, especially the young and the rural immigrants, the clichés are highly damaging: those portraying good characters in the movies are North American while the 'bad guys' are American Indian, German, Chinese, or from other countries. The 'good guys' are white, unmarried, rich, usually a detective, a policeman, or a soldier, while those portrayed negatively are frequently black or Indian, are poor, or are servants and workers.[46] Not surprisingly, the majority of stories that Third World children imagine take place in the United States and their heroes have English-sounding names.[47]

Yet the promotion of social change in the direction of Western values is not confined to entertainment or, for that matter, to the electronic media. News programmes in the Third World are filled with news of events and developments taking place in the West, with little attention being devoted to internal affairs or to news about other Third World countries.[48] (An exception to this and a source of considerable information about the Third World (though not Third World generated) is the news service of the BBC World Service on radio, heard in all Third World countries.) Preoccupation with what is happening in the West extends to the printed media as well, with much analytical commentary discussing not domestic issues but international developments such as European unification, space flights, and the like. Like the electronic media, most journals and magazines in the Third World devote much of their attention to promoting Western values and perceived notions of life. They at times demonstrate equal or even greater concern for rumours adrift in the Western entertainment industry than for local personalities or events. Domestic literature is similarly compromised. Novels and dramas are frequently translated from the major European languages, especially English and French, rather than produced domestically.

Travel, missionary activities, and education are other means through which alien values and norms are introduced to a culture and result in its alteration. Travel to other countries, especially to Europe and the United States, has largely the same effects that the electronic media and the cinemas have. Owing to the expense involved, however, the society-wide impact of travel is limited and encompasses only those social segments able to afford trips abroad. More consequential and far-reaching are the efforts of missionaries, whose religious teachings are invariably intertwined with their social and cultural backgrounds. The intense Christianisation of pre-independence Africa through missionary work had a profound effect on the social and cultural make-up of the continent. There were large Christian missions in Africa, operating like whole towns and running their own schools and hospitals. Through permeating most aspects of life, these missions dramatically affected and changed local culture, especially through stigmatising local rituals such as dances and ceremonies and ridiculing native deities.[49] Political independence in Africa and elsewhere has not halted the activities of Western missionaries, although it has in some cases led to greater sensitivity to the local culture on the part of the missionaries involved. Still, the social changes that result from missionary activity are profound. A case in point is the missionary activities of members of the Mormon church. Mormonism is a distinctly American religion that was born and has flourished in the United States and whose zion is located in Utah.[50] As a world-view, Mormon principles are designed specifically for an American way of life, although adaptation to local conditions is not ruled out.[51] Yet despite its decidedly American underpinnings, Mormonism continues to grow and to win converts in many Third World countries, especially in Latin America and East Asia.[52] Mormon missionaries from around the world, who receive their missionary training in Utah, cannot by nature help but act as agents of social change in the countries in which they operate.

Even more widespread than the effects of missionaries on social change are the ramifications of education in the Third World. The role of Third World universities as agents of social change is particularly acute, although education at all levels instils new values and challenges prevailing ones.[53] Throughout the Third World, education serves as a mean for the integration of foreign values into the indigenous culture in several ways. To begin with, a growing number of Third World educators and students alike study in the West and adopt Western values and assumptions, which they in turn pass on to their students and peers.[54] But even those who receive a domestic education are subject to exposure to foreign, mainly Western, values. The educational systems of almost all Third World countries are based on either the European or the American models, depending largely on the country's colonial legacy or its recent political history.[55] In fact, throughout Africa, Asia, Latin America, and even in the Middle East, most secular schools were first established by Christian missionaries from the West who were as much agents for Westernisation as they were teachers. Although the passage of time has led to the secularisation of most of these former missionary schools, it has not necessarily ended their adherence to and in turn inculcation of Western values, albeit through subtle and non-blatant mechanisms. Western assumptions about libertarianism, rationalism, and progress underlie the educational systems of many Third World countries, particularly at the university level.[56] The spread of literacy and education to increasing numbers of Third World inhabitants only accentuates the process of social change that is already under way with intensity.

Apart from missionary activities, which bring about social change largely through the execution of religious edicts and principles, travel, literature, and the media compel people to change their social and cultural values through the demonstration effect. New patterns of conduct and social relations are presented, idealised, and then emulated. Social change is brought about largely without the conscious efforts of those it affects. This mostly voluntary process is often complemented by the government's active promotion of policies that are designed to alter social values in specific directions. It is true that with few exceptions found mostly in Latin America, Third World governments dictate the contents of their media and determine what the public is allowed to read and to see. Complementing this somewhat concealed promotion of social change are policies and overt initiatives aimed at accelerating the process. The bluntness with which governments promote certain values over others varies from one political system to another. Post-revolutionary governments, seeking to instil their legitimacy through social and cultural links, are most vociferous in denouncing some aspects of their culture and praising others. China's Cultural Revolution is an extreme example of a massive and brutal campaign to 'purify' the

Chinese culture in the post-revolutionary era.[57] Similar but lesser-known campaigns followed the revolutions in Russia, Cuba, Algeria, and more recently Iran.[58] The purpose of such campaigns is more than to merely bestow popular legitimacy on the new political leadership. Rather, they are designed to alter the society's values and culture at the most fundamental levels in a manner supportive of the new leaders' ideologies and beliefs. In order to carry out their cultural indoctrination campaign, governments use whatever tools they have at their disposal, be it the media, the pulpit, the educational system, or, if need be, coercive bodies such as the army and the police.

In most contemporary Third World nations, however, the promotion of cultural values takes place with less intensity than it does in post-revolutionary states. Governments try to induce social change through policy initiatives rather than loudly proclaimed campaigns and ventures. This is not an easy task owing to the difficulties involved in designing and implementing plans and programmes that aim to change the daily lives of people.[59] The areas targeted for the most change are often villages and other rural areas least affected by social change. Frequently, professionals or paraprofessionals are sent into the countryside to initiate and oversee community development projects. These agents of change perform a number of basic functions such as community education, organisation and mobilisation of the community and its resources, demonstration of innovative technology, and the acquisition of goods and services not found locally.[60] In many instances, when government resources are scarce or the political will to bring about change is lacking, priests or other religious figures act as agents of social change. The assumption of temporal as well as religious duties by priests in the Third World is especially prevalent in low income urban neighbourhoods and in villages.[61] Although often inadequately trained and paternalistic in dealing with those they seek to help, priests have come to assume important roles in the community development of many Third World countries. They often act as a community's leader, doctor, manager, thinker, and planner.[62]

The effectiveness of these initiatives in bringing about social change varies from case to case and country to country. Development projects in the Third World are often designed by Western or Western-educated planners, usually with assistance from foreign donors, and are frequently impervious to local needs and necessities.[63] Even when the policies and plans that are carried out meet the objective conditions of their intended targets, their success is not guaranteed. The availability of development projects in rural areas, for example, do not necessarily lead to their use by local villagers. This is symptomatic of an incomplete process of social change, whereby local customs and traditions have not changed although industrialisation has led to significant material advancements. Western-style medical clinics in remote parts of Saudi Arabia and AIDS clinics in India are hardly used by local inhabitants, who in both cases prefer traditional healing methods over modern medicine. In these and in other similar cases, values have not changed to a sufficient degree as to make new practices socially acceptable. Social change might have occurred, though without having altered some of the more ingrained cultural beliefs and values of the population.

It is precisely this fragmentary nature of social change that calls forth the examination of another of its facets: which social groups are most susceptible to social change and how the process as a whole affects the various social classes. The selective adoption of values by specific groups and the broader ramifications of social change continually alter culture and society in the Third World. It is to these questions that we turn next.

MANIFESTATIONS OF SOCIAL CHANGE

The onslaught of social change and its extent and intensity have resulted in the development of several specific social and cultural characteristics in the developing countries. Although each is unique in its culture and values, Third World societies share a number of common social and cultural traits that have been the result of social change. In specific, social change has affected Third World societies at two particular levels. It has, on the one hand, resulted in a significant and continued alteration of Third World cultures and values. On the other hand, it has resulted in the appearance of a number of previously non-existent classes, each of which has its own social and cultural characteristics. These two developments, which complement and reinforce one another, give Third World societies the social and cultural features that they have.

Social change involves the transformation of values and beliefs among individual members of society. As such, it has far-reaching psychological ramifications for those effected. Changing values, particularly those that are deeply entrenched and legitimised through generations of acceptance, entail considerable psychological anguish and discomfort, often manifested in the form of counter-culture or escapist movements or sharp inter-generational disagreements. Anomie, cultural disorganisation, confusion, and tension are common psychological ramifications of social change.[64] More specifically, social change results in a fragmentation of attitudes and beliefs, the development of a sense of inferiority within and between societies, the appearance of social differences based on language and dialect, place of birth, gender, and status, and the emergence of new social classes.

Social change results in a weakening of prevailing social values and their growing ambiguity. The individual undergoing social change is confronted with values which place priority on different things and in fact often directly contradict one another. The pressures acting on the individual, which compel him to retain his previously held values or to adopt new ones, determine his overall attitude and cultural orientation. In the developing countries, where the conflicting forces of modernisation on the one hand and traditional values and cultural heritage on the other are by nature strong, the psychological dilemmas caused by the clashing of norms are even more tormenting. Thus confronted with conflicting values and compelled by the force of circumstances, the individual's values and attitudes are compartmentalised, applying one set of values at one time and another in a different circumstance. In a sense, he or she undergoes a fragmentation of attitudes.[65]

Fragmentation of attitudes is commonplace in Third World societies, particularly among groups most directly involved in the process of development. Industrial development and modernisation force these groups to apply certain values in their professional conduct, especially in so far as employment and economic matters are concerned. Yet the same individuals, who have adopted and vigorously apply modern values in their professional conduct, are often highly traditional in their private outlook and personal conduct. The Third World is full of examples of social actors such as merchants who adopt modern values in running their business but continue to remain authoritarian at home. The prevalence of fragmentation of attitudes is underlied by the ability of individuals undergoing social change to only partially reconstruct their normative values and patterns of social behaviour.

By introducing various rationalizations, [people fragmenting their attitudes] simply compartmentalize a difficult incongruity in [their] environment and behave as if the situation subsumed under the conflicting views were unrelated. However, where major social change is taking place there is less reinforcement for moderate compromise and less opportunity for evasion of social pressure . . . . In a very real sense, development means that evidence constantly piles up to remind the partially adapted individual of the contradictions and limitations of many attitudes.[66]

Fragmentation of attitudes allows the individual to hold and to practise two different sets of values without confronting him with moral and psychological dilemmas arising from his inconsistent beliefs. Once this fragmentation is accented and the contrast between values grows sharper, there is a tendency to change values completely and to acquire an entirely new frame of reference. A partial change of attitudes is overcome by a complete attitudinal change.[67] The individual is no longer confronted with conflicting values, his many beliefs and actions now being underwritten by principles that are consistent and non-contradictory.

Acceptance of new values is a matter of degree.[68] Even when the individual resolves his psychological dilemma by either fragmenting his attitudes or completely embracing one set over another, his adherence to the new values is not complete and unconditional. This resilience of values and beliefs is particularly evident in cases where they have been passed on by successive generations and retain their popular acceptance despite scientific advances that negate them. Beliefs in supernatural forces that govern various aspects of individual and social life predominate Third World societies and are commonly held by social groups regardless of their economic standing or degree of exposure to social change. 'Collective representation' is the term that some authors have given to these persistent beliefs and attitudes that often border on superstition.[69] These collective representations are transmitted to all or most of society from one generation to another. Often with no rational basis whatsoever, they revolve around mystic forces and arise from such items as myths, magic, occultism, religious practices, customs, habits, behaviour, and specific historical events. The individual is believed to stand in some sort of relationship with the universe. The universe is in turn considered to be an ensemble of hidden forces which influence and are influenced by man in a manner different from that which can be considered logical and empirical.[70]

Examples of collective representation can be readily found throughout Third World societies. In southeast Asia, people often consider themselves invulnerable against bullets, and in Malaya the failure of the rice crop is often attributed to the attitudes of government officials.[71] Throughout the Middle East, a temporary hesitation and rest is believed prudent after sneezing. African societies are particularly fertile with such ritualistic beliefs that have no scientific basis. Most often, such beliefs and attitudes are not conducive to industrial development or to the growth of social habits which encourage modernisation. Collective representations have an especially strong hold in rural areas and in low-income urban centres, where the process of social change has not had the same intensity that it does in other areas. Irrigation practices, planting seeds, seeking employment, finding buyers for one's products, or other economic activities are thus strongly affected by beliefs that arise from collective representation.[72] With the growth of scientific orientation inhibited owing to reliance on magico-animistic rituals, self-confidence for the mastery of nature is also curtailed and passive resignation is encouraged.[73] Maladies arising from illness, natural disaster, or inaccurate farming methods are blamed on oneself and little thought is given to their rectification in the future.

Another significant psychological ramification of social change in the Third World is the development of a society-wide sense of inferiority vis-à-vis other social classes and members of other societies. As a result of interaction among unequals, an inferiority complex grips not only those social classes who for one reason or another feel humble against others but also entire inhabitants of a country who consider themselves socially and culturally inferior to people from another nation. Insecurity about one's worth, whether individual or collective, arises when values ascribed to others are idealised and are striven for. A constant attempt is made to become or at least to emulate those whose values appear to be appealing. In so far as the Third World is concerned, a society-wide inferiority complex is extremely acute at both the international and the intranational level, but, perhaps not surprisingly, is rarely admitted or discussed by Third World scholars or political leaders.

Intranational inferiority complex in the Third World pervades all levels of society and is one of the most noticeable characteristics of each social class. Third World societies are, in fact, marked by ceaseless struggles of members of one social class to imitate and to eventually become part of a more prestigious class. Rural inhabitants try to become industrial labourers, members of the middle class seek to join the *upper middle class* and the *nouveau riche*, and the upper middle class try to break into the upper classes and become part of the elite. While economic motives and considerations are important, it is the *culture* of each succeeding group that the lower stratum seeks to imitate and their values that it tries to adopt. Each social class considers itself culturally inferior to those with higher social standing and economic power, primarily because the latter's greater exposure to social change has supposedly endowed them with superior values and has turned them into more 'cultured' individuals. A relationship that can be best described as 'psychological feudalism' exists between those in positions of power and their subordinates. Individuals in positions of power and/or with greater exposure to values that society idealises often expect others, whom they view as their sub-ordinates, to be loyal and faithful to them in a manner that often comes into conflict with professional norms.[74] People with economic power and more modern values often demand and frequently receive deference from others who are generally considered and who in fact consider themselves to be inferior.

The idealisation of certain values and efforts to become part of the classes that hold those values assume even more intensity in Third World countries owing to their governments' assumption of the role of cultural progenitor in addition to that of political protector. Through the media, literature, or official propaganda, a certain style of life is, with varying degrees of subtlety, portrayed as the ideal. As earlier discussed, the image that is most commonly portrayed and which subsequently shapes the cultural aspirations of countless Third Worlders is that conveyed through Western films and movies. And the more one is subjected to social change the more Westernised you are likely to become, having thus inched closer to embracing values that society idealises.

It is this idealisation of Western values and norms that in turn led to a feeling of inferiority in comparison to the West. Just as the lower social classes in the Third World try to imitate higher ones by embracing their values, so do the inhabitants of the Third World attempt to become more Western by embracing as many aspects of the West's culture as possible. This imitation of the West is apparent in three specific aspects of Third World culture: language, science and knowledge, and values. Linguistic imitations of the West are particularly prevalent in the Indian subcontinent and in Africa, where in many countries (depending on their colonial heritage) English or French are preferred over the native language.[75] Similarly, fluency in a Western language is a sign of great social prestige and a goal to which many in the Third World aspire. To some extent, this linguistic under-development can be blamed on colonial penetration, but the continued use of certain Western words in preference to their native equivalents is more a matter of social prestige today than colonial influence. Equally pervasive is a lack of congruity between one's knowledge of the West compared with awareness of one's own history and heritage. Third World elites and intellectuals often know much more about the West than they do about their own country. They have travelled more widely among Western capitals than through their own country's various towns, and are frequently better versed in Western philosophy and literature than in their own history and cultural heritage. Both of these aspects of cultural underdevelopment, the linguistic and the scientific, are symptomatic of a third facet, namely preference for Western values over indigenous ones.

What ensues are distorted cultural identities ridden with inferiority complexes and constant attempts to become better imitators of Westerners. Regardless of their merits, domestic cultural products are inevitably felt to embody some sort of flaw because they are not from the West. They are in any case seen as inferior to whatever cultural products have come from the West. Few domestic cultural items are consciously retained and even fewer are cherished. Pride is taken in one's degree of Westernisation rather than in the retention of identity and heritage. Because of their apparently superior values, average Westerners are believed to know more and to have more wisdom than the average citizen of a Third World country. Those Third World citizens who have had greater exposure to the West are considered luckier, wiser, and generally better than the rest, but they are still not true Westerners and thus continue to remain inferior to them. Never-theless, the closer contact one has had with supposedly superior cultures, the more willing you are to flaunt the values associated with them, and the more respect and prestige you are likely to get. In many Third World countries, for example, Western-educated physicians indicate on their office signs the name of the country where they received their degrees, a practice that domestically educated doctors refrain from. The foreign educated doctor is believed to be a better physician and the patient derives more prestige by going to him in preference to the one educated domestically. Similar deference is shown to foreign-educated engineers, teachers, economists, linguists, and the like.

Another significant ramification of social change is the acquisition of new norms and values by emerging social groups and classes. The class structure of contemporary Third World societies is manifested through industrial development and economic growth rather than social change. However, it is no longer sufficient to consider merely the economic bases of the various classes. Their cultural orientation and the degree to which they have been exposed to social change also need to be analysed.

Third World inhabitants can be divided into the two general categories of rural inhabitants and urban residents. In very broad terms, rural inhabitants can be broken down into tribes, landless labourers, small shopkeepers, land-owning peasants, and feudal lords. In the urban areas, meanwhile, most residents are either recent migrants from villages who exist on the fringes of society, or are industrial workers, belong to one of the layers of the middle class, or have reached elite status through economic mobility and wealth. Within these various groups, those residing in rural areas are least exposed to social change owing to their general geographic remoteness and the inaccessibility of means through which alternative values could be disseminated and popularised. Particularly excluded from the process of social change are nomadic tribes – numerous as they are in central Asia, the Middle East, and Africa – whose seasonal migration and lack of permanent residence largely precludes them from assimilating alien values. For values to change, extensive and lengthy exposure to alternative norms is necessary, a factor negated by the nomads' constant relocation from one place to another. In recent decades, the intensity of social change in Third World villages has drastically increased owing to official efforts aimed at community development and closer contacts with the cities. Electricity has brought with it radios, television, and recently even video cassette recorders to many remote villages.[76] Moreover, those landless labourers who, in search of becoming urbanised venture into the cities, themselves serve as means of social change for those they leave behind but with whom they remain in contact. The new values with which the migrants have become acquainted are passed on to the village community, where they gradually gain partial or even full acceptance.

It is in the urban areas where social change is most acute. All urban residents are entangled in the process of social change at one level or another. Each social class is attempting to overcome its sense of inferiority by adopting the values of those ahead of it: the upper and the middle classes constantly try to model their life on their counterparts in the West; the working classes and the lumpen-proletariat seek to enhance their social standing by adopting the values of the middle classes; and those partially exposed to urban values seek to become complete urbanites by permanently immigrating to the cities. In the process, each group hurriedly abandons its own values and norms and clings onto the values of the group of which it seeks to become a part. Not all old values can be easily compromised, neither can all of the new ones be understood or wholeheartedly embraced. Fragmentation of attitudes is one of the least socially disturbing developments that arise as a result. Equally likely in such circumstances of valuational adjustment are counter-culture movements, proclivity toward mass hysteria, confusion, and even rebellions.[77] It is within these contexts that the importance of social change transcends mere social and cultural matters and reaches into the political realm.

CONCLUSION

There is a direct correlation between social change and political instability. The connection between these two phenomena is all the more pronounced in developing countries owing to the particular characteristics that mark Third World societies and political structures. Social change leads to the transformation of values that prevail throughout society. It further compels people to actively seek the adoption of those values. People in the Third World seek to emulate the West by altering their own cultural frame of reference in a way that would correspond to the West's. Consumerism encourages the mass consumption of Western goods. Literature, the media, and government propaganda praise the virtues of Western ways and patterns of conduct. And the public itself formulates perceptions of what life in the West is like and tries to apply it to its own life. What is excluded from all of this are Western values governing political conduct. Third World governments try to expose the public to the social and cultural values of the West but not to its political principles. They want their peoples to become Westernised socially and culturally but not politically. The ensuing contradictions and conflicts are cause for much political upheaval and turmoil.

Attitudinal changes are by themselves insufficient to produce serious political crises. Several political dynamics need also be at work for concurrent changes to take place in the political structure.[78]

Nevertheless, social change has the potential of seriously undermining the values that legitimate the political leadership's mandate. Values change, some more so than others. Values pertaining to kinship, gender, and religion may demonstrate great resilience and continue to remain unchallenged among many sectors. But political values rarely have great strength of their own and have little resilience. In vast parts of the Third World, political legitimacy is derived from the barrel of a gun rather than from historically rooted practices and commonly respected beliefs.[79] Indeed, when exposure to the West takes place, dominant political principles are among the first values to be questioned and challenged. Social change challenges the legitimacy of the political establishment by bringing into question those values on which the body politic is based. By nature, social change is an inherently destabilising process, upsetting the dominant values, relationships, and habits of the societies it affects. Such destabilisation of values occurs not only in the social and cultural domains but in politics as well. In fact, the delegitimation of (all too often shallow) political values may be more acute than that affecting deeply rooted social and cultural norms. Social change brings into question the validity of those values with which the political establishment justifies its continued existence and its political agendas. The strength of the valuational challenge to existing political realities, and the forcefulness with which the public is prompted to enforce a congruence between differing political values and political realities, depend on the political culture within which these processes are taking place. It is this political culture which to a large extent determines the viability of new political values and the bereavement of the old.

NOTES

1 Hermann Strasser and Susan Randall. *An Introduction to Theories of Social Change*. (London: Routledge & Kegan Paul, 1981), p. 23.
2 See Wilbert Moore. *Social Change*. (Englewood Cliffs, NJ: Prentice-Hall, 1963).
3 Mehran Kamrava. *Revolution in Iran: Roots of Turmoil*. (London: Routledge, 1990), p. 96.
4 Wilbert Moore. *Social Change*. p. 3.
5 Hermann Strasser and Susan Randall. *An Introduction to Theories of Social Change*. p. 16.
6 See, for example, William Friedland. 'A Sociological Approach to Modernization', in Chandler Morse *et al. Modernization By Design: Social Change in the Twentieth Century*. (London: Cornell University Press,

1969), pp. 34–84; and J.E. Goldthrope. *The Sociology of the Third World, Disparity and Development.* (Cambridge: Cambridge University Press, 1984).

7 J.E. Goldthrope. *The Sociology of the Third World.* pp. 8–9.
8 William Friedland. 'A Sociological Approach to Modernization'. p. 37.
9 Ibid. p. 38.
10 Vicky Randall and Robin Theobald. *Political Change and Under-development: A Critical Introduction to Third World Politics.* (London: Macmillan, 1985), p. 79.
11 This line of thinking is particularly prevalent among a growing number of Third World political leaders and intellectuals, who, at times in collusion together, try to devise and implement cultural policies conducive to inculcating specific, Western values.
12 Vickey Randall and Robin Theobald. *Political Change and Under-development.* p. 59.
13 J.E. Goldthrope. *The Sociology of the Third World.* p. 165.
14 See Chalmers Johnson. *Revolutionary Change.* (London: Longman, 1983), Chapter 4, especially pp. 61–3.
15 William Friedland. 'A Sociologial Approach to Modernization'. p. 74.
16 Chalmers Johnson. *Revolutionary Change.* p. 65. Also see below, Chapter 5.
17 Majid Al-Haj. 'The Changing Arab Kinship Structure: The Effects of Modernization in An Urban Community'. *Economic Development and Cultural Change.* vol. 36, no 2, (January 1988), p. 254.
18 William Friedland. 'A Sociological Approach to Modernization'. p. 74.
19 Hermann Strasser and Susan Randall. *An Introduction to Theories of Social Change.* pp. 69–73.
20 W.F. Ogburn. *Social Change with Respect to Culture and Original Nature.* (New York: Viking, 1950), pp. 200–1.
21 For T. Parson's 'neo-evolutionary' theory of social change see his *Societies: Evolutionary and Comparative Perspectives.* (Englewood Cliffs, NJ: Prentice-Hall, 1966), and 'Evolutionary Universals in Society', in T. Parsons, ed. *Sociological Theory and Modern Society.* (New York: Free Press, 1967).
22 Herbert Blumer. *Industrialization as an Agent of Social Change: A Critical Analysis.* (Hawthorne, NY: Aldyne de Gruyter, 1990), p. 54, see also pp. 42–9.
23 See Chapter 2.
24 Armand Mattelart. *Transnationals and the Third World: The Struggle for Culture.* David Buxton, trans. (South Hadley, Mass.: Bergin & Garvey, 1983), p. 111.
25 Susan Marshall. 'Politics and Female Status in North Africa: A Reconsideration of Development Theory'. *Economic Development and Cultural Change.* vol. 32, no 3, (April 1984), p. 501.
26 Armand Mattelart. *Transnationals and the Third World.* p. 112.
27 W.F. Ogburn. *Social Change.* p. 200.
28 William Friedland. 'A Sociological Approach to Modernization'. p. 38.
29 A.L. Kroeber. 'Diffusionism', in Edwin R.A. Feligman and Alvin Johnson, eds. *The Encyclopedia of the Social Sciences III.* (New York: Macmillan, 1937), p. 140.

30 Wilbert Moore. *Social Change* p. 86.
31 William Friedland. 'A Sociological Approach to Social Change'. p. 39.
32 Jacques Ellul. *Propaganda: The Formation of Men's Attitudes.* Konrad Kellen and Jean Lerner, trans. (New York: Vintage, 1973), pp. 62–70.
33 Ibid. p. 64.
34 See below, Chapter 4.
35 An insightful essay on the subject appears in the anthology of works by Jalal Al-e Ahmad, the late Iranian intellectual. See Michael Hillmann, ed. *Iranian Society: An Anthology of Writings by Jalal Al-e Ahmad.* (Lexington, Ky: Mazda Press, 1982), pp. 116–21.
36 Douglas Boyd and Joseph Straubhaar. 'Developmental Impact of Home Video Cassette Recorders on Third World Countries'. *Journal of Broadcasting and Electronic Media.* vol. 29, no 1, (Winter 1985), p. 6.
37 J.E. Goldthrope. *The Sociology of the Third World.* p. 203.
38 Armand Mattelart. *Transnationals and the Third World.* p. 82.
39 Douglas Boyd and Joseph Straubhaar. 'Developmental Impact of Home Vieo Cassette Recorders on Third World Countries'. pp. 7–8.
40 J.E. Goldthrope. *The Sociology of the Third World.* p. 203.
41 Douglas Boyd and Joseph Straubhaar. 'Developmental Impact of Home Video Cassette Recorders on Third World Countries'. p. 12.
42 Ibid. p. 16.
43 Ibid. p. 11.
44 J.E. Goldthrope. *The Sociology of the Third World.* p. 200.
45 Nathan Keyfitz. 'Development and the Elimination of Poverty'. *Economic Development and Cultural Change.* vol. 30, no 3, (April 1982), p. 653.
46 Recollecting aspects of culture in pre-revolutionary Cuba, a Cuban intellectual writes: 'In Cuba you learn to watch films before you learn to walk, and I learned in the worst possible way, watching Tarzan taming blacks and wild animals and "honorable pale-faces" massacring "evil" Apaches.' Pedro Perez Sarduy. 'Culture and the Cuban Revolution.' *The Black Scholar.* vol. 20, nos 5–6, (Winter 1989), p. 20. In recent years, the American movie industry has taken some steps toward preventing the negative portrayal of racial and ethnic minorities, but stereotyping still continues, if not necessarily against more traditional minorities (African-Americans and women, for example), against new groups whose negative portrayal has yet to be taken up by the 'political correctness' (PC) movement (Arabs, Latinos, etc.). Moreover, most television stations and broadcasting corporations in the Third World continue to buy and to re-run older movies from the West made before steps were taken to rectify negative portrayals based on race, ethnicity, or nationality.
47 Armand Mattelart. *Transnationals and the Third World.* p. 83.
48 J.E. Goldthrope. *The Sociology of the Third World.* p. 199.
49 Ibid. p. 52.
50 For a balanced discussion on Mormonism see Leonard Arrington and Davis Bitton. *The Mormon Experience: A History of the Latter-day Saints.* (New York: Vintage, 1980).
51 Klaus Hansen. *Mormonism and the American Experience.* (Chicago, University of Chicago Press, 1981), Chapter 2.
52 Leonard Arrington and Davis Bitton. *The Mormon Experience.* p. 286.

53 Armand Mattelart. *Transnationals and the Third World.* p. 6.
54 See, for example, Hyung-Chang Kim. 'The Americanization of Higher Education in Korea'. *Asian Profile.* vol. 17, no 2, (April 1989), p. 132.
55 In West Africa, universities and institutions of higher learning tend to be based on the French model, a factor derived from the region's colonial experience with France. In South Korea, however, and in other countries whose recent political history has drawn them politically and culturally close to the United States, universities are mostly based on the American model.
56 Hyung-Chang Kim. 'The Americanization of Higher Education in Korea'. p. 133.
57 For a comprehensive discussion of China's Cultural Revolution see, Immanuel Hsu. *The Rise of Modern China.* (Oxford: Oxford University Press, 1990), Chapter 28.
58 See John Dunn. *Modern Revolutions: An Introduction to the Analysis of a Political Phenomenon.* (Cambridge: Cambridge University Press, 1972). On Iran's 'Cultural Revolution' see Shaul Bakhash. *The Reign of the Ayatollahs: Iran and the Islamic Revolution.* (London: I.B.Tauris, 1985), pp. 110–14.
59 Elizabeth Howe. 'Responsive Planning and Social Development Programs in the Third World'. *Journal of Planning Literature.* vol. 2, no 4, (Autumn 1987), p. 385.
60 Trudy Brekelbaum. 'The Use of Paraprofessionals in Rural Development'. *Community Development Journal.* vol. 19, (October 1984), p. 233.
61 Bidum Kuyunsa. 'The Priest as a Change Agent'. *Community Development Journal.* vol. 19, (October 1984), p. 259.
62 Ibid. p. 255.
63 Elizabeth Howe. 'Responsive Planning and Social Development Programs in the Third World'. p. 388.
64 Mahmoud Dhaouadi. 'An Operational Analysis of the Phenomenon of the Other Underdevelopment in the Arab World and in the Third World'. *International Sociology.* vol. 3, no 3, (September 1988), p. 227.
65 Douglas Ashford. 'Attitudinal Change and Modernization', in Chandler Morse *et al. Modernization by Design.* p. 158.
66 Ibid. pp. 158–9.
67 Ibid. pp. 159–60.
68 Ibid. p. 140.
69 Syed Hussein Alatas. *Modernization and Social Change.* (London: Angus & Robertson, 1972). p. 54.
70 Ibid. p. 56.
71 Ibid.
72 Ibid. p. 58.
73 Ibid. p. 61.
74 Ibid. p. 101.
75 Mahmoud Daouadi. 'An Operational Analysis of the Other Underdevelopment in the Arab World and in the Third World'. p. 220.
76 Douglas Boyd and Joseph Straubhaar. 'Developmental Impact of Home Video Cassette Recorders on Third World Countries'. p. 12.
77 Chalmers Johnson. *Revolutionary Change.* p. 65.
78 See below, Chapter 6.
79 See below, Chapter 6.

Chapter 5

Political culture

Social change induces alterations in the prevailing values of Third World societies and inevitably results in a certain degree of political instability. Through social change, the cultural orientations of a population are altered, with new norms of conduct and of thought, new ways of life, gaining increasing legitimacy among various social classes. The previous chapter discussed how these valuational changes affect the social and cultural characteristics of Third World countries. It is now important to examine the relationship between social and cultural values on the one hand and the body politic on the other. The nature and ramifications of the nexus between culture and polity can be best understood through political culture. By examining the role and significance of political culture in Third World countries, this chapter explores the popular political perceptions and orientations that prevail throughout the Third World, the means through which these attitudes are formed, and the effects they have on political behaviour and participation.

There has recently been considerable scholarly debate on the conceptual definition of political culture and the role it plays in the political process.[1] At the most elementary level, political culture refers to the cultural values that govern political behaviour. In their pioneering work on the subject, Almond and Verba defined political culture as the 'particular distribution of patterns of orientation toward political objects among the members of the nation'.[2] They saw political culture as the connecting link between micro- and macro-politics, with popular political perceptions and orientations having direct bearing on a country's political institutions and prevailing patterns of political behaviour.[3] Thus political culture affects 'the conduct of individuals in their political roles, the content of their political demands, and their response to laws'.[4] Along similar lines, a number of other definitions have also been put forward, seeing political culture as 'the particular pattern of political orientation to political action in which each political system is embedded',[5] 'the overall distribution of citizen's orientations to political objects',[6] or as 'all the important ways in which a person is subjectively oriented toward the essential elements in his political system'.[7] More recently, a somewhat different interpretation of political culture has been offered, arguing that it consists of 'all publicly common ways of relating' to political symbols.[8]

Regardless of the terminology used, political culture entails the collective political attitudes of a population, their views and orientations toward the body politic in general and toward specific political events, symbols, and activities. Political culture is part of the more general culture of a society and as such is deeply affected by it,[9] and its orientations are implicit, unconscious, and often taken for granted and treated as *a priori*. Political participants do not consciously reflect on the doctrinal orientations or political characteristics that are brought on by political culture, and are not even aware that political culture expresses itself in their daily activities and thoughts.[10] As such, political culture is a shared and society-wide framework for political orientation and encompasses the society in its entirety.[11]

The tenets of political culture are brought on and nurtured through political socialisation, the process whereby political values, attitudes, and beliefs are learned and adopted.[12] It is through this process of learning that political orientations are formed and political initiatives and responses formulated. Agents through which political socialisation typically occurs involve political institutions and experiences such as historical events, political parties, and the bureaucracy and other governmental organs (e.g. the police and the army), as well as non-political institutions such as family, school, and occupation. Political orientations are formed through daily experiences with these institutions or the memory of specific political events as maintained through symbols. Parades and celebrations marking the anniversary of military victories or revolutions, ceremonies to inaugurate a new president or to crown a monarch, and elections, plebiscites, and other political rites serve to instil specific values in a nation's political culture.[13] The early, largely latent socialisation that takes place through non-political organs such as the family and school is often more salient than the purposive socialisation one undergoes in

later years. Adults are, however, more likely to have definite orientations toward politics because of the greater likelihood that they come
into direct contact with specific political objects.[14]

Momentous or lengthy historical events are also important determinants of a nation's political culture, especially those that affect
great masses of people directly, tangibly, and profoundly. Wars of
liberation, revolutions, civil wars, lengthy periods of economic
depression or intense growth, and other similar events that cause
people to become deeply involved in the political process are
examples of historical experiences that dramatically shape the character of a nation's political culture.[15] In specific relation to the Third
World, history is replete with recurring instances of mass-based
political involvement. Even for younger generations who did not
directly participate in such events, the legacy of national liberation
movements (e.g. throughout Africa), international wars (Iran, Iraq,
Egypt, Syria, Jordan, Israel, India, Pakistan, Bangladesh, etc.),
intense industrialisation (South Korea and other nations of Southeast
Asia), military coups (throughout Africa and Latin America), or
internal revolutions (China, Cuba, Iran, and Nicaragua) are kept
alive through propaganda and political indoctrination. Moreover,
Third World governments frequently attempt to tailor a political
culture suited to their needs and objectives. The campaign to create
a new 'political man' and a 'political religion' takes many different
forms, from the Maoist extreme of Cultural Revolution to subtle
nuances embedded in school textbooks, the media, or, more
blatantly, in official propaganda. In fact, the process of transforming
an existing political culture or building a political culture entirely
anew is central to efforts by numerous Third World countries to
embark on nation building.

POLITICAL CULTURE IN THE THIRD WORLD

In the Third World, the forging of a new political culture is an
essential part of the process of nation building. More specifically,
political legitimation greatly depends on the strength and weakness
of cultural values which support political institutions and practices.
The internalisation of regime-approved norms and values is a crucial
requisite for gaining political legitimacy, and new orientations are
necessary to support new institutions and new forms of political
activity.[16] Moreover, political culture helps to define political roles,
expectations, and objectives, thus giving overall contextual

coherence to the political system and its relationships with the general population.[17] This contextual coherence is particularly important in the Third World, where political institutions are generally weak and political roles are vaguely articulated.[18] Thus official state ideology and propaganda have become pervasive facts of daily life in much of the Third World, permeating everything from lessons taught to school children to matters relating to personal life, such as marriage and death.[19] At a more fundamental level, political culture helps to construct a new national identity and averts an identity crisis. Through its use of symbolism and its role as legitimator of the polity, political culture helps bind together political systems that are otherwise torn by parochial allegiances, rapid social change, geographic space, and nationalist sentiments.[20] In countries where tangible or perceptual symbols of national identity are lacking or have little popular legitimacy, political culture strengthens prevailing political institutions and their links with the larger society.

Despite efforts at creating a new political culture or transforming the old one, and at times precisely because of such efforts, the political culture of most Third World countries is marked by discontinuities and lack of coherence. Fragmented political cultures are, in fact, one of the marked attributes of Third World political systems. Reforming political culture is a long and socially costly process, particularly if parochial units remain intact and serve as refuges from discontinuities in society, economy, and politics.[21] Partial and incomplete socialisation into a political culture makes new political values and institutions appear as alien and even hostile. The political culture becomes fragmented, with little consensus emerging as to the 'rules of the game' and the manner in which political life should be conducted.[22] Fundamental political principles are never agreed upon and thus major differences in political orientations and beliefs continue to persist. Under such circumstances, parochial loyalties maintain supremacy over national ones, often to the extent that the central government is unable to gain widespread popular legitimacy. There is also a lack of widely accepted and operative civil procedures for goal attainment and conflict management, thus increasing the likelihood of political violence, unreconciled conflicts, and repressive politics. Moreover, weak and unstable national governments co-exist side by side with social paranoia, political distrust, and civil disorder.[23]

In addition to the partial application and/or adoption of a political culture by the body politic and the society respectively, fragmented

political cultures result from a number of social and cultural characteristics. Divisive factors include the many facets of social pluralism,
such as a multiplicity of races, languages, ethnic and social groups,
and religions. Deferential allocation of resources, location of
administrative centres, and political movements and parties committed to furthering the causes of local constituents further accentuate differences in political orientations and lack of agreement over
fundamentals.[24] Rapid and intense industrialisation, wars and revolutions, and major and fundamental shifts in government policies are
also likely to disturb the coherence of cultural norms and upset the
uniformity of an existing political culture.[25] In these instances,
people are suddenly thrown into a political whirlwind and the
political orientations to which they have become accustomed are
disrupted by sudden and fundamental shifts in politics. Also, a fragmentation of political culture can occur due to the implementation
of new policies with far-reaching effects into the people's daily lives,
such as the Cultural Revolution in China or, even more dramatically, Nazi policies in the Third Reich. The establishment of new
political forms, such as Latin America's industrialisation-inspired
corporatism, or the prevalence of attitudes of self-sufficiency, at
times to the point of belligerence, in countries where wars have
'toughened up' public attitudes (especially, for example, in Israel),
can also potentially alter all or certain aspects of a prevailing political
culture and lead to its transformation. The more intact the tenets of
the prevailing political culture, the more resistant to transformation
it is likely to be and the more likely are parochial units to serve as
refuges from transformative powers or as institutional centres of
resistance.[26]

    A fragmented political culture, which the political cultures of
most Third World countries are, is more prone to political instability
and disruption than an integrated one. Unlike fragmented political
cultures, integrated ones are marked by diffuse political trust among
social groups and a conspicuous absence of the social paranoia that
characterise fragmented cultures.[27] Depending on the strength of
existing political institutions and the measures a regime is willing to
take in order to maintain itself, fragmented political cultures lead to
either strict conformity or intransigence and open revolt. The political system is inherently unstable, subject to violent overthrow or
maintained through highly coercive means.[28] Requiring considerable
energy and much sacrifice in terms of human life, submissive conformity to systems with fragmented political cultures are more likely

than their revolutionary overthrow.[29] In such circumstances, where coercion inhibits the possibility of open rebellion against the alien world of politics, a retreat into parochial units such as family, neighbourhood, and village community or tribe takes place.[30] The political establishment appears increasingly threatening, its institutions increasingly irrelevant, and its ideology and propaganda sophistical and even offensive. Politics becomes a field of practice for the vain. Official political activities bear little resemblance to accepted cultural practices, their underlying assumptions viewed as alien and inconsequential. Obedience to authority thus becomes ritualistic, arising out of compliance without commitment or cognition.[31] Opportunism and self-serving behaviour in politics replace dedication and commitment to political forms.

Yet cultural anomie is only one of the characteristics of political culture in the Third World. To begin with, within each Third World country, it is not uncommon to find a plurality of political cultures. Third World political cultures are marked by a sharp dichotomy into the political cultures of the elites and that of the masses, each differentiated from the other by its unique features and characteristics.[32] Mass political culture is formed by attitudes and orientations toward politics of the population as a whole, including the participating citizens and the rank and file members of both authoritative and non-authoritative structures which do not significantly control the output of the political system.[33] Elite political culture, on the other hand, 'involves the attitudes, sentiments, and behavior of those who through the operation of political recruitment function have been brought to active roles in the political system and have a direct effect on the output of the system. The elite political culture thus involves those in authoritative structures but also the leadership elements of the non-authoritative structures and processes'.[34]

The 'elite', with their distinct political culture, do not necessarily need to be political elites as the above definition implies. Throughout the Third World's differentiated societies, there are considerable differences between the masses of people on the one hand and economic, social, and intellectual elites on the other, each of whom have orientations that are markedly different from those of the popular masses.[35] Similarly, elite political culture may not necessarily be supportive of prevailing political forms, as it may belong to a growing nucleus of elite intellectuals who oppose the political establishment. The incompatibility of this intellectual elite's political culture with that of the masses leads to the former's psychological alienation from the general public, complicating their quest for identification with and leadership of the masses.[36] The affinity of the political elite's culture with that of the masses depends largely on the degree to which the polity has undergone popular legitimation. The weaker the link between state and society, and the more fragile the legitimacy of political institutions and practices, the sharper are the differences between the elite and the mass political cultures. The state–society nexus is in fact weak in much of the Third World (see below) and there are, as a result, often stark differences between the political cultures of the elites and those of the masses.

In addition to its divisions into fragmented and integrated, mass and elite, political cultures can be divided into the three variations of parochial, subject, and participant.[37] In parochial political cultures, there are no specialised political roles (e.g. leadership, headmanship, etc.), and political orientations toward these roles are the same as religious and social ones.[38] Increasingly rare in the contemporary world, parochial political cultures can be found in tribes and tradi-tional polities with extremely diffuse and unformulated political structures, or in religious sects for whom religious leadership is closely linked with community and political leadership. In subject political cultures, the type most commonly found in the Third World, the person is aware of specialised government authority but does not take part in it and is merely subject to the government's administrative output. There is only a one-way flow of information between the political establishment and the larger society, and people's negative or positive orientations toward political objects matter little.[39] Subject political cultures are prevalent in countries ruled by authoritarian regimes, where conformity and blind obedience to administrative directives reign supreme. In participant political cultures, on the other hand, social classes take an essentially activist role in the political process, whether in its support or its defiance.[40] Participatory democracies, populist governments, and even authoritarian regimes on the brink of revolutionary overthrow, in all of which there is a high rate of cognitive public participation in politics, all have participant political cultures.

The degree to which the public is cognitively aware of politics and is active in it is key to whether a political culture is parochial, subject, or participant. In parochial political cultures, the public is unaware or is only dimly aware of politics and is largely detached from the political system. In subject political culture, the public's awareness of and participation in the political process is limited to the system's outputs as meted out through the bureaucracy, the executive, and the judiciary. In participant political cultures, however, the public is highly aware of the intricacies and nuances of the political system and actively participates in the process of politics.[41] Of course, these different political cultures are not mutually exclusive and do not exist in complete isolation from one another. Especially in the Third World, parochial tendencies often coexist side by side with subject or participant political cultures. This is particularly the case in urbanising societies, where participant or subject political cultures among the urban population may coexist with widespread parochial tendencies in the countryside. What determines the overall character of a political culture is the predominance of one form over another.

Given considerable variations from one country or region to another, Third World political cultures are often highly fragmented, are marked by either extremes of participant, subject, or parochial tendencies, and are frequently sharply divided between the political culture of the elite and that of the masses. Throughout the Third World, there is a striking absence of a shared understanding as to what the generally expected limits and potentialities of political action should be.[42] The fragmentation of political cultures arises out of incomplete or misdirected political socialisation, the resistance of old orientations to the onslaught of new political forms, and the resulting emotive nature of political conduct. Fragmentation is accentuated by the persistence of traditional values and the slow legitimation of new political principles and institutions, despite massive and at times even violent attempts by Third World governments to transform the existing political culture. More commonly, however, the methods used to inculcate a new political culture include latent propaganda or overt mobilisation through the mass media, the official party, the bureaucracy, and the school system. Through these efforts, Third World governments hope to discredit old political orientations and instil new ones in their place.[43]

Most studies of political culture have concentrated on Western, predominantly democratic, political systems.[44] Taking the collective political orientations of the population as the axiom of political culture, most scholars have thus concentrated on open manifestations of political sentiments such as patterns of voting behaviour in order to examine the political culture of a particular country.[45] The political characteristics of most Third World countries automatically disqualify many of these studies as applicable methodological guides to the study of their political cultures. Except in a few isolated instances, true political sentiments and orientations in the Third World are hardly expressed through institutionalised means such as voting patterns or public opinion polls. It is through more subtle medians of expression, not merely political expression but also cultural, folkloric, and even artistic expression, that political sentiments and orientations are expressed. Literature, music, films, and even religion are some of the powerful carriers of political messages in the Third World. When open political expression is inhibited, such alternative means of expression become heavily impregnated with political symbolism. As a result, in many Third World countries there is more meaning to cultural idioms than meets the eye. Within such a context, an examination of political culture in the Third World needs to focus not merely on the orientations underlying political behaviour but on the more subtle tools that serve as proxies for overt political sentiments. Only through an examination of popular idioms such as literature and religion can an adequate understanding of political orientations in the Third World be reached.

POLITICAL ORIENTATIONS

A study of political culture involves examining public sentiments and orientations toward political objects. In this endeavour, a distinction needs to be made between orientations toward politics in general and toward existing political arrangements in particular. Although at times the two may converge, *political orientations* and *regime orientations* in the Third World are not necessarily always the same. A fine distinction separates the two. Political orientation refers to those collective sentiments that govern the public's general outlook toward politics as a field of practice, as an abstract science, and as a general guideline for the attainment of community or national power. Regime orientation, however, refers to public sentiments toward the specific political actors who currently hold the reins of power, the institutions they have established, and the laws they have devised. The objects of attention are tangible and currently at work. Orientations toward politics, on the other hand, are orientations toward the *field* of politics rather than toward specific, existing objects. Admittedly, one's general views toward politics are heavily influenced by the prevailing political environment. That is why it only makes sense to talk of such a distinction in closed, authoritarian political systems, where outwardly manifest orientations toward the political system are almost invariably different from sentiments toward politics as a field. For this reason, the distinction between political orientations and regime orientations is particularly significant in the Third World. There, orientations and sentiments toward politics are primarily expressed through three main idioms: ideology and doctrinal beliefs; religion; and popular cultural forms such as music, the arts, and literature. Through these mechanisms, sentiments and orientations toward political objects (including political institutions and practices) are expressed, often in codified language but at times expressly.

Within the three idioms for the expression of political sentiments, ideology has particular significance. This significance arises from ideology's express concern with politics, thus bestowing it with particular importance in providing a conceptual frame of political thought and orientation toward society at large. Throughout the Third World, as elsewhere, ideologies and doctrines are viewed as systematic blueprints which lay out procedures for the attainment of political power and the dispersion of that power once acquired. To the politically minded, ideology provides the conceptual framework within which political objectives can be formulated and initiatives toward their achievement launched. Ideology is an 'all-embracing political doctrine, which claims to give a complete and universally applicable theory of man and society, and to derive therefrom a programme of political action'.[47] Moreover, within Third World societies, ideology helps to define values, both political and otherwise.[48] To the politically diehard, ideologies are more than purely political blueprints; they are guidelines to social and cultural values as well. They provide universes around which constellations that govern one's life revolve. As such, in closed and authoritarian political systems, which predominate in the Third World, non-official ideologies are often perceived by the political establishment to be highly threatening conceptual frameworks for political opposition.[49] They provide for alternative methods of thinking about political objects and do not endorse, if not necessarily negate, the valuative justifications with which political incumbents justify their rule.

Largely because of the circumstances under which they are formulated, political ideologies in the Third World are marked by high degrees of dogmatism, intolerance for competing ideologies, and a lack of in-depth understanding by their propagators. Particularly in countries where political liberties are severely curtailed, public familiarisation with 'unofficial' ideologies takes place in a clandestine and haphazard fashion. Secret meetings and underground 'discussion groups', pamphlets and protracted speeches, banned books and essays, and association with students or returning immigrants from abroad with different political outlooks often sum up the means through which most Third World residents come into contact with ideologies other than the state's. At best, only a superficial understanding of an ideology could hence be attained. Catchphrases and fragmented notions thus become the embodiment of the public's understanding of a particular ideological framework. Yet this superficiality does not inhibit an ideology's acceptance by certain social groups and even its widespread popularity. Ideologies are adopted and followed not necessarily because of their deep understanding and dynamic applicability to local conditions, but because they are for the most part in contradiction to the prevailing mode of political thinking. Intellectuals and political activists adopt a certain ideology as much for its rejection of the existing polity as they do for its principles and valuational merits. Ideologies provide an alternative to existing political principles and values. That much is understood and appreciated. It is hardly clear, and frequently even unimportant, what the intricacies of these conceptual alternatives that are being followed are.[50] Moreover, nuances in human nature, which enhance the appeal of that which is forbidden, further accentuate the attraction of non-official and politically suppressed ideologies. This is particularly true of ideological alternatives in the Third World, where adherence to a doctrinal framework other than the regime's often symbolises political opposition and open-mindedness.

A more fundamental reason for the legitimation of alternative ideologies in the Third World lies in the social and cultural ramifications of rapid industrialisation and a realisation of economic backwardness vis-à-vis the West. In instances where rapid social change has disrupted traditional cultural norms, and diffusion and industrialisation have brought on feelings of inferiority and backwardness, extremist ideologies offering quick and radical solutions find a ready and eager mass of believers.[51] Feelings of inferiority are compensated for by dogmatic denunciation of the existing order and promises of a future more glorious than what the West has. Whether through religious imagery and theological reasoning (as in Iran), or through the 'science' of Marxism–Leninism or the warped logic of Nazism in the Third Reich, the extremist ideology finds adherents because it offers a precise and codified blueprint for the attainment of the earthly heaven that it promises.[52] More important, it is a means through which a lost sense of identity could be regained. With social and cultural values in disarray, with indigenous sources of identity ravaged by the unrelenting forces of social change, an ideology could offer the median through which the self can once again be discovered and asserted.[53] How this ideological self-assertion is articulated depends on various historical, national, and social and cultural characteristics. Depending on specific features and experiences, greatness may be found in a race (as in the cases of Nazism, Apartheid, Negrotude, and Jewish Zionism), a religion (witness Islam's role in the Islamic world), a political doctrine (communism and Arab socialism), or an identity forged across international boundaries (Pan Africanism, Pan Arabism, and the *Ummat* – Islamic community). In each case, they restore a lost sense of identity, and even more than that, an identity inflated by greatness and chauvinistic ego.

The risks involved in believing in ideologies other than the one advocated by the regime are often too great in many Third World countries for any meaningful segment of the population to openly adopt and adhere to. Additionally, strict government control of the mass media, coupled at times with unrelenting police repression, often significantly curtails the means through which political aspirants can formulate and then propagate their ideologies among the population. Yet political factors are not alone in curtailing the spread of alternative political ideologies. Social and cultural considerations weigh equally heavily in determining whether a particular society is receptive to alternative, non-official ideologies at all, and, if it is, what those ideologies are most likely to be. Can, it is necessary to examine, any alternative political doctrines be nurtured in societies like those of the Third World, where illiteracy and repression inhibit political education, organisational mobilisation, and the introduction and spread of ideologies which do not have official backing? Are Third World social conditions conducive to the mass-based popularisation of ideological frameworks that are different from, if not necessarily opposed to, the regime's? In mass-based movements, a plethora of political dynamics, in particular the hegemony of ideological standard-bearers over the masses, determine the ideological orientations of the dominated social classes.[54] When, however, political circumstances make the social acceptability of alternative ideologies unfeasible, much less allow for their growth and popularity, ideologies find expression through other socially accepted norms.

In many parts of the Third World, religion fulfils exactly this surrogate function. The political importance of religion in the Third

World arises out of its socially pervasive character. Religion is a perennial source of political action and meaning because of the ability of religious metaphors, places, and rituals to sum up and intensify popular experiences.[55] Moreover, religion performs a pivotal role as a social unifier, providing the language and sets of ideas which people across all social levels can readily hear and easily understand. The fusion of political objectives into religious practices is at times an inadvertent development arising out of prevailing social conditions. Latin American priests' assumption of responsibility aimed at rectifying social and economic injustice inflicted against peasants testifies as much to the acuteness of prevailng social circumstances as it does to an inter-marriage of religion and political convictions.[56] No doubt, however, many political activists in the Third World also find in religion a convenient mechanism for popular legitimation and mass mobilisation. The specific political character and orientation that a religion may acquire depends most of all on the interpretation of religious principles by those preaching them to the masses. Thus the specific direction of religion's political legitimation is up for grabs and is determined by the patterns of domination in culture, politics, and economy.[57] Expressly revolutionary political interpretations of religion, notably Liberation Theology in Latin America and the beliefs of the Moslem Brotherhood in Egypt and in other Arab countries, are just as likely to be countered by strict conservatism of the kind preached and practised by the Vatican and by the House of Saud. Similarly, in the Third World and elsewhere, religion has been as much a tool for political oppression as it has been for political dissent and agitation. Thus the fusion of religion and politics does not necessarily guarantee the former's doctrinal colouring one way or another. Religion may be, and in fact in recent years it often has been, used as a language of political discourse. Such a language is not, however, inherently revolutionary or conservative. Such characteristics vary depending on the social, political, and historical contexts within which the coalescence of religion and politics takes place.

Despite the absence of a systemic relationship between religion and political orientation, a number of factors in the Third World have pushed religion into a politically oppositional role. Political repression, corruption, feelings of exploitation at the hands of foreigners, and other similar political grievances have combined to shape religion's political ethos overwhelmingly in the direction of political opposition. This politically oppositional posture is especially true of religions that have so far not attained institutional, political power, such as Catholicism in Latin America or Islam in pre-revolutionary Iran. The more politically institutionalised a religion, or the closer the affinity of religious institutions to political ones, the more politically conservative a force is religion likely to be. Israel, Saudi Arabia, and post-revolutionary Iran all offer examples of cases where the close amalgamation of religious and political institutions reinforce the conservative character of both religion and the body politic. Conversely, the greater the gap between religion and politics, the more is religion likely to be opposed to the political establishment and be of a revolutionary nature. Ostensibly secular societies – such as pre-revolutionary Iran, present-day Egypt, and the ones in South and Central America – are most amenable to religious radicalism.

In countries where repression predominates and civil and political liberties are non-existent, religion's growing concern with actual or perceived injustices has been gradual and for the most part implicit. Massive outbursts of religiously tainted political sentiments, of the kind that erupted in Iran in the late 1970s and that sporadically flares up in other parts of the Middle East, are the exception not the rule. For the most part, religion's concern with political themes in the Third World has occurred through a re-evaluation of core theological principles and their application to everyday life. From Africa and Asia to Latin America, religious doctrines have been re-interpreted in order to more adequately fit the life patterns and the daily concerns of those they affect. In the Philippines, for example, religious authorities have attempted to portray a more activist character of Christ in recent years, emphasising his role as a sub-versive trying to create a new brotherhood and a new era.[58] Similar reinterpretations of religious doctrines have occurred throughout Africa, where an ongoing process of religious indigenation is aiming to make religion more attuned to the continent's cultural and political realities.[59] In South Africa, where political repression is at its extreme, the politically oppositional role of religion is even more accentuated.[60]

Nowhere has the politically oppositional role of religion been formulated in such a comprehensive and systematic manner as has been the case in Latin America. In countries otherwise as different as El Salvador, Chile, and Brazil, the common concern of religion with political repression has heralded in a brand of Catholicism known as Liberation Theology. Liberation Theology's concern has been the welfare of the masses at the most local level, in villages and in neighbourhood communities most dramatically afflicted with political injustice and economic inequity.[61] The basic interlocutor of Liberation Theology is not the unbeliever but the poor, its problem less atheism and idolatry than suffering.[62] Its emphasis on grassroots movements is accentuated by the proliferation in recent years of Base Ecclesial Communities, groups that meet regularly to read and discuss the Bible, pray, and celebrate liturgies.[63] Both developments, however, have come to spearhead causes such as literacy, leadership, initiative, and self-help, thus undermining the pervasive influence of the Catholic church and its more conservative priests. Liberation Theology has emerged as an indigenous language of political discourse, indeed of political dissent, aided to a great extent by the relentless political repression which much of Latin America experienced in the 1970s and most of the 1980s. Once an alternative conceptual framework within which political sentiments could be formulated was found, i.e. Catholicism, a number of developments helped transform it into a mass-based ideology. Agrarian proletarianisation, large-scale urbanisation, and the growth of literacy and mass communication combined to provide circumstances that were conducive to Liberation Theology's growth as a mass-based, non-official political ideology.[64] The growing political democratisation of Latin American countries beginning in the 1980s is likely to lessen Liberation Theology's concern with political repression, secular ideologies and organisations, increasingly assuming the functions with which Liberation Theology entrusted itself. Nevertheless, continued economic growth and development, and the resulting perpetuation of inequities and economic miseries, will keep Liberation Theology alive as an agenda for opposing the (economic) status quo.

In more subtle and less discernible ways, political orientations and sentiments are also expressed through various cultural forms, especially through music, literature, and the arts. Unlike religion and ideology, the political message embedded in cultural forms is often implicit and coded. Unable to voice their political sentiments openly, political aspirants and agitators use cultural means to communicate their message across to the people, using diverse tools like music, films and plays, novels and short stories, and even paintings. Frequently, the perpetrator is an artist renowned for his or her work, an intellectual who has to rely on artistic abilities to bypass government censors and get across to the people. The decipherer, meanwhile, needs to be equally skilled in order to be able to look beyond the surface appearance of the art and grasp its deeper meaning. Thus the whole affair of using cultural forms as mediums of political discourse, as links between ideological protagonists and the larger society, is a decidedly elitist affair. Yet political sentiments are in fact often expressed through art and their message is indeed understood by many. Not every work of art in the Third World is, of course, the bearer of some deeper meaning and message. To the contrary, disillusionment over phenomena such as political repression, economic and social dislocation, and cultural alienation have resulted in a proliferation of escapist forms of entertainment in many Third World countries.[65] Nevertheless, especially in countries where the open expression of political sentiments is a risky venture, it is worth looking to see if a work of art, especially in the literary field, is trying to convey more than its obvious message. Third World countries are inundated with artists who use their talents to express their political sentiments, albeit in coded and disguised language. Often, the artists use their essays, films, plays, or songs to merely comment on their society and culture, eschewing from political commentary for fear of prosecution. But such concealed political expressions are still prevalent. During the height of repression in Turkey in the 1960s and the 1970s, Aziz Nassin managed to write a plethora of biting commentaries on the state of Turkish society and politics. Ahmad Shamlu had achieved similar literary feats in Iran in the 1950s and the 1960s. Before the wave of democratisation that swept across eastern Europe in the late 1980s, the Czechoslovak playwright and future president Vaclav Havel was in a similar predicament. Egypt's Najib Mahfuz continues to this day to elude government censors and write piercing commentary on aspects of Egyptian life. And the list continues.

A further characteristic of political orientations in the Third World is their highly emotional nature. In almost all Third World countries, ordinary, everyday experiences with politics have resulted in intensely emotional political sentiments. The coercion experienced at the hands of the police and the army, the anguish and disillusionment arising from the government's economic and industrial policies, and the frustrations stemming from the bureaucracy's inertness and inefficiency all combine to make sentiments toward politics in the Third World intensely emotional. This emotive nature of political expressions is reinforced through the absence of organised, institutionalised ways through which political sentiments and feelings could be expressed. To avoid the risks involved, political sentiments are often expressed through double-talk or in secret meetings and clandestine groups. Such methods by nature involve considerable emotional intensity. Moreover, political education, clandestine as it is, often takes place through participating in or observing mass-based, emotionally charged movements that are often spurred by dramatic, extreme, and even violent language.[66] Although the frenzy of a politically excited mob is an extreme example, the basic undercurrents remain the same. Political aspirants frequently dramatise the deeds of their past heroes, often to the point of mythicising them, and using them as models for themselves and for those they call to action. Melodrama becomes an important part of their political dogma and a main *modus operandi*. In cases where there has been a personalisation of the political system by incumbents, a similar glorification of personalities resonates into opposing aspirants. The contest for political power becomes as much a contest between myths and personalities as one between differing systems of thought and belief. Men become goals in themselves, viewpoints become ideologies, and emotions replace principles.

The intense, emotional nature of political sentiments in the Third World leaves little room for meaningful discourse and mutual respect among those with varying political orientations. Mention has already been made of the highly dogmatic nature of ideologies in the Third World, being largely viewed by their believers as inflexible and unchangeable sciences. The believers are rigid in their doctrinal outlooks, seldom seeing the need or the rationale for the existence of other ideologies and political persuasions. A similar dogmatic sectarianism permeates political orientations. Everyone thinks that others with different orientations are hopelessly misguided and un-informed. Within a society, in fact, competing tendencies and orien-tations may sharply divide collective political perceptions and sentiments. Adherents of communist ideologies look with extreme contempt at those who give religion political colourings, and vice versa. Those who favour liberal economic policies find virulent opposition from, and themselves sharply oppose, those advocating centralised economic planning. Among the masses at large, at least, there is little room for ideological compromise or even mutual understanding.[67] An ideology and a set of views about the larger world of politics is expressed and only partially understood through clandestine or heavily refined medians (such as religion or the arts), and then it is largely viewed as the unchangeable truth. The circum-stances within which these orientations are formed, such as the necessity to conceal them to avoid persecution, in turn reinforces their sectarianism. As a result, sectarianism is an endemic character of political orientations in the Third World.

REGIME ORIENTATIONS

While *political orientations* denote the public's perceptions of and tendencies toward the world of politics in general, *regime orientations* entail the more specific feelings and sentiments that are directed toward existing political incumbents. The two reinforce one another and are at times even indiscernible. One's understanding of *politics* is, indeed, shaped and heavily influenced by prevailing political institutions and practices which govern society and determine its laws and regulations. In parochial and subject political cultures especially, there is seldom the ability or the necessity to differentiate between orientations toward current power-holders and orientations toward politics in general. Yet the two are indeed different and have different characteristics. Political orientations are seldom expressed openly and often find expression through religion or various culture forms, are often highly emotional, and are, consequently, largely sectarian. Regime orientations, on the other hand, are for the most part tied to the fulfilment or the frustration of expectations. They are marked by reductionist tendencies which see politics as a game controlled by forces far more powerful than those which people can collectively influence. Moreover, rumours play an important part in the understanding of and perceptions toward the prevailing power structure. Lastly, political cultures throughout the Third World demonstrate a striking lack of interpersonal trust, itself symptomatic of political repression and the ensuing apprehensions and fears that mar attitudes toward political structures and institutions.

Third World political cultures are extensively influenced by long periods of disappointed expectations and resulting dissatisfied political attitudes. Such negative attitudes toward the existing polity arise from prolonged periods of economic uncertainty coupled with political repression.[68] The economic flux that is an inescapable facet of Third World development, and the predominance of restrictive and oppressive political institutions there give rise to a general sense of economic and political dissatisfaction. In few political systems, with the exception of populist regimes, is there any degree of genuine public support for the establishment. Most people are either politically passive or hold highly cynical views toward political incumbents. Cynicism of this sort is historically perpetuated and is passed on from generation to generation through pre-adult social-isation, becoming part of distinctive cultural patterns.[69] Such patterns transcend more than mere political cynicism and lead to a host of characteristics involving the broader tenets of political culture. Inter-personal distrust and scepticism, the perception of politics as a con-trolled and cruel game played by giants at the expense of the masses, and the consequent dogmatism of such vitriols as communism or anti-Americanism are all derived from the predominance of negative perceptions toward existing political arrangements.

The example of anti-American sentiments merits further elabora-tion. The anti-Americanism that has become an ingrained part of Third World political culture is most directly traceable to negative dispositions toward local regimes in power. In most parts of the Third World, anti-American sentiments have grown because of American over-identification with unpopular local rulers.[70] In the Middle East, the friendly ties between the United States and unpopular regimes like the Iranian monarchy or President Sadat in Egypt is cause for the widespread resentment toward American policies found in the region.[71] In Africa, anti-Americanism results largely from the cordial relations between the United States and the South African government, whose racial policies of apartheid stir passionate hatred throughout the continent.[72] American heavy-handedness in Central America and the Caribbean to sustain un-popular regimes, especially during the Reagan administration, also accounts for the prevalence of anti-American sentiments in Latin America.[73] American policy-makers' tendency to personalise relations with foreign heads of state, who in the Third World are mostly despised at home, does not help the United State's image.[74] There are, of course, anti-American sentiments in the Third World that are issue-specific (e.g. the Palestinian question and apartheid), ideologically inspired, or are the result of government propaganda.[75] Yet the United States' close identification with local regimes, which are already subject to much public resentment anyway, reinforces anti-American feelings and sentiments throughout the region.

To a large extent, political cynicism and anti-American senti-ments have combined to inject into Third World political cultures analytically reductionist tendencies. Politics is reduced to a con-spiracy between overbearing forces which are impervious to local demands and indigenous movements. It is seen as a conspiratorial game, with the principal adversaries being the global superpowers and their puppets, the local rulers. Political activism is considered to be futile, unable to influence the tide of events which shape the nation's political structure and destiny. Domestic affairs are viewed as reverberations of international deals conspired and struck in Washington, London, Paris, or Beijing. This line of thinking is a much less scholarly, home-brewed version of the dependency theory of economic development, seeing politics in much the same light as economy, as the dictates of powerful patrons to helpless clients. The protagonists of such thinking, however, are not merely scholars and intellectuals but the people at large, from the working classes upward, especially those who have reached a level of social, economic, and political sophistication sufficient to express political sentiments. Ironically, many of these social classes are themselves beneficiaries of the government's economic policies (e.g. bureaucrats and civil servants, teachers, entrepreneurs and merchants, physicians, and the like), and are, for the most part, uncritical, even perhaps unaware, of the overwhelming influence of multinational corporations in their country's economy.

The widespread currency of politically reductionist sentiments is largely the product of the political history of those countries in which colonialism was most prevalent. The Middle East and Africa have especially been arenas in which colonial giants have shaped history and have at one point or another ruled as they pleased. Whether it was the Ottomans, the French, or the British, the omnipotence of colonial power in yesteryears has left an indelible impression in the minds of most Third Worlders. The lingering inability of most post-colonial countries to stand on their own economic and political feet after independence has merely accented the public's suspicion of colonial hands at work. Blatant and covert actions by the American Central Intelligence Agency, the British Secret Service, and the former Soviet Union's KGB in carrying out their agendas in various parts of the world have further given credence to the perception of Third World politics as a superpower game.[76] These operations have over the years given a measure of justification to the conspiratorial vision of politics in the Third World. But to discount every political development and turmoil as a plot conspired by an intelligence agency is as misdirected as is an uncritical endorsement of the dependency theory of economic development. Much of the reason for the prevalence of conspiratorial political views in the Third World is the public's inadequate understanding of the social sciences (see below). Unable to comprehend the complex economic, political, and social dynamics at work in their societies, most Third

Worlders see a convenient culprit in the superpowers, using their countries' tumultuous history to justify their views.

A further characteristic of political culture in the Third World is the lack of interpersonal trust, which in turn displays itself in public orientations toward the existing regime. Political repression, manipulation, corruption, instability, and insecurity have all combined to nurture a strong sense of distrust among the politically-minded in the Third World. The omnipresence of state intelligence agencies in many Third World countries is hardly conducive to the flourishing of trust among the people and between people and the political establishment. People have little faith that their desired political ends can be achieved through existing institutions, do not trust political aspirants to invest their energies in positive directions if they were to attain power, and have little faith on the fruitfulness of political activism altogether. The political cynicism arising out of reductionist thinking reaches into and affects interpersonal relations, particularly on the political plain. The scarcity of economic resources and fierce competition for greater access to them, practised by all social classes alike, further accentuates the sense of interpersonal distrust and scepticism.

A final factor in the analysis of regime orientations in the Third World is the role played by rumours. As impersonal communication systems are not adequately developed in the Third World, rumours play an important role in disseminating information and ideas.[77] More specifically, rumours proliferate where information and data on political personalities and events is either completely non-existent or fragmentary at best. The very secretive nature of political elites in most Third World countries invite speculation about their intentions, actions, and personalities. In many Third World countries, for example, little is known about the personal lives of political leaders, such as their marital status, number of children, or wealth, or about their personal rapport with one another.[78] Any slight indication that may lead the public to form an opinion one way or another can also cause much elaborate theorising and speculation. In many Third World countries, rumours are equally prevalent in relation to the government's policy intentions. This is particularly evident in countries where the public is kept in the dark about the government's intentions, with officials either being impervious to public opinion or not having developed institutions through which they could effectively articulate their intended policies for the people. The prevalence of conspiratorial views toward the political establishment only helps to reinforce the forcefulness of rumours. A road expansion project may be seen as a means to further enhance the favourable position of a government minister (or his tribe), or viewed as a tool for extending government control in previously remote areas.

Whether through manipulation by political actors or by exposure to the writings and speeches of intellectuals, the process of forming ideas and orientations toward political objects takes place through political socialisation.[79] It is through political socialisation that one becomes aware of the prevailing political environment and forms orientations toward existing political arrangements as well as toward politics in general. Much of political socialisation, especially in the Third World, where the state tends to be omnipresent, takes place through specific governmental organs charged with instilling a certain political outlook among the population. Some Third World governments have bureaus and departments which are specifically designed for creating politically supportive attitudes among the population. Post-revolutionary Iran's Ministry of Islamic Guidance is an example of a government body entrusted with the specific task of augmenting the regimes' ideological base of support among the population.[80] The Information or Interior ministries of a number of other Third World governments perform similar functions. In these and in other instances, the media are particularly instrumental in shaping the public's orientations toward current political incumbents and their doctrines. Even in those countries where the media have traditionally enjoyed a measure of independence from the government, as in India and a growing number of Latin American countries, they still continue to serve as tools for political socialisation by creating political sentiments among the public. Even if the intent of a given article in a newspaper or an entertainment show on television is not expressly political, the implied message is in one way or another frequently supportive of the status quo, unless, of course, the artist is using those medians to express opposition to the system.

EDUCATION

Parallel and concurrent with all of this is the role of the educational system, from the most elementary level to university, which plays a paramount role as an agent of political socialisation. Through the educational system, Third World governments try to socialise children and students into the official political culture and to familiarise them with political norms that are supportive of the regime.[81] This was most widely practised by colonial powers who used the educational systems of their colonies as mechanisms for recruiting civil servants and bureaucrats.[82] This they did without trying to assimilate the local population into the colonial culture.[83] However, their enduring legacy of indigenous political cultures cannot be denied. Formal, linear education (advancing from one level to the next) has become commonplace in the Third World while traditional methods of non-formal education have been almost completely uprooted.[84] Moreover, there is heavy emphasis on learning things that are 'Western', even in the sciences, while indigenous and proven advances in fields such as animal husbandry, herbal medicine, and local techniques are discarded and ridiculed.[85] Publishing has become a field dominated by Western giants, and an understanding of the Western languages has become essential for keeping up with the latest scientific and technological advances.[86] For their part, Third World governments have discovered the overwhelming importance of education in shaping orientations toward politics and have turned their educational systems into tools for perpetuating their own stability and longevity.

The most blatant efforts at political socialisation take place at the elementary and middle school levels of education. Considerable emphasis is placed on curriculums that introduce children to basic facts about politics and important political leaders. Memorising of the national anthem and the names of the capital, the ruling party, and principal political actors is often an important part of early formal education. The teaching of an officially approved version of history assumes paramount importance, with highly selective emphasis on those aspects or eras supportive of the existing regime at the neglect of darker, less flattering periods. In instances when monumental historical events contradict the current regime's ideologies, merely different interpretations are applied. Auxiliary disciplines which further support the status quo are also created and made part of the school curriculum. Religious studies is one such typical subject, as are somewhat less prevalent courses such as civic sciences and social studies. These and other similar subjects, which inundate Third World college and high school classrooms, are designed to create politically supportive orientations among students.

Efforts at moulding the political orientations of university students have been somewhat different. By nature, university students have always been prone to questioning the state's authority and have consistently been among the first groups to voice their displeasure over the political establishment, often not hesitating to use extreme and violent measures. In restrictive polities such as those in Iran, Egypt, Turkey, South Korea, and China, universities and even high schools have at one time or another been an oasis of political activism and discontent. In fact, in countries with a long tradition of student activism, such as South Korea, taking part in student demonstrations and sit-ins is considered to be a rite of passage and a sign of intellectual maturity. Part of the reason for this activism on the part of students lies in their exposure to alternative political ideologies and to doctrines which call into question the legitimacy of current officeholders. Students have relatively easier access to banned or restricted books which are almost impossible to find outside university campuses. The very fact that they are students also puts them in greater contact with like-minded peers, enabling them to acquire a sense of community and togetherness which they would not have otherwise had. Moreover, by the virtue of their elitist position as university students, they see themselves as entrusted with a mission to rectify the wrongs of their society. This sense of mission is clearly evident through the clandestine publications of those Third World university students who have risen in revolt against their countries' leaders. Among Iranian students in 1978, 1979, and 1980, Egyptian students through the late 1970s and the early 1980s, and Chinese students in summer 1988, the establishment of social justice, democracy, and economic equity were of primary importance.[87] In South Korea, similarly, university students have been the forerunners of the call for reunification with North Korea.[88]

Containment of the university student population and control over what they read and think is thus of paramount importance to virtually all Third World governments. However, because of their greater intellectual sophistication, official efforts to influence their political orientations have also been more sophisticated and less blatant. Most commonly, university students are discouraged from studying the social sciences and, often through special grants and scholarships, are encouraged to study technical and scientific subjects. The fact that Third World universities have consistently demonstrated greater eagerness to train students in the natural and technical sciences rather than in the social sciences only partially reflects their desire to catch-up with the West technologically. Keeping students ignorant of the social sciences in order to lessen the likelihood of their political activism is also part of the equation. That is partly why over threequarters of all political scientists and two-thirds of all psychologists are from the United States.[89] Most Third World universities which do have active programmes in disciplines other than the natural sciences, meanwhile, concentrate on largely non-political subjects such as philosophy, law, jurisprudence, literature, ancient history, and economics. In cases where instruction in the social sciences does take place, concepts and notions are imported from the West and are taught without much modification, thus being largely irrelevant to indigenous circumstances.[90] A deliberate effort is made to present subjects such as political science and sociology as almost purely abstract and irrelevant to prevailing social and political circumstances.

The difficulties of attaining a viable and academically credible education at both primary and higher levels are compounded by a lack of sufficient and relevant textbooks and the general weakness of the publishing industry in the Third World. Third World countries have neither the massive literate population nor the well developed library facilities that provide the demand for large-scale book publishing. Furthermore, only in recent years have most of the basic elements necessary for publishing, such as equipment and editors, been built and developed having been largely non-existent before.[91] Only a few Third World countries with long literary traditions, most notable of which are Mexico, India, and Egypt, have made some inroads in publishing. Otherwise, publishing remains a largely infant industry in the Third World. According to one estimate, some eighty per cent of the world's book titles are published in the industrialised countries of the West.[92] Moreover, major European languages have come to dominate publishing, discouraging publishers from aggressively translating titles into the languages other than English, French, and Spanish. As a result, more than half of total published titles are produced in only eight European countries.[93]

It is within the context of manipulated curriculums and controlled schools, large-scale and institutional discouragement of the social sciences, and inadequate literary resources and fledgling publishing industries that Third World intellectuals, those merchants of ideas, emerge. It is their role, as traders in the market of ideas, which makes them instrumental in shaping a nation's political culture and the orientations of its people toward things both political and otherwise. As a distinct social class, Third World intellectuals share a number of characteristics with their Western counterparts. Broadly, intellectuals have been defined as those 'qualified, and accepted as qualified, to speak on matters of cultural concern'.[94] They are, however, inherently different from academics and scholars. While intellectuals 'predicate societal action', academics focus on the 'seminal diffusion of ideas to students'.[95] There is also a distinction between intellectuals and the intelligentsia. Intellectuals are usually a part of the intelligentsia: while the intelligentsia are simply better educated, intellectuals trade in and reflect on ideas. The intellectual, therefore, is essentially defined by virtue of his or her relationship to social and cultural values. Through the utilisation of ideologies, intellectuals elicit, guide, and form the expressive dispositions of a society,[96] thus either reshaping or reinforcing certain norms and values around which matters of social and political controversy revolve. Intellectuals speak against their society's dominant cultural frame of reference and choose deliberately to estrange themselves from the cultural superstructure. Such estrangement often arises out of the intellectuals' alienation from their surrounding environment and from other social groups with whom they cannot communicate and for whom they largely remain enigmatic and little understood. As a result of their social alienation and psychological frustration, intellectuals often become politically oppositional and view themselves as future leaders of a political movement.

The role that intellectuals play in modernising societies differs from that of intellectuals in more advanced, industrially developed ones. As modernisation requires the transformation of both the industrial infrastructure and the cultural values that govern a society, intellectuals in such a polity acquire a special relationship to the rapidly changing body of social and cultural values. In modernising societies, intellectuals' support for or opposition to the values at hand is at a more fundamental and grass-roots level. Such values have either not been fully adopted by the general population, or their adoption and popular social acceptance can be easily challenged by other, contending values. In modern societies, in contrast, where values have long been adopted and form an integral part of the accepted norms of society, the intellectuals' support for or opposition to such values is not as fundamental to their popular acceptability or rejection as is the case in modernising societies. In modernising countries, therefore, intellectuals exert a much higher degree of social influence. As the contention between values is more polarised in countries that are undergoing rapid social change, so is the influence of intellectuals, owing to the nature of their position in relation to those values. The more polarised the divergence among values, and the more fragile their acceptability among members of society, the greater is the significance of intellectuals.

Despite the theoretical definitions attached to them as a social class, Third World intellectuals have for the most part become politically passive, socially isolated and uncaring, and intellectually indolent. Even if they were to be seen as 'social commentators' or as '"microjournalists" who perforce (have) a development orientation',[97] they still fail to live up to their theoretical definition. Throughout the Third World, 'intellectualdom' has become a nominally impressive but realistically ineffectual domain for the exertion of social and political influence. Intellectuals have indeed estranged themselves from the dominant social and cultural frameworks of their societies, but they make little or no efforts to bring themselves closer to the population through 'social commentary' or 'macrojournalism', much less by political activism or social engineering. This indolence is brought on partly by the prevailing political and social circumstances in the Third World and partly by the intellectuals' own lethargy and inaction. Repressive politics and manipulated educational systems throughout the Third World have severely stunted the growth of intellectuals as a social class.[98] Moreover, most Third World countries are notorious in lacking the resources and the infrastructure within which intellectual activity can flourish and independently grow. In practically no Third World country has there been much investment in building libraries, promoting reading habits, glorifying past thinkers, patronizing lectures and scholarly debates, or encouraging publishing.[99] As a result, there is not an environment within which intellectualdom as a field can grow and flourish. In fact, some observers have even gone so far as to assert that as a social class, Third World intellectuals do not really exist.[100]

But to blame the absence of an intellectual spirit in the Third World entirely on political circumstances and infrastructural inadequacies is somewhat tautological. Third World intellectuals are themselves as much to blame. Their social and political inactivism is due not only to the political environment within which they operate but also to their own elitism and inadequate understanding of their society. The elitist attitudes of Third World intellectuals are most noticeable in countries where the rate of illiteracy is especially high and education is one of the few tools for upward mobility. Most intellectuals deliberately abstain from efforts that would bridge the gap between themselves and the larger society. Disgusted and disillusioned with the narrow-mindedness, sterility, and idleness of their countrymen, most succumb to existing vile realities, suppress their inspirations, and turn themselves into 'superfluous men', like those enlightened pre-revolutionary Russians who became increasingly uncomfortable with themselves for seeing the misery of the masses but were incapable of doing a whole lot.[101] Not being understood by the masses, and frequently also unable to understand them, Third World intellectuals become increasingly condescending toward their fellow compatriots. Perhaps this is an escape mechanism, enabling them to retain their uniqueness and educational superiority vis-à-vis the larger society. Or, perhaps, they merely feel contempt for those whom they consider to be intellectually and educationally inferior. Whatever the underlying cause, the psychological and thus the social distance between intellectuals and the masses in the Third World is a great and as yet unabridged one. It should not be a surprise, therefore, to discover that a high percentage of immigrants from developing countries to the United States are highly educated and skilled.[102] Greater employment opportunities are only part of the reason for this 'brain drain'. Psychological alienation and social and cultural frustration are also determining factors.

It is within these overall social contexts that political and regime orientations in the Third World are formulated. Specifically, Third World governments use the education system as a viable and potent tool for political socialisation, tailoring it to maximise their political longevity and augment their ideological and doctrinal legitimacy. Most notably, primary education is often taught through thick doctrinal lenses in an effort to ensure the continued adherence of future generations to prevailing political arrangements. In higher levels, especially at the university level, the educational system becomes selective in the disciplines it covers, encouraging natural and technical sciences at the expense of fields which invite independent thinking and social and political inquisitiveness. The result is a population largely ignorant of the social sciences and an intellectualdom vastly separated from the rest of society. The intellectuals, who are in charge of enlightening the people about their miseries and introducing them to alternatives, have become mostly apathetic, preferring to undergo oblivion or to emigrate rather than risk the dangers of social and political involvement. A few, as will be later discussed, have indeed attempted to create a sense of political awareness among their peoples. But their efforts, rather inadvertently, have been largely limited to first creating a viable national identity within which political orientations can be formed and expressed. It is to this aspect of political culture which we next turn.

NATIONAL IDENTITY

National identity is the way in which we view our national self-worth and is the measure of pride in our nationality. It is an integral part of political culture, affecting the way we perceive dominant political arrangements and the broader field of politics in general. Political culture is heavily influenced by the sense of national identity which people have of themselves. A perception of themselves as a collective political community, as a nation, heavily influences the way in which people perceive their roles and relationships vis-à-vis political objects. The orientations and sentiments people have toward politics in general and toward existing political arrangements in particular are formulated within the context of the views they have of themselves and their concept of their own identity. It is this sense of identity which largely determines how people behave politically and in turn view their political environment. To an extent, political and regime orientations are captive to, or are at least heavily influenced by, our sense of national identity.

The connexion between national identity and orientations toward political arrangements assumes special importance in the Third World, where both developments are highly fluid and in constant flux owing to changing social and political circumstances. The lack of a persistent set of norms and social values, a result of social change, makes it difficult to form solid opinions about what exactly our identity is, both at a personal level and nationally. The ensuing identity crisis finds equal disillusionment on the part of political and regime orientations, which are by nature fragmented and incoherent, sectarian, and highly changeable. An examination of national identity in the Third World is thus key to understanding the political cultures prevalent in the region.

It is often asserted that development entails a cultural transformation in the direction of reaffirmation of national identity and tradition.[103] Growing economic advancement and political sophistication are assumed to foster a sense of life satisfaction and lead to generally positive attitudes about the prevailing social and political environment.[104] However, such developments have almost completely bypassed the Third World and have instead taken place in Western democracies.[105] In fact, the social and political characteristics of the Third World not only have failed to result in a strong sense of national identity and life satisfaction, but have, adversely, fostered feelings of disappointment and identity crisis. Political repression, rapid industrialisation, the growth of the urban-based populations, economic dislocation, and social change prompt people in the Third World to question not only their prevailing social and political values but, more important, their very identity as a nation. The development of a national identity crisis in Third World countries is in fact seen by some as 'a phase of growth that the political system must inevitably experience whenever its basic forms are substantially changed. It is a sign of growth and change, not of weakness and abnormality'.[106] Whether an impediment to development or an inevitable and necessary part of it, national identity crisis has become an endemic character of Third World politics.[107]

There are three fundamental causes for the development of national identity crisis in the Third World. Most commonly, crises of national identity can occur when there is not a unanimous and clear appreciation of the geographic boundaries of a nation and a common acceptance by people that they share a distinctive and common identity.[108] This is a particularly pressing problem for a number of African countries, whose boundaries were drawn arbitrarily and without great concern for their inhabitants' socially and culturally varied heritage. Even in highly developed and centralised states (such as India, Pakistan, Afghanistan, Iran, and Turkey in Asia and Honduras, Guatemala, Nicaragua, Colombia, Peru, and Bolivia in Latin America), national boundaries mean little to peripheral ethnic groups who periodically migrate across international borders. The problem is most acute in Africa, however, where national identities have not effectively been formed yet. In cases where geographic boundaries have long been formed and nationalist sentiments have gained strength, parochial allegiances and loyalties to sub-national groups can still create crises in national identity.[109] The division of your loyalty between the central state on the one hand and your ethnic background and race on the other can throw into confusion the sources with which you identify. Again, Africa provides numerous examples of nations torn by sub-national loyalties. The continent is, however, by no means alone. Ethnic strife has become a regular feature of life in India, the Commonwealth of Independent States, central and eastern European states, and several countries in

Central America, where Mosquito Indians frequently clash with central governments in an effort to maintain their unique, indigenous identities.

Another prevalent cause of national identity crisis in the Third World is the ongoing process of social change and industrial development.[110] Social change leads to feelings of rootlessness and uncertainty over which values to choose. Incomplete processes of political institutionalisation on the part of the regime and political socialisation by the population add to the difficulty of developing a coherent identity toward political objects and, in fact, even toward one's nationality. Constant comparison with other countries and nationalities, disappointment and often resentment against existing sources of identity, and the inability to pinpoint a coherent set of characteristics to various social classes all combine to impede the development of a strong sense of national identity. This is a problem that is endemic to all modernising societies, regardless of the popular acceptability of their geographic boundaries or the strength or weakness of their parochial tendencies. It is an inevitable ramification of social change and, more specifically, of cultural diffusion. The development of an almost uniform 'middle class culture' throughout the Third World, which has as its cornerstone the emulation of Western social practices and cultural norms, is further cause for the questioning of indigenous sources of identity.[111]

Periodic attempts have been made by social and political actors in the Third World to alleviate identity crises and to forge a strong sense of national identity. Most blatant have been the efforts of various governments which, often through coercive means, try to foster a sense of identity among the population which is compatible with their political agendas and doctrines. Monuments are erected, national leaders and past heroes are glorified, nationalist sentiments are stressed, national sports teams are cheered on, and ethnic and parochial loyalties are supplanted by nationalist ones.[112] Nationalist sentiments are engineered with the express intent of supporting the political *status quo*. The emergent national identity is consequently tailored to fit a political culture most supportive of existing political arrangements. In this sense, the relationship between national identity and political culture assumes particular importance. The former becomes a tool for the maintenance of the latter, an artificial creation suited to particular, narrow political needs.

More independent efforts at asserting national identity or in forging new ones are made by a minority of Third World intellectuals. Despite the passionate beliefs and writings of some of these scholars and literary figures, only a few have gone on to attain national fame and become able to express their views to a wide range of audiences. For the most part, political repression has prompted Third World intellectuals to eschew discussing sensitive political topics such as national identity and self-assertion. There is also a marked tendency toward lethargy among Third World intellectuals themselves which has over the years led to their social and political passivity.[113] There are, nevertheless, a few who have assumed the responsibility of critiquing their societies and have tried to foster new national identities. Mexico's Octavio Paz is a prime example. Through studying the Mexican character, Paz criticizes the inferiority complex of his countrymen and urges them to become aware of their heritage and unique identity.[114] 'To become aware of our history,' he writes, 'is to become aware of our singularity.'[115] For Mexicans, Paz argues, the uniqueness of their identity lies in their Indian heritage.[116]

Few Third World scholars and intellectuals have gone on to achieve the fame and recognition in their societies that Octavio Paz has achieved in Mexico and even beyond. Yet such identity-conscious intellectuals do exist, albeit few in numbers, and their cries of 'return to the self' do occasionally gather steam in their respective countries.[117] But despite the passionate writings and speeches of these and other nameless intellectuals who try to make the public aware of their national identity and heritage, often at great risk, their efforts remain largely ineffective in forging a national identity or in overcoming their country's collective identity crisis. Political repression often prompts them to either tone down their social criticism or to abandon the subject altogether. In cases where their commentary is formulated in relatively free environments and openly expressed, as is Paz's case in Mexico, they find themselves addressing audiences who are overwhelmingly illiterate and are either suspicious of their intentions or impervious to its message. It is one thing to pinpoint identity crisis and write about it; it is quite another to get the message across to disillusioned and lost masses.

It is within the context of ambivalent and uncertain national identities that Third World political cultures take shape and are formulated. For the most part, Third World inhabitants feel ambivalent about their identity and national self-worth, viewing themselves as inferior to the West. In their desperate search to find sources with which to identify, they blindly emulate the culture and the norms of the West. Yet emulation at best resolves their sense of cultural inferiority. Their alienation from the act of governance still remains. They are, meanwhile, manipulated, their sentiments and orientations tossed around by politicos hoping to further their own legitimacy. For its part, intellectualdom remains mostly on the sidelines, its infrequent cries of self-discovery seldom heard and rarely understood. What emerges is a political culture tainted by contempt for the political self and disdain for existing, politically dictated identifications.

CONCLUSION

Political culture is the bond between politics and society, the median through which the two interact and interconnect. It is that aspect of culture which specifically deals with politics, be it particular political objects and arrangements or the broader field of politics in general. In examining Third World political cultures, varied as they are, one factor consistently stands out. Regardless of social, cultural, and political characteristics that are unique to individual countries, throughout the Third World there is an almost uniformly weak nexus between state and society. Consequently, regime orientations are extremely weak despite often massive efforts to inject political acculturation through bureaucratic and even coercive means. The regime's ideology and doctrine have little genuine acceptability among the population and are often forced on them by various means. Most commonly, people need to prove their ideological 'purity' through special exams which are designed to filter out non-believers from government jobs and universities and to bar them from access to other privileges. Similarly, participation in the political process is often merely perfunctory, taking place out of fear or opportunism rather than a genuine sense of civic duty and obligation. Voting for pre-approved candidates is compulsory, if not by law by the fear of what may ensue if one refrains from it. Taking part in government-sponsored marches and demonstrations also become part of a ritualistic allegiance to the political system.

Within this context of forced loyalties to the state and to its principal figures, two important ramifications arise. Firstly, the ensuing orientations that emerge within the population are usually extremist. The public is often either completely apathetic toward politics, is highly supportive of the regime, or, given a chance, is violently opposed to it. The majority of people refrain from politics, believing 'unseen hands' to be at work and viewing politicians as mere pawns in the hands of others. They are, for the most part, either caught up in the economic struggle to survive the tumults of industrialisation or are pre-occupied with seeking its benefits. Alongside the politically apathetic majority are minority groups who are either actively supportive of the regime and wholeheartedly believe in its legitimacy and doctrinal agendas, or are quietly opposed to it and will work for its overthrow if given an opportunity. Those who are vociferous in their support for the regime are motivated either by sheer opportunism or by a genuine adherence to the regime's doctrines, or, as is frequently the case, by a convergence of the two. Regardless of their doctrines or structural features, regimes always find support among a certain segment of the population, even though that segment may be extremely small and in a socially disadvantageous position. Such bases of support can be found among merchants and industrialists who favour certain economic policies, or civil servants who find job security through the existing bureaucracy, or youths who support a regime's extremist ideology. On the opposite extreme, there are those who see through the regime's manipulations and are not only unimpressed but are prompted to advocate a radical overthrow of the system. What prompts these political aspirants to oppose the system, openly or quietly, varies from case to case. They are, however, mostly driven by the same factors that motivate the regime's supporters: ideological beliefs and a desire to wield power. The extremism that divides opponents and supporters of the regime extends even to cases where there are open and free elections, as in Latin America, with support for candidates being sharply divided along highly polarised, ideological lines.

The second ramification that tends to ensue from political cultures in the Third World, and directly linked to the first one, is the proclivity toward the development of revolutions. The tendency to lead to revolutionary circumstances is, in fact, the most enduring and significant by-product of political culture in Third World countries. The weak links that bond the political system to society at large, the general cynicism that pervades the population, the predominance of dogmatism and sectarian tendencies, and the ready existence of a group eager to articulate its opposition to the regime, albeit at times small, all combine to make Third World governments susceptible to being overthrown by revolutionary movements. However, despite this built-in susceptibility, full-scale revolutions are the exception rather than the rule since they involve considerable energy, anguish, and human sacrifice. The incumbents' determination to maintain power at all costs also impedes the development of revolutions and instead harshens the already perilous political arena. Instead of revolutions, political instability, arising out of legitimacy crises and raw inter-elite political competition, has become endemic to Third World polities. Palace coups and personality changes have become commonplace, while revolutions occur with striking rarity. Yet Third World political cultures are indeed conducive to the development of revolutionary circumstances and the overthrow of existing political arrangements. The exact developments that bring about revolutions are products not only of political culture but of existing social arrangements, cultural dynamics, and, of course, political forces as well. Combined with and occurring within political culture, these developments provide the appropriate contextual environment within which revolutions take place.

NOTES

1 See Stephen Chilton. 'Defining Political Culture'. *Western Political Quarterly*. vol. 41, no. 3, (September 1988), pp. 419–45.
2 Gabriel Almond and Sidney Verba. *The Civic Culture*. (London: Sage, 1989), p. 13.
3 Ibid. p. 32.
4 Ibid. p. 25.
5 M. Margaret Conway. 'The Political Context of Political Behavior'. *Journal of Politics*. vol. 51, no. 1, (February 1989), p. 4.
6 Denis Kavanagh. *Political Culture*. (London: Macmillan, 1972), p. 11.
7 Walter Rosenbaum. *Political Culture*. (New York: Praeger, 1975), p. 8.
8 Stephen Chilton. 'Defining Political Culture'. p. 427.
9 Dennis Kavanagh. *Political Culture*. p. 12.
10 Walter Rosenbaum. *Political Culture*. p. 8.
11 Stephen Chilton. 'Defining Political Culture'. p. 422.
12 Walter Rosenbaum. *Political Culture*. p. 13.
13 Dennis Kavanagh. *Political Culture*. p. 33.
14 Ibid. p. 35.
15 Walter Rosenbaum. *Political Culture*. p. 17.
16 Dennis Kavanagh. *Political Culture*. p. 40.
17 Lucian Pye. 'Identity and Political Culture', in Lucian Pye *et al. Crises and Sequences in Political Development*. (Princeton, NJ: Princeton University Press, 1971), p. 109.
18 See above, Chapter 1.
19 The paying of homage to Lenin's mausoleum by bridal couples and group marriages sponsored by the Communist Party in China are two of the more extreme examples of routinized efforts to instil officially sponsored political cultures.
20 Lucian Pye. 'Identity and Political Culture'. pp. 111–12.

21 Harry Eckstein. 'A Culturalist Theory of Political Change'. *American Political Science Review.* vol. 82, no. 3, (September 1988), p. 798.

22 Walter Rosenbaum. *Political Culture.* p. 37.

23 Ibid. pp. 44–7.

24 Ibid. p. 41.

25 Stephen Chilton. 'Defining Political Culture'. p. 769.

26 Harry Eckstein. 'A Culturalist Theory of Political Change'. p. 799.

27 Walter Rosenbaum. *Political Culture.* p. 54.

28 Lucian Pye. 'Identity and Political Culture'. p. 106.

29 Harry Eckstein. 'A Culturalist Theory of Political Change'. p. 797; see also below, Chapter 6.

30 Ibid.

31 Ibid.

32 Walter Rosenbaum. *Political Culture.* p. 103.

33 Lucian Pye. 'Identity and Political Culture'. p. 103.

34 Ibid.

35 See above, Chapter 4.

36 Walter Rosenbaum. *Political Culture.* p. 145.

37 Gabriel Almond and Sidney Verba. *The Civic Culture.* pp. 17–19.

38 Ibid. p. 17.

39 Ibid. p. 18.

40 Ibid.

41 Ibid. p. 45.

42 Lucian Pye. 'Identity and Political Culture'. p. 106.

43 Dennis Kavanagh. *Political Culture.* pp. 44–5.

44 Gabriel Almond and Sidney Verba. *The Civic Culture*; M. Margaret Conway. 'The Political Context of Political Behavior'; Walter Rosenbaum. *Political Culture*; Harry Eckstein. 'A Culturalist Theory of Political Change'; Stephen Chilton. 'Defining Political Culture'; Ronald Inglehart. 'The Renaissance of Political Culture'. *American Political Science Review.* vol. 82, no. 4, (December 1988), pp. 1203–30; Gabriel Almond and G. Bingham Powell. *Comparative Politics: Systems, Processes, and Policy.* Boston: Little, Brown, 1978.

45 See, especially, Gabriel Almond and Sidney Verba. *The Civic Culture.*

46 The growing tide of democratization across Latin America since the 1980s has resulted in the establishment of a number of political systems in which sentiments and orientations toward ruling incumbents can be expressed with a measure of liberty (e.g. Argentina and Brazil). Also, a few other Third World countries, such as India and Pakistan, have historically had a more tolerant political tradition.

47 Roger Scruton. *A Dictionary of Political Thought.* (London: Macmillan, 1982), p. 213.

48 Douglas Ashford. 'Attitudinal Change and Modernization', in Chandler Morse, ed. *Modernization by Design: Social Change in the Twentieth Century.* (London: Cornell University Press, 1969), p. 180.

49 A distinction needs to be made between the *official* state ideology and doctrines and beliefs independent of the political establishment.

50 Mehran Kamrava. *Revolution in Iran: Roots of Turmoil.* (London: Routledge, 1990), p. 117.

51 Howard Wiarda. 'Political Culture and the Attraction of Marxism-Leninism: National Inferiority Complex as an Explanatory Factor'. *World Affairs*. vol. 151, no. 3, (Winter 1988–9), p. 145.
52 Ibid. p. 148.
53 Frantz Fanon discusses this importance of ideology, but, addressing a black audience, argues for the blacks' discovery of 'Negrotude'. See Frantz Fanon. *Black Skin, White Mask*. Charles Lam Markmann, trans. (New York: Grove Press, 1967).
54 See below, Chapter 6.
55 Daniel Levine. 'Religion and Politics in Contemporary Historical Perspective'. *Comparative Politics*. vol. 19, no. 1, (October 1986), p. 97.
56 Daniel Levine. 'Assessing the Impact of Liberation Theology in Latin America'. *Review of Politics*. vol. 50, no. 2, (Spring 1988), p. 246.
57 Daniel Levine. 'Religion and Politics in Contemporary Historical Perspective'. p. 100.
58 Ibid. p. 102.
59 Terence Ranger. 'Religion, Development, and African Christian Identity', in Kirsten H. Petersen, ed. *Religion, Development, and African Identity*. (Uppsala: The Scandinavian Institute for African Studies, 1987), p. 50.
60 Daniel Levine. 'Religion and Politics in Contemporary Historical Perspective'. p. 106.
61 For a study of Liberation Theology in Brazil, where the impact of the movement has been strongest, see Thomas Bruneau and W. E. Hewitt. 'Patterns of Church Influence in Brazil's Political Transition'. *Comparative Politics*. vol. 22, no. 1, (October 1989), pp. 39–61.
62 Daniel Levine. 'Assessing the Impact of Liberation Theology in Latin America'. p. 245.
63 Ibid. p. 253.
64 Ibid. p. 249.
65 S.C. Dube. *Modernization and Development: The Search for Alternative Paradigms*. (Tokyo: United Nations University, 1988), p. 89.
66 Lucian Pye. 'Identity and Political Culture'. p. 106.
67 Douglas Ashford. 'Attidudinal Change and Modernization'. p. 174.
68 Ronald Inglehart. 'The Renaissance of Political Culture'. p. 1209; as earlier mentioned, Inglehart discusses Western democracies rather than Third World political systems.
69 Ibid. p. 1207.
70 Richard Parker. 'Anti-American Attitudes in the Arab World'. *The Annals of the American Academy of Political and Social Sciences*. vol. 497, (May 1988), p. 53.
71 For two excellent treatments of this subject see Fouad Ajami. *The Arab Predicament: Arab Political Thought and Practice since 1967*. (Cambridge: Cambridge University Press, 1981), and James Bill and Robert Springborg. *Politics in the Middle East*. (Boston: Scott Foresman/Little, Brown, 1990), pp. 360–8.
72 Alvin Rubenstein and Donald Smith. 'Anti-Americanism in the Third World'. *The Annals of the American Academy of Social and Political Sciences*. vol. 497, (May 1988), p. 39.

73 Riodan Roett. 'Anti-Americanism in the Southern Cone of Latin America'. *The Annals of the American Academy of Political and Social Sciences.* vol. 497, (May 1988), p. 71.

74 Richard Parker. 'Anti-American Attitudes in the Arab World'. p. 53. Parker has served as a US ambassador to various Middle Eastern countries.

75 Alvin Rubinstein and Donald Smith. 'Anti-Americanism in the Third World'. p. 35.

76 Examples of such overt interventions include the Soviet Union's military invasions into Czechoslovakia, Hungary, and Afghanistan, and American-sponsored coups in Iran and Chile and its invasions of the Dominican Republic, Grenada, and Panama.

77 J.E. Goldthrope. *The Sociology of the Third World.* (Cambridge: Cambridge University Press, 1984), p. 199.

78 This is not necessarily the case with all Third World leaders, especially those like Ferdinand Marcos in the Philippines, who wish to portray to the masses a certain style of life and do not mind being emulated by others.

79 Walter Rosenbaum. *Political Culture.* p. 79.

80 Indonesia, as a random example of a Third World country, has cabinet level ministries for 'public welfare', 'education and culture', 'home affairs', 'information', 'religion', 'social affairs', 'role of women', and 'youth and sports'. In most Third World countries, it is not uncommon to find separate cabinet portfolios for such departments as 'culture', 'religious affairs', 'youth development', and 'internal affairs'. See, Central Intelligence Agency. *Chiefs of State and Cabinet Members of Foreign Governments.* (Washington, D.C.: CIA, 1987).

81 Dennis Kavanagh. *Political Culture.* p. 31.

82 Ibid. p. 35.

83 Keith Watson. 'Educational Neocolonialism – The Continued Legacy', in Keith Watson, ed. *Education in the Third World.* (London; Croom Helm, 1982), p. 10. A similar argument is made by Phillip Foster. 'The Educational Policies of Postcolonial States', in Lascelles Anderson and Douglas Windham, eds. *Education and Development: Issues in the Analysis and Planning of Postcolonial Societies.* (Lexington, Mass: Lexington Books, 1982), pp. 3–25.

84 Keith Watson. 'Educational Neocolonialism – The Continued Legacy'. p. 184.

85 Ibid. p. 193.

86 Ibid. p. 199.

87 See Mehran Kamrava. *Revolution in Iran.* Chapter 3, for Iran; Immanuel Hsu. *The Rise of Modern China.* (Oxford: Oxford University Press, 1990), Chapter 40 on China; and Nazih Ayubi. 'The Politics of Militant Islamic Movements in the Middle East'. *Journal of International Affairs.* vol. 36, no. 2 (Fall/Winter 1982–83), pp. 271–87 for an examination of political activism by Egyptian students.

88 See, for example, J. Cotton, 'From Authoritarianism to Democracy in South Korea.' *Political Studies*, vol. 37 (June 1989), pp. 244–59, and S.J.

Han, 'South Korea in 1988: Revolution in the making.' *Asia Survey*, vol. 29 (January 1989), pp. 29–38.

89 Fredrick Gareau. 'Another Type of Third World Dependency: The Social Sciences'. *International Sociology*. vol. 3, no. 2, (June 1988), p. 173.

90 Ibid. pp. 172–3.

91 Philip Altbach and S. Gopinathan. 'Textbooks in the Third World: Challenge and Response', in P. Altbach, A. Arboleda, and S. Gopinathan, eds. *Publishing in the Third World: Knowledge and Development*. (London: Mansell, 1985), p. 15.

92 Philip Altbach, Amadio Arboleda, and S. Gopinathan. 'Publishing in the Third World: Some Reflections', in P. Altbach, A. Arboleda, and S. Gopinathan, eds. *Publishing In the Third World*. p. 2.

93 Ibid. p. 6.

94 J.P.Nettl. 'Ideas, Intellectuals, and Structures of Dissent', in Philip Rieff, ed. *On Intellectuals*. (Garden City, NY: Anchor Books, 1970), pp. 89–90.

95 Ibid. p. 90.

96 Edward Shils. 'The Intellectuals and Power: Some Perspectives for Comparative Analysis', in Philip Rieff, ed. *On Intellectuals*. p. 30.

97 Jay Weinstein. 'The Third World and Developmentalism: Technology, Morality, and the Role of Intellectuals', in Raj Mayhan, ed. *The Myth-makers: Intellectuals and the Intelligentsia in Perspective*. (Westport, Conn.: Greenwood, 1987), p. 115.

98 Mehran Kamrava. 'Intellectuals and Democracy in the Third World'. *Journal of Social, Economic, and Political Studies*. vol. 14, no. 2, (Summer 1989), pp. 231–2.

99 Syed Hussein Alatas. *Modernization and Social Change*. (London: Angus & Robertson, 1977), pp. 49–50.

100 Ibid. p. 9.

101 Ibid. p. 72–3.

102 Ransford Palmer. 'Education and Migration from Developing Countries', in Lascelles Anderson and Douglas Windham, eds. *Education and Development*. p. 117.

103 Alejandro Portez. 'On the Sociology of National Development: Theories and Issues', in Janet Abu-Lughod and Richard Hay, eds. *Third World Urbanization*. (Chicago: Maaroufa Press, 1977), p. 109.

104 Ronald Inglehart. 'The Renaissance of Political Culture'. p. 1207.

105 Ibid. pp. 1215–16.

106 Lucian Pye. 'Identity and Political Culture'. p. 111.

107 Identity crisis is indeed an impediment to political development and inhibits the growth of a sense of political community and nationhood. It is, however, an inevitable stage through which all developing polities must pass in order to overcome the force of parochial identities. See Lucian Pye. 'Identity and Political Culture'. p.124.

108 Ibid. p. 112.

109 Ibid. p. 117.

110 Ibid. p. 118.

111 Nathan Keyfitz. 'Development and the Elimination of Poverty'. *Economic Development and Cultural Change*. vol. 30, no. 3, (April 1982), p. 651.

112 See above, Chapter 1.

113 Mehran Kamrava. 'Intellectuals and Democracy in the Third World'. p. 231.
114 See Terry Hoy. 'Octavio Paz: The Search for Mexican Identity'. *Review of Politics*. vol. 44, no. 3, (July 1982), pp. 370–85.
115 Octavio Paz. *The Labyrinth of Solitude: Life and Thought in Mexico*. Lysander Kemp, trans. (London: Evergreen, 1961), p. 10.
116 Terry Hoy. 'Octavio Paz: The Search for Mexican Identity'. p. 385.
117 See the case of Iran's Ali Shariati, in Mehran Kamrava. *Revolution in Iran*. pp. 73–6. Shariati repeatedly acknowledged his debt to Fratz Fanon for his concept of 'return to the self'.

Chapter 6

Revolutions

The dynamics which lead to the appearance of revolutions and revolutionary movements in the Third World are engendered by evolving political structures and by social and cultural arrangements and dynamics. More specifically, as discussed in previous chapters, the particular characteristics of Third World states, coupled with the broad, contextual ramifications of social change and the dynamics inherent in political cultures, combine to give rise to conditions conducive to the outbreak of revolutions. However, despite the widespread prevalence of such conditions, revolutions have become decidedly rare occurrences in the Third World and indeed everywhere else. Why, it is thus important to ask, have revolutions not taken place with their supposed frequency given the existence of their social and political requisites? Moreover, exactly how and what social and political dynamics lead to revolutions and at which specific junctures? It is to these questions which the present chapter turns.

Broadly, revolutions denote rapid and fundamental changes in political arrangements and leaders, principles and orientations.[1] They entail the transformation of the very political fabrics on which a government is based. Palace coups and changes in leadership and in personalities do not necessarily constitute a 'revolution' in the fullest sense, despite what the coups' protagonists often like to think, although it is quite conceivable that a coup may set in motion a chain of events that could lead to the outbreak of a revolutionary situation. Revolutions are much more fundamental developments. They turn the world of politics around, change the basic premises on which political culture is based, and transform the guidelines and the intricacies with which political conduct is governed. In this respect, revolutions are distinctively political episodes, although their precise occurrence is brought on by a coalescence of not only political but also social and cultural factors as well.[2] As past and recent experiences have demonstrated, to say that revolutions are 'political struggles of great intensity'[3] and that they invariably entail considerable violence[4] has become somewhat of a truism, although the decade of the 1980s did bear witness to the budding of 'negotiated revolutions' in some parts of eastern Europe.[5] Yet by and large revolutions still remain mass-based affairs of great magnitude, brought on and carried through by the mobilisation of masses of people against specific political targets. Even Hungary's largely 'negotiated revolution' was precipitated and in turn fuelled by the vocal protestations of mobilised Hungarians in Budapest and in other cities.[6]

REVOLUTIONARY CAUSATION

It follows that any credible attempt to explain revolutions needs to consider the conditions under which mass mobilisation is achieved.[7] This includes an analysis of the prevailing *social* as well as the *political* conditions that are conducive to the attainment of revolutionary mass mobilisation. Revolutions are *political* episodes to the extent that they denote the crumbling of an old political order and its replacement by new political objects, arrangements, and structures. Exactly how this collapse and the subsequent replacement are brought about are manifestations of not only political dynamics but also of all those other factors, such as social and cultural, which also influence mass mobilisation and political activism. Thus to see revolutions as only political events is to grasp only half of the picture. Political dynamics need to be considered in conjunction with social and cultural developments.

It is within this type of a multi-disciplinary framework that theories of revolutionary causation need to be constructed and put forth. Ancient and contemporary scholarship bears witness to ceaseless and at times highly impressive efforts to examine the root causes of revolutions and to grasp the full extent of the social and political dynamics which result in revolutionary episodes.[8] Theories of revolutionary causation and consequences abound in social sciences literature, some of which have had far greater explanatory success than others. Nevertheless, these theoretical explanations for the most part suffer from a number of highly significant analytical deficiencies.[9] To begin with, most existing theories ignore the inherently varied nature of revolutions and attempt to explain such diverse phenomena in one, all-embracing framework. What results are theories which in their attempt to find applicability to *all* revolutions become at best too generalised.[10] The need for specificity is both historical and contextual. Revolutions vary from one another according to the different historical contexts within which they occur.[11] Thus a theoretical framework which explains the causes of, say, the French revolution may not necessarily apply to more contemporary examples.

Yet a theory of revolution's necessity for historical specificity pales in comparison with the importance of its attention to the significant role that human agency plays, which is by nature reflexive and changeable. A theory of revolution needs to consider the intrinsic changeableness that is imparted to revolutions because of human initiative.[12] More than anything else, the actual success or failure of revolutions depends on the specific actions taken by revolutionary participants, actions which are inherently varied according to the context, the timing, and the manner of their execution.[13] The decisions which revolutionary leaders make, the manner in which those decisions are implemented and pursued, and the specific consequences that may arise from them differ from one case to another. It is precisely these vital details that make each revolution different from another one. Even in cases where deliberate attempts are made to emulate previous models, as, for example, Che Guevara tried in Bolivia, the striking differences in the detailed mechanisms with which revolutions are carried forward become plainly clear. It is precisely this lack of attention to contextual specificity, at the heart of which is the variable nature of human conduct and initiative, that has led to the demise of so many emulative revolutionary movements around the world.[14]

In addition to their overly ambitious and thus highly generalised nature, most theories of revolution put too much emphasis on one aspect of revolutionary eruption at the expense of other, equally significant ones. Among the theories of revolution which in recent years have gained widespread respect and currency within the academic community, emphasis has been placed either on the 'dissynchronisation' of value systems and the ensuing 'disequilibrium' of pre-revolutionary societies;[15] on the inability of social actors to fulfil their wants and aspirations;[16] on the regime's incapacity to absorb emerging groups into itself[17] or to mobilise them to its own benefit;[18] or on the state's inability to withstand the pressures brought on it by structural weaknesses and by class-based revolts.[19] In virtually all of these approaches, overwhelming emphasis is placed on one facet of

social and/or political developments while the simultaneous contribution of other dynamics to revolutions are undermined or completely ignored.[20] In a few instances, emerging developments have
forced a revision of earlier, one-faceted theories.[21] But the tendency
to give primacy to one aspect of analytical examination while under-
estimating the importance of others still pervades current scholarship
on revolutions.

The study of revolutions, whether classic or contemporary, in the
Third World or elsewhere, requires a multi-disciplinary, multi-
dimensional approach. The dynamics that result in the appearance of
revolutionary circumstances are political as well as social. Politically,
the outbreak of revolutions require a significant weakening of the
powers of political incumbents and their growing incapacity to hold
on to the state's powers and its various other resources. These
include loss of control of the means of economic hegemony over the
general population, discontinued control over not only the coercive
organs of the state such as the army and the police but also over the
regime's propaganda networks such as the electronic and the printed
media, and a steady loss of privileged access to socially valued goods
and institutions. In general, the primary precondition of revolutions
is the loss of previously held powers and privileges on the part of the
elite. This reduction in the elite's powers may be caused by any
number of domestic or international developments which could
adversely affect the powers of the state. Internationally, such a
weakening could occur through inter-state disputes and military
conflicts, or excessive diplomatic pressures or conditional relations.[22]
Internally, the elite's hold on power may be weakened by such
events as the demise of a central, authoritarian personality, or excessive and naked competition over power resources. Concurrently,
however, the political exigencies thus created need to be exploited
by the efforts of groups who initiate specific acts in order to bring
about the regime's ultimate collapse. Unless and until such groups
exist, and acquire powers sufficient to overwhelm those of the dying
regime, a revolution will not occur. In essence, revolutions are raw
power struggles of the highest order: on the one hand exist the
political elite, in control of the state, their powers and privileges
steadily declining owing to a variety of internal and/or international
developments; on the other hand there are revolutionaries,
increasingly belligerent and with more specific demands, gradually
achieving enough size and strength to overpower and replace the
elite.

These political dynamics cannot occur in a social vacuum. The growing momentum of the contenders for power, who are gradually seen as – and who come to see themselves as – revolutionaries, and the withering of the state, both take place within and in fact are precipitated by social and cultural dynamics. Social developments help in the structural weakening of the state in a number of ways. Most fundamentally, social change and industrial development lead to the creation of various social classes and values which the existing system cannot absorb into itself.[23] Thus, especially in modernising societies, where new classes are continually emerging and where old and new values are in constant flux, the state assumes an essentially conflictual relationship with emerging social groups and seeks constantly to sever their access to sources of political power. Regardless of the eventual outcome of this state–society conflict, even if society has been subdued and subjected to the state's full control, the very existence of such an adversarial nexus weakens the basic foundations of the regime and increases the likelihood of its collapse.

A more important contribution that social dynamics make to revolutionary outbreaks is in augmenting the extent of popular support enjoyed by revolutionaries among the general population. By their very attempts to communicate with the masses and to get their increasingly revolutionary message across, emerging revolutionary groups employ various social medians, some of which they may not even be aware of. The existence of a number of social and cultural factors can either significantly enhance or curtail the legitimacy of political contestants and influence their respective longevity and political viability. Depending on the specific conditions within a given society, apathy and conservatism may drown a revolutionary group into oblivion, with its cries of injustice and calls to revolt falling on ears deafened by passivity and content. Yet at the same time, social conditions may invoke in people senses of injustice, deprivation, and nationalist and religious sentiments which make them highly amenable to revolutionary mobilisation. The prevalence of specific social conditions that conduce revolutionary action, and the exact nature of the link between the existing conditions and the types of responses evoked, are context-specific and vary from society to society. What is clear is that social conditions do in fact influence revolutions, more specifically revolutionary mobilisation and action, in highly significant and far-reaching ways.

In analysing the causes, the course, and the outcome of revolutions in the Third World, a multi-disciplinary approach of the type laid out above finds particular applicability. In contrast to the West, throughout the Third World social and political forces confront each other nakedly, in their most brutal form, seeking aggressively to implant themselves and to supplant others.[24] This polarisation is further accentuated by the fragility of norms that govern political conduct, underwrite social relationships, and support existing institutions.[25] Within this context, while the state–society links in the Third World are more tenuous, their relationship with each other is a much more consequential one. In the Third World, changes occurring in the state can far more dramatically affect society than is the case in the West. Adversely, changes taking place in Third World societies can have far more dramatic political ramifications than they would in Western countries. Examining revolutions in the Third World thus requires detailed analysis of political dynamics that lead to the state's weakness and to the emergence of its avowedly revolutionary foes, in addition to the development of social and cultural conditions conducive to popular revolutionary mobilisation. State breakdown is only one facet of revolutionary episodes. The social and cultural milieu within which it occurs is just as important.

STATE BREAKDOWN

Revolutions are brought about through a confluence of political developments and social dynamics which weaken the powers of governing incumbents and at the same time augment the capabilities of those aspiring to replace them. The political dynamics at work involve the incumbents' loss of legitimacy, the growing weakness and vulnerability of the structures and the organisations they have at their disposal, and the concurrent activities of revolutionary groups aimed at exploiting these emerging exigencies and the resulting mobilisation of masses toward revolutionary goals. Equally significant are the prevailing social and cultural conditions that are conducive to revolutionary mobilisation, be they a general sense of deprivation among various social strata or disenchantment over emerging social values. Also important are the means of access which revolutionary groups have to the general population, determined in turn by either existing social organisations or by alternative nexuses that are specifically forged for this purpose.

It is only through a concurrent appearance of all of these dynamics, from legitimacy crisis and structural breakdown to revolutionary activism and socially and politically conduced mass mobilisation, that a political revolution in the fullest sense takes place. Otherwise, in instances where emerging political weaknesses and vulnerabilities are not exploited by revolutionary groups, or when self-proclaimed revolutionaries operate in a social vacuum and seek to overthrow a strong and viable state, what occurs is merely political instability and upheaval but not revolution. It is important also to distinguish between a revolution and a palace coup, the latter resulting merely in a change of personalities while the former denotes an all-encompassing change in political arrangements, institutions, and practices. Coup leaders all too often proclaim themselves to be revolutionaries and declare their reign to be the start of a revolutionary era. It was indeed a military coup that brought the Ethiopian revolution to a head and caused the dawn of the post-Haile Selassi era.[26] However, the Ethiopian example has not been widely repeated, and the vast majority of military coups, especially in Latin America and Africa, result in a change of political personalities rather than principles. Politicians are only actors in the political drama. Their replacement by other actors does not necessarily affect the outcome of the play. It is the institutions which they create and which they in turn occupy, and the ideologies and principles which they espouse, that constitute the political drama itself and affect society at large. Revolutions involve changing not only political actors but the entire scenario on which the drama of politics is based.

With this in mind, it is important to remember that the key to all successful revolutions, the catalyst that sets into motion all the other dynamics which produce revolutionary circumstances, is the political incapacitation of the ruling elite. Revolutions are in the first order developments that result from the political crises that engulf those in power. This centrality of state power arises out of the state's control of the various prized resources in society. Especially in the Third World, the state not only has power over the army, the police, and the bureaucracy, it also controls, directly or indirectly, various aspects of economic life, including resources, services, and general economic activity. In short, the state controls most if not all of the essential tools and resources that are necessary for the running of the country. Unless and until this control is somehow weakened and is in turn transferred to centres outside of the state, then aspiring revolutionaries will not find sufficient resources with which to mount and to maintain a political takeover.

The political weakening of pre-revolutionary states can be caused by the appearance of three broad categories of developments. Most directly consequential in bringing about revolutionary situations, and by far the most common set of developments weakening state power, are those with direct negative bearings on the state's cohesion and organisational viability. These are developments which lead directly to the structural collapse of state organisations and institutions. Developments as diverse as wars, economic bankruptcy, or the death of a central figure in a personalised system are among those categories of events which can dramatically reduce the state's continued ability to control the resources needed to stay in power. Similar consequences may arise from partial and incomplete processes of political modernisation, thus leading to over-stretched bureaucracies incapable of dealing with evolving circumstances, unfulfilled demands for increased political participation, and a general absence of society-wide political entrepreneurship. Lastly, there is the development of a situation best described as a 'crisis of legitimacy', engulfing political leaders and hence reducing their ability to rule and to stay in power.

These developments are not mutually exclusive and in fact often occur in connection with one another. The relationship between crises of legitimacy and structural collapse is especially a strong one. In fact, these two developments are naturally interrelated and reinforce one another. This relationship of mutual reinforcement assumes particular importance in Third World countries, where the very process of development denotes crises of legitimacy for political incumbents. Questioning the legitimacy of political leaders is an inevitable ramification of the intertwined processes of industrial growth, social change, and political development. The development syndrome results in a widening of perceptions on the part of ever greater numbers of people and, therefore, an increase in sensitivities about possibile alternative ways of doing things in all phases of life.[27] What occurs is a 'dis-synchronisation' between the values that political leaders hold on the one hand and those of the general population on the other.[28] More specifically, crises of political legitimacy arise when the claims of current leaders to power are based on socially unacceptable historical or ideological interpretations, when the degree of political socialisation has not been sufficient to convince the people of the legitimacy of existing political arrangements, and when there is excessive and uninstitutionalised competition for power.[29] In essence, legitimacy crisis arises out of inadequate and incomplete political institutionalisation, itself an endemic mark of Third World political systems.[30] Thus a structural analysis of the collapse of pre-revolutionary states must necessarily examine legitimacy crises that concurrently accompany them.

A legitimacy crisis is basically a crisis of authority. It signifies the inability of political leaders to justify their continued hold on power.[31] As earlier mentioned, legitimacy crisis is inherent in the process of development. However, a number of specific dynamics exacerbate the withdrawal of the proverbial 'mandate of heaven' and heighten a regime's sense of illegitimacy among the population at certain historical junctures. The problem is one of inability to deliver the goods promised or in demand, be they economic, political, or emotional.[32] Lack of dynamic leadership and political acumen, continued and persistent demands for greater political participation or increased economic gratification, or a neglect or abuse of sources with symbolic importance, such as religion and nationalism, can all significantly accentuate popular perceptions about a regime's illegitimate claims to power and unfitness to govern. Structural weaknesses in turn augment the potency of legitimacy crises by compounding the difficulties faced by supposedly incompetent leaders and by giving added purchase to people's negative feelings about the regime. Moreover, the sense of illegitimacy that prompts people to demonstrate their displeasure with political leaders has important consequences for mass mobilisation, when prevailing circumstances allow. Here again, the relationship between structural variables and legitimacy crisis is crucial in pushing forward the eruption of revolutions.

Within the plethora of social and political developments which bring to a head the eruption of legitimacy crisis, the role of political leadership is central. This centrality arises from the fact that it is the legitimacy of political leaders that is at the very heart of legitimacy crisis. This propensity toward a sense of leadership illegitimacy is even stronger in countries subject to intense social change, where, through diffusion or imitation, the populace is constantly striving to attain political liberties prevalent in the West. With varying degrees, Third World leaders need constantly to react to or at least to justify not abiding by the standards which underlie the Western world because their populations are inclined to criticise, albeit often implicitly, the basis of political authority based on such foreign standards.[33] It is no accident that revolutions have historically taken place in decidedly anti-democratic, authoritarian states.[34] Within the specific context of the Third World, exclusionary regimes, which do not bother to mobilise popular support in order to justify their narrowly-based sources of authority, are seen as particularly illegitimate and are most vulnerable to the outbreak of revolutions.[35] Such regimes are often based on the rule of a single, all-powerful political figure and have an increasingly narrow base of support.[36] The blatant elite corruption that is frequently endemic to these regimes, their tight control over education and the press, the control of economy by a few families, and their frequent neglect of national interests in preference to the interests of the superpowers, all combine to significantly increase the likelihood that such polities fall victim to crises of legitimacy.[37] Nevertheless, even these brittle political systems can stave off revolutions if they acquire the patronage of a sufficiently strong segment of the population, especially the middle classes.[38]

Yet the relationship between political leaders and legitimacy crisis extends to more than the mere maintenance of popularly acceptable political practices and interpretations. Political leaders can significantly enhance or harm their popular legitimacy depending on how they treat the various symbols that are held in high value by important social classes. Most notably, the political leaders' neglect or offensive treatment of nationalist values and sentiments, historical traditions and cherished cultural values, and religious beliefs and symbols can dramatically reduce their legitimacy. In order to bring the prevailing social and cultural principles in concert with their political doctrines and ideologies, political leaders often interpret socially pervasive symbols in a manner that would fit their narrow purposes, regardless of how twisted or even offensive those interpretations may be. Interpretations ascribed to specific historical episodes and to religious values are particularly used extensively in augmenting the legitimacy of existing political institutions and practices.[39] Manifestations of nationalism are even more determinant in accentuating the popular sense of illegitimacy ascribed to political leaders in developing countries.[40] Colonial or neocolonial relations generate the most potent sense of nationalism and are most conducive to legitimacy crises for colonial powers or their local proxies. Other forms of less dependent relationships are also instrumental in bringing into question the legitimacy of existing elites by heightening a perception of their subservience to foreign powers.[41] Yet the linkage between legitimacy crisis and nationalism is more than one of political sensitivity. Nationalist sentiments can be offended through the appearance of economic and industrial subservience to a foreign country. A group of elites may effectively cultivate a sense of political nationalism and in fact exploit it to their benefit. However, the economic policies that they pursue, especially if their strategy of economic development is one of import-industrialisation substitution,[42] can give rise to sentiments of economic nationalism and discredit their legitimacy as genuinely national leaders. Similarly, intense propagation of Western values and norms by governing elites and ensuing backlashes among social classes can have similar effects.

In addition to demands for greater political participation and the upholding of values with symbolic importance, crises of legitimacy can arise out of a government's inability to meet evolving economic demands and expectations. The inability to 'deliver the goods', politically and emotionally, represents only two of the shortcomings that lead to legitimacy crisis. A government's inability to deliver more tangible goods, those which directly affect the economic well-being of the population, can have even more direct bearing on its perception as legitimate or illegitimate. Similar to anti-democratic, authoritarian states, those countries that are in a comparatively disadvantageous economic position are more prone to revolutions.[43] Not unlike growing demands for greater political participation, often arising out of diffusion with or exposure to Western political practices, the transitional nature of economic development breeds rising expectations, thus accentuating the legitimacy crisis of those regimes unable to meet such expectations.[44] In instances where 'there is the continued, unimpeded opportunity to satisfy new needs, new hopes, new expectations', the legitimacy of political leaders is greatly enhanced and the probability of a revolutionary outbreak is reduced to a minimum.[45] When there is widespread economic deprivation, however, whether actual or perceived, real or relative, the likelihood of opposition to a regime is significantly increased, especially when that regime is seen as an obstacle to continued economic mobility.[46]

Lastly, the sources and the means through which a sense of the illegitimacy of political leaders is instilled and popularised among the people is important. A general feeling of unacceptability regarding the political and ideological justifications of political incumbents may already exist among a population. But how are these negative sentiments given sufficient potency and direction to be usefully channelled into revolutionary agitation? The issue is not merely one of overt revolutionary mobilisation. Before large-scale mass mobilisation toward avowedly revolutionary goals can be achieved, and even before the social and cultural conditions conducive to mass mobilisation can appear in a society, there must be voices of dissent, no matter how faint and silent, bringing to light the illegitimate premises on which the current leaders' rule is based. Legitimacy crisis is based on the perception that current political values and practices are not legitimate whereas some other alternatives are. It is more than coincidental that almost all legitimacy crises that precede revolutions occur along with a general 'intellectual rebelliousness', a 'foment of ideas' which sharply criticise the status quo and propose ideological and valuative alternatives. The proliferation of intellectual activities that occurred before the revolutions in France,[47] Russia,[48] Cuba,[49] Iran,[50] and Hungary,[51] to mention a few, all had the affect of heightening popular perceptions of illegitimacy attributed to incumbent regimes. All too often, these sudden outbursts of intellectual activism are scattered, unorganised, and uncoordinated, without a coherent doctrine or theoretical framework emerging until some time later. In France, for example, there was little agreement before 1789 between the many *philosophes* and *physiocrats* who were theorising about various political concepts.[52] Russia's pre-revolutionary 'foment of ideas' in the 1910s was expressed mostly through a highly amorphous literary movement. In Cuba what occurred was not a coordinated attempt to formulate a new theory but essentially 'a guerrilla war of concepts, objectives, and abstractions'.[53] And in Iran the evolution of 'political Islam' as an alternative frame of ideological reference was only piecemeal and gradual.[54] Yet the cumulative effects of these alternative values and conceptual frameworks in undermining the legitimacy of political incumbents is undeniable.

Precisely why the flourishing of intellectual activity, which is part of the process of legitimacy crisis, occurs before revolutions is related both to social and to political dynamics. On the one hand, the characteristics that are inherent in Third World political cultures, coupled with the intense social change under way there, breed an environment which is conducive to the appearance of intellectuals propagating comparatively revolutionary ideas and concepts. In societies where merely speaking one's mind or even satirical writings are considered 'revolutionary', any meaningful steps toward commentary and analytical writings can have a magnified social and political affect. At the same time, on the other hand, the structural weaknesses that engulf pre-revolutionary states add a special significance to the works of intellectuals and other men of letter. Even if purely artistic in value, works done by intellectuals in such an atmosphere add to the overall sense of scepticism regarding the legitimacy of the current order in general and that of the political establishment in particular.

The growing sense of unease with the legitimacy of the body politic is further compounded by the structural breakdown of the political system itself. A group of politicians who are unable to deliver the political, social, and emotional goods that are in demand are considered as even less justified in their rule when the very organisations through which they govern start to break apart. Again, the contextual relationship between legitimacy crises and structural weaknesses assumes crucial importance. Revolutions, as mentioned earlier, are in large part a product of the breakup of the political establishment. Only after the state has already lost a substantial part of its coercive abilities due to various debilitating developments, such as military defeats or bureaucratic collapse, have revolutionary groups found an opportunity to carry forward their agendas and to gain widespread popular support.[55] Reinforcing and in fact expediting this breakup is the popular perception of political elites as unfit to rule and unjust in holding on to the reins of power.

In analysing the structural breakup of pre-revolutionary regimes, equal attention needs to be paid to domestic as well as to international factors. With the growing complexity of evolving national agendas and international circumstances, economic and even political interdependence between modern nation-states has become an inseparable part of contemporary comparative politics. 'Every modern state', it needs to be remembered, 'if it is to be understood accurately, must be seen just as fundamentally as a unit in an international system of other states as it must as a key factor in the production of social and economic power within its own territorial purlieus.'[56] Consequently, the types of developments and relations necessary to analyse within pre-revolutionary states are not merely those between the pre-revolutionary state and society but also those between the state itself and other states.[57] Specifically, it is important to see what negative ramifications arise from a state's inability to meet the challenges of evolving international circumstances as, for example, the French, Russian, Chinese, Iranian, and more recently the governments of eastern European countries experienced.[58]

Various types of domestic developments have the potential of causing the paralysis of pre-revolutionary states and subsequently expediting the appearance of revolutionary movements. Such developments occur fundamentally within the purview of the state's organisations and its structures. In specific relation to Third World countries, the breakdown of state structures assume particular importance owing to the peculiar manner in which an overwhelming majority of such structures have evolved. Third World countries are inundated with states that have variously been called 'praetorian', 'neo-patrimonial', or 'Sultanistic'.[59] For reasons discussed below, the structures supporting these states are particularly brittle and un-reformable and are thus prone to being subsumed by revolutionary movements. Such regimes are inherently weak, for they cannot substantially penetrate their respective societies regardless of their cumbrous bureaucracies or the fear and awe they instil in their populations through their armies and secret police. The fragile and often compulsory bonds that link the state to society are easily broken when the very seams that hold the state together begin to disintegrate, and the social energy released through this breakage often has devastating revolutionary consequences. It is not wide-spread poverty and misery but rather this endemic fragility of state institutions in the Third World, and in turn their inability to control and to penetrate civil society, that is the most preponderant cause of revolutions in Third World countries.[60]

Third World governments are particularly susceptible to revolu-tions because they tend to breed an atmosphere which politicises grievances that may otherwise be completely non-political. Those who are excluded from the political process and are not recipients of its patronages are especially likely to blame the political system for shortcomings that may or may not be politically related, such as economic difficulties or sudden social and cultural changes that cause widespread disillusionment and resentment. Particularly in closed, authoritarian systems, political leaders are seen as the primary protec-tors of the social and economic good, the all-embracing force from whom all power emanates. Eager to ascribe to themselves all benefits accrued through their rule, they are similarly blamed through popular eyes for discomforts that may not necessarily be of their doing. Precisely because of this overwhelming role played in all affairs of the country, or at least due to popular perceptions of such predominance, these elites represent highly visible and resented symbols of authority, targets that are not only easily identifiable but also serve to unify protestors with different grievances and from diverse backgrounds.[61] Also important is the tendency of such regimes to valorise political opposition and, by virtue of their repres-sive characters, to turn even moderate opposition into radical revolutionism.

Unlike personalised political systems, military dictatorships and bureaucratic-authoritarian regimes are not as readily susceptible to revolutions, although they are inherently just as unstable politically. The accentuated instability of personalised systems as opposed to bureaucratic or military dictatorships arises from structural characteristics as well as the functional attributes of the different systems. Structurally, the varying roles of the armed forces and the police in different systems are central to the extent of their political survivability. In all three types of political systems, repressive organs such as the military and the police play a pervasive part in maintaining the status quo. In fact, coercive organisations in such systems tend to be the most sophisticated and organisationally viable of the institutions.[62] Nevertheless, in military dictatorships and in authoritarian bureaucracies, the police and the army are often more capable of supporting the political order in times of crisis and turmoil than they are in personalised systems. This discrepancy in the effectiveness of coercive organisations in maintaining the status quo arises out of the different structural relationships that they have with the various governing bodies. In bureaucratic and military dictatorships, the army and the police are often the very organisations that occupy the seat of power and themselves form the governing elite. Even if not directly part of the establishment themselves, the relationship between these organisations and the ruling elite is at a much more intimate level than is the case in personalised systems. There is thus a lot more at stake for them in ensuring the survival of the political order than it might be in different circumstances. Moreover, dictators in personalised systems often govern through creating and then manipulating cleavages between various organisations, even within various factions of the army, and are highly dependent on the loyalties they forge through patronages and manipulations.[63] They are thus constantly on guard against possible conspiracies or at least a waning of loyalties, loyalties that frequently wear thinner as crises set in.

Domestic developments are, nevertheless, only one category of events that bring about the structural collapse of an existing state. International factors can be as equally potent determinants of the viability of domestic structures and organisations. The prevalence of unequal economic and political relationships between Third World governments and the more powerful Western countries only compounds the sensitivities of domestic Third World political institutions to changes in the international environment. The extent of domestic structural responsiveness to international fluctuations varies according to the degree of economic and political dependence. In overtly dependent Third World countries, several factors make the domestic power structure particularly brittle and exposed to revolutionary situations. To begin with, the over-identification of the elite with one or more foreign powers substantially increases their sense of illegitimacy in the public eye and makes it difficult for them to justify their rule on historical and nationalist grounds. More specifically, dependence on a foreign power reduces the political manoeuvrability of incumbent elites and circumscribes the range of their potential responses in times of crisis.[64] For the elite, the conduct of domestic politics becomes diplomatically conditional: domestic responses rely heavily on the diplomatic nuances of the more powerful state.[65] Thus incumbent regimes in Iran, in the Philippines, and in Hungary felt compelled, for one reason or another, to pursue domestic policies that were being explicitly or implicitly advocated by their stronger, respective patrons.[66] Whether actual or perceived, these regimes felt pressured by international constraints from pursuing policies which they otherwise might have pursued in order to remain in power.

In instances of outright colonial domination, ruling colonial structures are not necessarily any less prone to revolutions as are weaker, dependent states. Like personalised and bureaucratic-authoritarian regimes, direct colonial rule often disperses economic and political privileges to very few elite groups, often to settlers, and thus generates considerable anger and resentment especially among the middle and upper classes.[67] As if the granting of special privileges on the basis of racial characteristics, often the case in colonies, is not a sufficient precondition for widespread animosity toward the colonial establishment, nationalist sentiments and demands for political self-government further fan the flames of anti-colonial revolutions.[68] Furthermore, again like personalised regimes, colonial administrations are both highly visible targets for economic and political frustrations as well as unifying elements which draw together groups with diverse social, economic, and ethnic backgrounds whose unity would not have been so easily achieved otherwise.[69]

The external relations that can potentially lead to revolutions need not necessarily be of the type found between patron and client states. The outbreak of revolutionary circumstances in one country may lead to similar developments in another through imitation, instigation, or even contagion.[70] Insecure about the extent of their newly acquired powers and paranoid about the conspiratorial designs of outside forces, revolutionary regimes often try to foment revolutions in neighbouring countries in order to enhance their own legitimacy and power-base both at home and abroad. Similarly, domestic revolutionaries, for lack of indigenous role models or an ideology of their own, often idolise revolutionary heroes in other countries and try to follow their teachings and replicate their actions. Fuelled by such revolutionary myths as Latin American continentalism, Arab unity, and Pan-Africanism, the 'echo effect' of revolutions is amplified by the verbal inflation of what is usually no more than a handful of guerrillas.[71] Also prevalent are the contagious effects of revolution in one country on events occurring in another, a development further fuelled by the unrelenting propaganda of most revolutionary states and the tendency to imitate foreign revolutionaries. As the changes in the former Soviet Union in the late 1980s and their reverberations in the rest of Eastern Europe demonstrated, also important are the cumulative effects of gradual changes in world-historical contexts. These accumulated developments often give rise to 'slow, secular trends in demography, technology, economics, religion, and worldly beliefs that set the stage for the rise and decline of core hegemonic orders, which in turn create opportunities for peripheral and small groups to gather situational advantage and revolt'.[72]

In so far as dependent regimes are concerned, relations with a more powerful foreign patron can have either negative consequences for the viability of domestic structures or, as the case might be, a reinforcing, positive effect. For decades, for example, the overwhelming diplomatic force of the Soviet Union, backed up with military might under the Brezhnev doctrine, kept together the seams of Eastern European regimes and repeatedly suppressed emerging revolutions such as the one in Hungary in 1956 and in Czechoslovakia in 1968. In the 1960s, the Kennedy administration's policy of 'Alliance for Progress' was similarly designed to contain the embryonic emergence of revolutionary circumstances in the Latin American continent.[73] This policy of containment was once again pursued with great zeal in the 1980s under the auspices of what came to be known as the 'Reagan Doctrine'. In speech after speech, President Reagan warned of 'a mounting danger in Central America that threatens the security of the United States' and spoke of the necessity to contain it.[74] 'Using Nicaragua as a base', he declared,

> the Soviets and Cubans can become the dominant power in the crucial corridor between North and South America. Established there, they will be in a position to threaten the Panama Canal, interdict our vital Caribbean sealanes and ultimately move against Mexico.[75]

The pursuit of a foreign policy thus shaped in turn resulted in heightened American economic, diplomatic, and even military presence throughout Latin America, from Mexico down to Grenada, El Salvador, Honduras, Panama, Colombia, Chile, and Brazil and Argentina. In one way or another, whether militarily or through economic aid, American efforts in Latin America were designed to strengthen incumbent regimes and to stem the tide of revolutions threatening the governments of the region.[76]

In addition to crises of legitimacy and to domestic and international sources of structural weakness, states can lose a substantial degree of their cohesion and organisational viability owing to incomplete and partial processes of political modernisation. Thorough and complete political modernisation involves the progressive rationalisation and secularisation of authority, the growing differentiation of new political functions and specialised structures, and increased participation in the political process.[77] In almost all Third World countries, however, there has been a persistent reluctance on the part of existing centres of power to undergo growing secular rationalisation and to open the system to unsolicited and undirected political participation.[78] The negative ramifications of skewed political modernisation thus figure particularly prominently in Third World polities, where centralised political structures strive to pursue parallel but contradictory goals of increased consolidation and accommodative participation. Political modernisation is, in fact, inherently destabilising politically as it undermines loyalty to traditional authority, creates a need for new loyalties and identifications, and increases the public's desire for wider participation in the political process.[79] When demands for greater participation are not met, the accentuation of unfulfilled aspirations substantially increases the likelihood of political instability.[80] The absence of any meaningful means and institutions through which political objectives and demands for participation could be channelled only aggravate the inherent fragility of the system.[81] Even those groups which gain entry into politics do so without becoming identified with established political institutions or acquiescing in existing political procedures.[82] Under repressive regimes, where political demands cannot be comprehensively formulated, much less expressed, the result is a further polarisation of the inherently antagonistic relationship that in such countries exists between the state and society.[83] Moreover, partial political modernisation further hampers the cohesion of the political system and impedes the growth of political entrepreneurship and national integration.[84] The political context remains hopelessly unevolved, exacerbating the rawness and nakedness with which political forces and dynamics confront each other. Such a persistent absence of 'normative regulations of the means of competition', as one observer has put it, results in heightened political instability and a growing proclivity toward revolutionary eruption.[85]

In addition to structural attributes, functional characteristics are equally important in determining the longevity of various political systems. Personalised systems are comprised of highly visible, widely feared and resented, manipulative political figures whose longevity is determined by their vigilance, political will, and sheer wiliness. Patrimonialism pervades and there is a predominance of inter-elite and inter-organisational rivalries manipulated by the person of the ruler.[86] Bureaucratic and military dictatorships, along with other types of 'corporatist' regimes,[87] are, however, more likely to extend patronages to the various social groups and try to incorporate them into the system.[88] The vulnerability of such regimes to widespread, mass-based revolts is thus reduced, at least so long as the extension of patronages continues uninterrupted and the popular goods in demand, political and otherwise, are delivered.

REVOLUTIONARY MASS MOBILISATION

The political dynamics that bring about revolutionary circumstances are by no means limited to the structural breakdown of pre-revolutionary states. Equally important are the deliberate efforts of avowed revolutionaries in bringing down the existing political order, as too are the situational possibilities of such groups that enable them to achieve the widespread support and mobilisation of the masses. Revolutions, it must be remembered, are as much products of human initiative as they are the result of the political and structural demise of incumbent elites.[89] The existence of oppositional groups with the specific purpose of exploiting the state's evolving difficulties is an integral part of any full-blown revolution.[90] What varies from one historical example to another is the exact timing of the forma-tion of such groups. Some revolutionaries predate the start of the regime's structural difficulties, while others begin to collect into cohesive organisations *after* the regime's atrophy has begun.[91] The crucial difference, especially in so far as the starting point and the nature of revolutionary activism are concerned, is that some revolu-tions are *planned*, signified by the premeditated actions of revolu-tionaries based on previous calculations, whereas others are more *spontaneous*. Planned revolutions are typically formulated and carried

out by revolutionary organisations which, due to the force of circumstances, rely on guerrilla warfare in overthrowing existing
regimes. Thus the revolutions in Vietnam, China, Cuba, Algeria, and
Nicaragua were all planned revolutions.[92] Spontaneous revolutions,
on the other hand, acquire their leaders only after the revolutions are
well under way. The revolutions in France, Russia, Iran, and the
ones that swept across eastern Europe in the late 1980s were all of the
spontaneous variety. In all instances, nevertheless, the active initiatives of groups aiming to compound and to exploit the political
difficulties of regimes are essential in bringing revolutions into
fruition. Otherwise, what results are weakened states, lingering and
in disarray, but unopposed and unchallenged.

Spontaneous and planned revolutions differ most significantly in
the manner in which the revolutionary mobilisation of the masses is
achieved and in the role of the revolution's leadership cadre. In both
types of revolutions, the paramount weakness and vulnerability of
existing political institutions are necessary preconditions. In planned
revolutions, however, a clear, identifiable cadre of revolutionary
leaders exist who seek to expedite the regime's collapse through their
activities. In the process, they hope, their stature and legitimacy
within the public will increase, enabling them to augment their
popular support and following. Such groups are actively revolutionary, both in name and in their goals, and seek specifically to
bring about revolutionary circumstances. They in fact proclaim
themselves to be revolutionaries long before actual revolutionary
circumstances set in. In spontaneous revolutions, on the other hand,
leaders of revolution ascend to that position gradually and only
through the progression of revolutionary circumstances instead of
the other way around. In planned revolutions, revolutionary leaders
expedite the appearance of revolutionary situations. In spontaneous
revolutions, it is through the progression of revolutionary developments that its ultimate leaders are determined.

In planned revolutions, the role and initiatives of professional
revolutionaries are highly important. These revolutionaries do not
necessarily 'make' revolutions by themselves, but are instrumental in
mobilising, organising, and arming revolutionary masses.[93] Their
specific purpose is to compound the structural deficiencies of the
regime by turning the political frustrations of the masses into
organised revolutionary action.[94] In their efforts, self-proclaimed
revolutionary leaders recruit an army of their own and wage a war
aimed at overwhelming the state. They have two pressing concerns:

the formation of an army that would at least be comparable in strength to that of the regime; and the strategic and tactical man-oeuvres of this revolutionary army aimed at bringing about the regime's military defeat. It is only through a successful combination of these two tasks that a revolutionary organisation can succeed in overthrowing the state.[95] For reasons discussed below, the leadership cadre of this revolutionary army is frequently drawn from the ranks of the urban middle class, while the rank-and-file foot-soldiers, the majority of the troops, are made up of rural inhabitants and peasants.

The efforts of revolutionary leaders in mobilising and directing peasant activism require more than anything else a solid and viable organisational apparatus. In addition to an aroused and mobilisable peasantry, guerrilla revolutions require a disciplined army and a party organisation that can provide the coordination and tactical vision necessary for peasant unity and ultimately for control of national power.[96] Peasant-based revolutions depend directly upon the mobil-isation of peasants by revolutionary organisations, making the sheer availability and effectiveness of such groups a necessary precondition of revolutionary situations.[97] Often times, spontaneous political acts by peasants have forced a scramble for the mobilisation and forma-tion of its would-be leadership.[98] The degree of interaction between peasants and the leadership, and the extent to which leaders can absorb the peasantry into their organisation and to expand their power-base, determine the viability and success of the revolutionary movement. Absence of firm links between revolutionary leaders and followers, especially in guerrilla revolutions where planned revolu-tionary initiatives play an extremely important role, can substantially reduce a movement's chances of success.[99] Moreover, for guerrilla organisations to succeed in achieving their revolutionary goals, they need to have a sustained ability to recruit new members, to struc-turally and organisationally evolve and develop, and to endure the adversities of military confrontation with the regime.[100]

The social composition of the leadership of peasant-based revolu-tionary movements is often decidedly non-rural. It is, in fact, fre-quently the disaffected members of the middle classes, most notably urban-educated students and intellectuals, who occupy most of the leadership positions in guerrilla organisations. Disjointed processes of social, political, and economic development turn the middle classes in the Third World into inherently revolutionary groups, groups whose oppositional inclinations are likely to rise along with their level of education and social awareness. Given their greater sensitivity to their surrounding environment, the most revolutionary of groups in the Third World are middle-class intellectuals, and the most revolutionary of intellectuals are students.[101] These are dissatisfied literati elites who have turned into professional revolutionaries. They have entrusted themselves with the task of establishing solid revolutionary coalitions and alliances which can not only overcome social, ethnic, and economic divides but which are also capable of eventually replacing the current regime.[102] In search of an audience willing to follow and to obey them, they most frequently find the peasantry.

The preponderant role of the peasantry in guerrilla organisations arises out of a combination of rural conditions that are conducive to oppositional mobilisation, as well as to the political and ideological inclinations of revolutionary leaders themselves. To begin with, urban-based political activists are drawn to the peasantry by a number of practical political considerations. A lack of political penetration by the government machinery into distant towns and villages has in most Third World countries resulted in the alienation of the countryside from the rest of society. Despite detailed and large-scale control over various aspects of urban life, most Third World governments at best pay scant attention to the countryside and for the most part neglect not only the economic development of rural areas but, what is politically more important, their political mobilisation or at least pacification as well. Even in instances where concerted efforts aimed at the political mobilisation of rural inhabitants have been launched, large numbers of peasants continue to remain outside the influence of what often turn out to be only half-hearted campaigns. The political vacuum thus created offers potential guerrilla leaders ample opportunity for recruitment and mobilisation. In an environment of little or no official political presence of any kind, guerrilla leaders can not only recruit followers with relative ease but can also conduct revolutionary acts which, even if only symbolically important, may have a magnified effect. For guerrilla organisations, mere survival can be politically as important as it is to win battles. In the eminently political types of wars they wage, survival for the guerrillas is a victory in itself.[103]

Another reason for the attraction of revolutionary leaders to the peasantry is the supposed 'ideological purity' of peasants brought on by their geographic and political distance from centres of power. Alienation from civil society also entails ideological and valuative estrangement from the political establishment. Mao, who was perhaps the most astute observer of the peasantry's revolutionary potential, went so far as to label peasants (not the communist party) as 'the vanguards of revolution', 'blank masses' uncorrupted by the bourgeois ideologies of the city.[104] Moreover, not only is the peasantry ideologically unassimilated into the political establishment, its predicaments and objective conditions often closely match the revolutionaries' ideologies. Most revolutionaries declare their aims to be the alleviation of misery and injustice, poverty and exploitation, the very conditions which in one way or another pervade Third World rural areas. Coupled with greater possibilities for recruitment and mobilisation, ideological compatibility with objective conditions draws most leaders of planned revolutions to remote rural regions and areas. There is thus a strong connection between the revolutionaries' ideology and dogma and circumstances prevailing in the countryside.

The development of the actual links that bond revolutionary leaders and guerrilla organisation to the mass of peasants are important in determining the extent and effectiveness of revolutionary mobilisation. The establishment of such nexuses and the resultant mobilisation are dependent upon several variables, some indigenous to local conditions and others dependent on the characteristics of the guerrilla leaders themselves. Chief among these determining factors are the degree of the hegemony of the local ruling classes, the nature and extent of rural coalitions and alliances, and the ability of guerrilla leaders to deliver the goods and services which others cannot. In most rural areas in the Third World, pre-capitalist peasant smallholders, sharecroppers, and tenants are likely to enjoy cultural and social (as well as organisational) autonomy from ruling elites, despite their tendency toward localism and traditionalism.[105] This relative, built-in resistance to elite hegemony and consequently receptivity to ideological and organisational alternatives arises out of a sense of economic security and independence, as inflated as it may be, vis-à-vis the more dominant rural classes such as big landlords and estate owners. The spread of capitalism and the subsequent commercialisation of agrarian society is also important in bringing about peasant rebelliousness.[106] This increasing propensity toward revolutionism is not necessarily because of the increased exploitation of peasants due to the spread of capitalist relations, but, rather, is derived from a general breakdown of 'prior social commitments' to kin and neighbours and thus greater flexibility and independence to act as desired.[107] Even more important, however, is the extent of direct government control over a region, or indirectly through landed proprietors acting as government proxies. Favourable political circumstances, most important of which are the existence of weak states, are crucial in determining the feasibility of revolutionary activism and possibilities for peasant mobilisation.[108]

Another significant factor which determines the success of guerrilla leaders in mobilising peasants in their support is the guerrillas' ability to deliver goods and services, both actual and perceived. People will join or abstain from opposition groups based on the rewards they receive, both individually or as a collective whole, rewards that may be emotional as well as material.[109] In specific relation to rural areas, revolutionary movements have won broad support when they have been willing and able to provide state-like goods and services to their targeted constituents. The establishment of 'liberated areas' secure from government attacks, the provision of services such as public education, healthcare, and law and order, and the initiation of economic reforms in the form of land redistribution or tax reductions are particularly effective measures in drawing peasants closer to guerrilla leaders.[110] The success of revolutionary groups in peasant mobilisation becomes even more tangible when they provide local goods and services with immediate payoffs before attempting to mobilise the population for the more difficult task of overthrowing the government.[111]

The provision of goods and services may not necessarily be material. For most peasants and rural inhabitants, participation in an army-like guerrilla organisation offers a way of escaping from disillusioning surroundings and finding purpose and meaning in a greater cause. Membership in an organisation becomes an end in itself, a mean to fulfil desires of assertiveness and beliefs in higher goals and principles. To command and in turn to be commanded, to hold a gun in hand, and to aspire to dreams and ideals are often mechanisms through which peasant revolutionaries, especially younger ones, try to shatter their socially-ascribed, second-class image and, in their own world, attempt to 'become somebody'.

While planned revolutions frequently take the form of organised, peasant-based guerrilla attacks on specific targets, spontaneous revolutions are more elusive in their start and in their objectives, especially in their earlier stages, and tend to be centred more in urban as opposed to rural areas. Spontaneous revolutions typically begin with a drastic decline in the coercive powers of the state, followed in turn by a simplification of the political process and the subsequent growth of polarisation among various segments of society.[112] Political simplification and polarisation are inter-related: the growing dichotomy of society into two crude and simplified camps of political supporters and opponents polarises the political environment and leads to the politicisation of traditionally non-political groups.[113] Crisis-initiating events, exacerbating responses by the regime, and the increasing weakness of the elite in the face of the revolutionaries' growing momentum all combine to bring about a revolution.[114] In this sequence of events, political mobilisation takes place outside the state's purview and in fact it occurs precisely because the state itself was unwilling or unable to sanction popular political participation. Precipitating events force the hands of those claiming the revolution's leadership mantle, prompting them to be more reactive rather than initiative in their manoeuvres. These emerging leaders exploit rather than create the situational opportunities that arise as the revolution progresses.

Clearly, to minimise the role and importance of revolutionary leaders and their actions in spontaneous revolutions would result in a gross misunderstanding of the revolutionary process. The role of leaders in spontaneous revolutions increases as the course of events progresses and as the revolution's features and goals become clearer. Leaders of spontaneous revolutions do in fact call the shots, but only after it becomes clear that they are indeed the ones commanding the adherence of the masses in the streets. How these leaders achieve their exalted position vis-à-vis the protesting masses depends on a number of developments. Most notably, they include a coalescence of their organisational and verbal skills, the cultural communicability of their revolutionary message and ideology, and their effectiveness in exploiting the opportunities presented them by the regime's collapse. Also important are the viability of the social and/or political organisations through which they establish their links with the larger society and relay their beliefs and propaganda to their ever-growing mass of followers.

It is here that the crucial role of social organisations in spontaneous revolutions becomes evident. Focus must be on the groups and classes that comprise a society's strata, the various groups that seek to overthrow the state by mobilising popular support, and the connections that are forged or which already exist between the social classes on the one hand and the oppositions groups on the other. In planned revolutions, the links between revolutionary leaders and the masses are established through the political parties that have been established for this very purpose. The ideology, structure, and initiatives of these parties are designed in a manner not only to capture political power but also to acquire popular support as a necessary starting point. In contrast, in spontaneous revolutions avowedly revolutionary organisations initially play only a marginal role and operate on fringes of the larger social and political setting. In fact, as exemplified in one historical case after another, the revolutionary organisations that evolve under the eventual leaders of spontaneous revolutions are at best highly amorphous and rather unstructured.[115] It is instead through existing social organisations that the necessary links between revolutionary leaders and the masses are established. Before having even acquired the support and sympathy of the population, the revolution's leaders are determined by virtue of their dominant position within society and by the strength of the social institutions they have at their disposal.

Whereas the success of planned revolutions greatly depend on the viability of the political parties and organisations involved, it is mostly through highly fluid, non-formal, and society-wide institutions and means of communication that the leaders of spontaneous revolutions communicate with their emerging followers and push the revolution forward. Gatherings in churches, tea-houses, community meeting places, social or ritualistic ceremonies, and other occasions in which intense inter-personal interactions at the local level are conducted can all serve as instruments through which messages and instructions can flow from revolutionary organisers to street protesters. The accessibility of various revolutionary groups to these instruments of communication and mobilisation determine which ones can call on the most followers more effectively, enabling them to eventually assume the leadership of a mounting revolutionary movement. Other factors significant in the nexus between the leaders and followers thus established include, among others, the depth and social salience of the informal and society-wide institutions involved, the sheer numeric size and popular availability of these organisations, and their degree of immunity from government reprisals. Equally important are the ideological and strategic compatibility of these social organisations with those of the opposition groups. While priests and religious activists may fully exploit the advantages of churches and other religious institutions in communicating with the masses, for instance, communist activists, most of whom reject religious aesthetics on doctrinal grounds, are likely to shun their use and thus circumscribe the scope of their mobilisational efforts.

It is this differing role of social organisations as opposed to revolutionary parties that has led to a historical paucity of spontaneous revolutions in Third World countries. Examples of planned revolutions spearheaded by guerrilla organisations, or at least intended revolutions, inundate Third World countries, especially those in Latin America.[116] Planned revolutions occur most frequently where relatively strong (often military-based) regimes coexist side by side with bifurcated societies plagued by social, cultural, economic, and ethnic divisions. In such settings, revolutions could not possibly take place without the deliberate efforts of revolutionary organisations. Spontaneous revolutions, however, require strong social organisations and comparatively homogeneous societies, characteristics that are not readily found in many Third World countries. As it happens, throughout the Third World the most viable social organisations that have not been fully absorbed into the state are religious institutions, especially those with a history of political independence. It is primarily due to this reason that in non-Western countries where spontaneous revolutions have taken place, as in Iran and in eastern European states, religious institutions have played such vital parts in the revolutionary movement.[117] Politically independent social organisations, of which religious institutions have been prime historical examples, have afforded emerging leaders of revolutions access to the popular classes, both in terms of communication and organisation, and have thence enabled them to popularise their beliefs and propagate their revolutionary actions among the population at large.

A final feature that separates spontaneous and planned revolutions is the role of ideology. Ideology plays a much greater role in planned revolutions than it does in spontaneous ones. By nature, planned revolutions are far more dependent on the deliberate revolutionary mobilisation of the masses than are spontaneous revolutions, in which state breakdown and mass oppositional activity largely occur spontaneously and with little encouragement from designated leaders. As such, ideologies form an intrinsically more important part of planned as opposed to spontaneous revolutions. Planned revolutions, brought on by the efforts of organised guerrilla organisations, are often guided by strict interpretations of specific ideologies. They are, in essence, as much ideological movements as they are revolutionary. Spontaneous revolutions, however, initially lack ideological specificity, especially in their embryonic stages when revolutionary leaders have not yet been fully determined. Leaders of planned revolutions know exactly what they want, i.e. to wrest political power, and have clear targets and objectives. In their pursuit, they develop or adopt an ideology most suited to their ends. In furthering their cause and efforts, the adoption of an ideology by guerrilla leaders is particularly important in representing an alternative frame of reference to that of the regime. Since they do not hold power, revolutionary leaders must convince their audience that what they believe in holds greater promise than what the regime has done. A revolutionary ideology is needed, therefore, to further the legitimacy of the revolutionaries and to delegitimise the views and beliefs of those in power.[118] In spontaneous revolutions, on the other hand, the ideology of the revolution becomes clear only with the emergence of its cadre of leaders. Most spontaneous revolutions are, in fact, free of any specific ideological characters until well after the ultimate winners of the revolution have become clear and have established their reign over the country. During the course of the revolution itself, differing ideologies are as much in competition with each other as are various opposition groups who find themselves at the helm of a brewing revolution. For protesting crowds, and for the emerging leaders of the revolution themselves, an ideological under-standing of the revolutionary movement is summed up in dogmatic slogans promising vague ideals and rejecting the present. Specific doctrines with detailed outlines for future courses of action are conspicuously absent, at least until after one revolutionary group has completely dominated the movement. Even then, the ideological character of many post-revolutionary states does not become clear until well after their initial establishment. Post-revolutionary ideo-logical orientations often emerge out of strategic, diplomatic, and organisational considerations which may not necessarily be the original ones that the revolutionaries held.[119]

Considering that spontaneous revolutions start out as non-ideological movements, the existence of precise factors and condi-tions that specifically facilitate mass mobilisation assumes particular importance. A regime's popular social base among those it governs, its ability and willingness to use coercion to quell the expression of anti-state sentiments, and the degree to which the popular classes are allied together against the governing elite all determine the extent and depth to which a population is spontaneously mobilised against a political order. A most important factor is the extent to which various social classes have been co-opted into the regime and identify with it both politically and valuatively. It is precisely those groups unincorporated into the system, often unidentified and alien from it, that are most amenable to anti-state persuasions.[120] They have very little or nothing at stake in the prevailing political arrangements, and indeed frequently view them as a source of misery and grief. Given the existence of favourable social and political circumstances, such as a permissible political environment and a general willingness to revolt, these groups waste little time in showing their displeasure over the state of affairs. These expressions of anti-state sentiments by one group are greatly strengthened when joined by those of other groups, enhancing the size and forcefulness of an emerging alliance united in its dislike of the prevailing polity. An alliance of the middle classes, who in the Third World are most prone to political opposition, and other, less well-placed social groups like the peasantry or the protoproletariat is particularly threatening to the political order.[121] Such a coalition not only enjoys the raw social and economic powers that stem from middle-class participation, it also has the numerical strength and size of the lower classes, who, not having a whole lot to lose anyway, are more prone to taking risks and partaking in acts of political violence.

Also influential in shaping the depth and the nature of anti-state mobilisation are a number of otherwise politically unimportant logistical factors. Variables that in one way or another affect popular conduct, such as the weather, availability of recreational facilities, transportation routes, and opportunities for fact-to-face communication all influence the extent of mobilisation and the manner in which it comes about and is conducted.[122] Expressly political factors are equally important. The mere existence of anti-state grievances and sentiments is not sufficient in resulting in mass mobilisation.[123] The political space provided by the state and by the efforts of existing or emerging revolutionaries are equally important. The extent to which the state is willing and capable of using coercion to maintain itself in power contributes most directly to the nature of oppositional mobilisation. Often, pre-revolutionary states lack the strong willpower necessary to withstand the onslaught of an evolving revolution, wavering between which options to adopt and unwilling to bear the costs of heavy-handed repression. In other instances, where expressions of opposition are met by determined responses, only sympathizers are intimidated into silence and become passively obedient. For the most part, activists are not discouraged but are rather radicalised, and the political atmosphere is more polarised than stabilised.[124]

The breadth of mass mobilisation is in turn determined by the existence of specific, society-wide conditions which are conducive to revolutionary developments. Several developments, not all of which are specifically political in origin and in context, arise within the larger society which make various social strata prone to revolutionary mobilisation and, concurrently, have the potential of further exacerbating the regime's political difficulties. In a broad sense, these developments provide the contextual background within which the widespread mobilisation of emerging revolutionaries is made feasible and takes place. More determinedly, the ramifications of these developments or at times their mere existence often serve as the main impetus for popular opposition against ruling elites, manifestations of which are made possible by permissive prevailing political circumstances. People will not revolt against a regime unless there is a compelling reason for them to do so.[125] Political incapacitation by incumbent regimes simply provides the space and the breathing room necessary for the articulation and expression of political antagonisms. It is not, however, by itself a sufficient *cause* for the co-ordinated expression of anti-establishment sentiments by a reasonably large segment of the population. The specific sentiments and grievances that prompt populations into political activism *may be* political, but they may just as likely be non-political, at least in genesis if not in the actual form of expression. What is needed is a thorough examination and understanding of the underpinning characteristics and features, both political and otherwise, of societies in which revolutionary mobilisation takes place. Then an identification can be made of those factors and dynamics which, individually or in conjunction with one another, invite an otherwise inert mass of people to demonstrate their collective displeasure when political circumstances allow.

Three specific sets of developments in any society have the potential of leading to the mobilisation of large numbers of people. They are, broadly, those developments that give rise to economically-based grievances, to social and cultural grievances, and to political grievances. In their own way, each of these developments produce feelings of resentment and opposition against those who are popularly perceived as responsible for society's ills. Feelings of economic unease and grievance can potentially arise out of the many consequences of industrial development and technological modernisation, such as scarcity of essential goods resulting from demographic growth, feelings of deprivation and inequality vis-à-vis others, and class structures conducive to antagonistic behaviour. Social and cultural grievances, meanwhile, become most acutely pronounced during periods of intense social change, particularly when prevailing social values become disjointed and clash with one another. Lastly, political grievances, which are both frequent and which form an integral part of almost all revolutionary movements, arise out of such developments as alienation and desires for wider participation in the political process, nationalism, and growth of alternative ideologies.

Various facets of economic development substantially increase the potential, in one way or another, of widespread protests among the different social classes. The precise causal connections between economic development and political instability and violence are blurred and varied at best.[126] Nevertheless, under specific circumstances, development invokes certain reactions among people that can have potentially politically threatening results. On the most elementary level, industrialisation expands the numerical size of some economic classes at the expense of others: rural inhabitants, most notably the peasants, find their numbers increasingly dwindling while the industrial and the middle classes often rise steadily. Property-less and unemployed villagers mushroom into lumpenproletariat, and domestic migration becomes an uncontrolled, integral part of the development process.[127] Depending on specific economic policies, traditionally-based elites and upper classes are also often weakened, both politically and economically, and are replaced by newly emerging elite groups. In most Third World countries, it is thus not uncommon to find long-established landed or commercial elites and other aristocratic families who gradually fade into political oblivion and give way to new groups who owe their status to modern economic relations such as banking, international trade, and modern industries. How these consequences of industrial development and economic growth on class composition affects the stability of political elites varies from one specific instant to another. Nevertheless, shifting class structures can and in fact often do influence the viability of a political system, particularly in cases where the state is dependent on and, in turn, patronizes a specific class. The close political and economic affinity of numerous Third World regimes with one or more of the elite classes has frequently been one of the main sources of dissent and grievance by both the public at large and by emerging or existing revolutionary groups.

Another potential source of economic grievance that can increase the public's propensity toward revolutionary action is a feeling of deprivation from desired economic objectives. This syndrome is not unrelated to the development process and is, in fact, most accentuated in countries undergoing rapid economic growth and modernisation. Modernisation brings with it new needs, outlooks, and desires. It engenders new hopes and fosters rising expectations. Those who experience continued increase in wellbeing develop expectations about continued improvement.[128] In the promotion of society-wide economic grievances:

> The crucial factor is the vague or specific fear that ground gained over a long period of time will be quickly lost. This fear does not generate if there is continued opportunity to satisfy continually emerging needs; it generates when the existing government suppresses or is blamed for suppressing such opportunity.[129]

What occurs is a sense of economic deprivation, one that is relative to either one's past, to future aspirations, or to lesser capabilities than before but higher aspiration for the future.[130] People who feel deprived and are frustrated in their goals and aspirations have an 'innate disposition to do violence to its source', which, especially in the Third World, is perceived to be the government.[131] In instances when the sources of deprivation are obscure and cannot be attributed to specific political targets, alternative doctrines and ideologies which justify violence gain increasing currency and appear as more and more plausible to ever-growing segments of population.[132]

Also related to the general process of development and more specifically to feelings of deprivation are growing rates of inequality among various classes. Economic inequality by itself does not necessarily lead to political violence and the relationship between the two developments is context-specific.[133] In accented forms, however, inequality, whatever its causes, leads to a reduction of identification between the rulers and the ruled. In the face of continued immiseration and little or no identification between the body politic and the rest of society, widespread expressions of political discontent become highly likely.[134] In countries entangled in the complicated and multi-faceted web of industrial development, a variety of factors can potentially heighten existing economic inequalities and create new ones. Unequal access to economically valuable goods due to social or political influence, especially those goods whose value rises with the pace of industrialisation, exacerbate differences in class standing, power, and prestige. The spread of commercialism across social and class lines polarises competition over valued goods, especially those that are often in scarce supply, such as arable land and water. In instances where normative means of competition are lacking and there are permissive class structures and political circumstances, the potential for political violence is greatly magnified.

Economic inequality can also arise from demographic growth, albeit indirectly, which similarly increases the scarcity of prized resources both in urban and in rural areas, particularly in the latter. Although the connection between the two developments is not universal, under certain circumstances population growth severely strains state capabilities and can bring it to the brink of collapse, as was the case immediately prior to the English revolution.[135] Reduction of state revenues and irregularities in finances, elite competition and turnover, and other negative ramifications that can arise out of population growth may in one way or another propel a weakened state toward breakdown.[136] The connection between population growth, inequality, and revolutionary action is even more direct. 'Given a finite set of resources, a bifurcation process takes place in which many persons have very little and a few persons have much. This process has been shown to occur in instances of mass revolution.'[137] In fact, those revolutions that have involved the extensive mobilisation of peasants have taken place in countries where there has been a scarcity of land and its concentration in strikingly few hands.[138]

The last category of economic grievances which can potentially lead to revolutionary mobilisation stem from the predominance of particular class structures. These class-based mobilisational dynamics may or may not necessarily be exacerbated by the industrialisation process. The prevalence of specific structures and patterns of intra- and inter-relations within each class can significantly determine its potential for revolutionary mobilisation. The middle and the lower classes, including the peasantry, are most directly amenable to grievances arising out of class structures and relations. As earlier discussed, the primary source of grievance among the middle classes in the Third World is the frustration of their aspirations and feelings of relative deprivation. In so far as peasants and other rural inhabitants are concerned, their revolutionary mobilisation is most feasible when the peasant community as a whole is strong and they enjoy some sort of economic and political autonomy, and when landlords or proxies of the establishment lack direct economic and political control at the local level.[139] Peasants with small holdings are normally conservative and quiescent, reluctant to risk losing their paltry goods and heavily dependent on rich peasants and landed upper classes.[140] Share-croppers and property-less labourers, who have little to lose and much to gain by risking the adversities of violent action, along with middle-income peasants frustrated by their inability to break into the ranks of large estate proprietors, are most apt to partake in revolutionary action. An equally inert conservatism similarly pervades in the upper echelons of the industrial working class, especially among highly skilled technical workers who form part of a 'labour aristocracy'.[141] Having finally secured stable and relatively comfortable positions, skilled industrial labourers are less willing to engage in the risky and often violent political activities in which the lumpen-proletariat readily participate.

Despite their preponderant role, economic grievances are not the only category of dynamics that are conducive to mass mobilisation. Society-wide grievances with deep roots among the population can arise out of the appearance of certain social and cultural factors as well. The many and varied ramifications of social change are examples of the developments that can propel an otherwise quiescent group of people into revolutionary mobilisation. Socially-aroused political opposition is often attributed to an absence of 'harmony' between a 'society's values and the realities with which it must deal'.[142] Disparities between the way people feel and behave and their surrounding environment may indeed lead to their disillusionment and the subsequent focusing of their anger on political targets. But, at least in so far as Third World countries are concerned, social antagonisms are more likely to arise out of an incoherence in the very values that people hold and cherish. Specifically, deeply felt feelings of trauma and anguish are likely to occur when the prevailing values of society themselves are sharply divided, incoherent, and at times outright contradictory. Social and cultural homogeneity is hardly evident in any contemporary modern society. In some societies, however, especially those undergoing rapid modernisation and development, values are so disjointed and contradictory that valuative heterogeneity turns into what are almost completely separate and unrelated clusters of different cultures. When sufficient numbers of people subscribe to these differing value systems, and they all demand equal shares of the available cultural and political resources, then there is potential for violent action, especially if normative means of political competition are non-existent.

Yet the mutual incompatibility of desired and cherished values may not even transcend social and class lines. People, especially citizens of Third World countries, who are constantly bombarded with ever-changing norms and values, can become disillusioned within themselves and in turn vent their anger on political objects. They become torn between the values that they have traditionally come to adopt and cherish and those contradictory ones which they either feel compelled to adopt or willingly desire.[143] The greater the intensity of the conflict among prevailing social values, the greater is the extent of individual and collective disillusionment, and thus the higher is the probability of politically threatening behaviour. Similarly, the more acutely aware of the conflict between the values to be adopted, the higher is the disillusionment of Third World residents and thus the likelihood of their political activism. That is primarily why in the Third World, students and intellectuals, whose job it is to examine prevailing social values, are more prone to political opposition than are other groups.[144]

Lastly, a series of developments can give rise to politically-originated grievances. Because those grievances that are derived from social and economic developments are expressed in political terms, it is frequently difficult to distinguish between singularly political dynamics which prompt mass protests as opposed to those with social or economic roots. Nevertheless, there are several explicitly political developments which are by themselves sufficient causes for widespread political mobilisation. In fact, they are for the most part the same set of dynamics which bring about crises of legitimacy for incumbent elites and nullify their justifications for continued hold on power. The same factors that lead to a regime's growing political weakness have the potential of bringing about mass mobilisation. They include, among others, growing demands for greater political participation, increasing awareness of nationalist sentiments, and the widespread acceptance of ideologies other than that of the regime. There is, none the less, a fine and subtle difference between legitimacy crisis as such and politically-induced mass mobilisation. Legitimacy crisis is one of the conditions through which states are weakened and are pushed to the brink of collapse. It is only then, well after a permissive political environment has appeared, that the same set of factors that had led to legitimacy crisis result in mass-based revolutionary mobilisation.

A full examination of the grievances that provide the main impetus for mass mobilisation is important not only in acquiring a more accurate picture of the causes of revolutions but also in understanding the dynamics which result in the emergence of specific revolutionary leaders and their particular followers. The depth and preponderance of one particular form of grievance throughout society can by itself determine the composition of the revolution's leaders and their followers. More than anything else, the leaders and followers of a revolutionary movement are determined by the virtue of their relationship with the various sources of grievance that exist throughout society. Those who can most aptly discern the sources that aggrieve people, who are ideologically and organisationally capable of exploiting this aggrievement, and who offer precise remedies or vague promises for their alleviation rapidly ascend to the leadership of the revolution. At the same time, those masses who are most acutely afflicted by a certain form of actual or perceived misfortune, who are organisationally and situationally most accessible to groups promising to alleviate those very misfortunes, and who are emotionally and valuatively receptive to the appeals and cries of revolutionary leaders form the bulk of mobilised protestors. In short, the very dynamics which set into motion the onslaught of revolutions to a great extent determine the character and nature of their leaders and followers.

It is precisely for this reason that the overwhelming participants in revolutions in the Third World are made up of displaced and dispossessed peasants, disillusioned and unassimilated rural migrants, and the aspiring but frustrated segments of the middle classes. Given the right political circumstances, increased inequality and bifurcation due to a growing scarcity of goods or skewed commercialisation can promote an appropriate environment within which peasants become politically active and mobilised. The discovery by self-proclaimed revolutionaries of the merits of peasant-based revolutions, derived either from practical realism or from doctrinal idealism, provides a nexus between the two groups that has been a recurrent feature of many Third World revolutions. The less-than-successful peasant-based revolutionary movements that frequently flourish throughout Latin America attest to the centrality of peasants-revolutionaries' bonds in causing considerable political havoc, if not necessarily outright revolutions. The successful revolutions which occurred in China, Cuba, Vietnam, and to some extent in Nicaragua all did, none the less, entail considerable peasant participation.[145] At the same time, the cultural disillusionment, economic frustration, and political alienation of ever-growing lumpenproletariats turn them into readily mobilisable foot-soldiers for various revolutionary causes, the full meanings of which they may not necessarily grasp or even endorse. Their participation in revolutionary movements is not so much a result of deep understanding of and adherence to specific revolutionary ideals but more a result of their readiness and availability, both emotionally and organisationally, to partake in politically oppositional activities. Those who do hold revolutionary hopes and aspirations and who do not hesitate to voice them are mostly drawn from among the ranks of the middle classes. By the virtue of their social and economic positions, their education and background, and their political aspirations, the middle classes are much better positioned to assume the mantle of a revolutionary movement, and when revolutions do occur in the Third World it is indeed the middle classes who are frequently in the forefront and are their most vociferous leaders. The politics of exactly what groups become mobilised and by whom are in turn determined by the prevailing social and cultural dynamics that bond the various social strata together.

CONCLUSION

Revolutions are clearly multi-faceted phenomena arising out of the interplay of an array of diverse political, economic, and social developments. They are, in the first place, products of skewed political development, of inherently unstable processes in which the body politic passes through, voluntarily or involuntarily, on its way toward becoming a modern polity. Revolutions are, in essence, violent struggles aimed at achieving a fuller and more developed political establishment that is supposedly more capable of delivering popularly desired goods and services than those which the present regime can offer. This struggle is in fact an imminently political one, with its genesis, direction, scope and magnitude all dependent on the specific political configurations that happen to prevail at the time. However, the contextual environment within which the wilful leaders and the receptive audience of this struggle emerge is heavily influenced by dynamics which may be fundamentally apolitical, particularly those that are social and cultural or economic in nature. The polarising effects of this contextual environment are all the more accented in the Third World, where industrial development, rapid urbanisation, and intense social change simultaneously take place at dizzying pace and breed an atmosphere that is highly conducive to the eruption of full-blown revolutions or at least to the appearance of revolutionary movements.

Where revolutions lead is a question largely dependent on whether they are more planned in genesis and execution or involve greater spontaneity. Planned revolutions are based largely on premeditated programmes devised by wilful revolutionaries who know precisely what they want and have a clear idea of the ways and means to achieve their goals. Their efforts are undertaken with clear goals in mind and, if successful, there is thus often little disparity between their previously proclaimed goals – apart, of course, from their boisterous and at times manipulative and false promises – and newly initiated policies. Spontaneous revolutions, on the other hand, are more often the outcome of developments that at first look hardly revolutionary. They involve neither formulated programmes nor planned initiatives. Their leaders emerge relatively late, and the ultimate goals of those leaders are formed and pronounced even later. The revolution's goals and ideals are initially elusive at best, summed up in dogmatic slogans and vague promises. Each cadre of leaders promises such appealing alternatives as democracy and equality, principles that are left open to differing interpretations once it is time for their implementation. In these instances, the ideals and purposes of revolutions often appear vastly contradictory to their eventual outcomes, a contradiction which is more the result of the inherent looseness of the revolutionary process itself rather than the sinister manipulation of revolutionary turn-faces.

Nevertheless, with remarkable uniformity and regardless of whether spontaneous or planned, revolutions give rise to populist, inclusionary regimes. By nature, revolutions involve the patronage of masses of people. The relationship between revolutionary leaders and followers is essentially one of patrons and clients, with the group most capable of catering to the needs and wishes of the widest spectrum of people emerging as their leader in opposing the establishment. Once the revolution has succeeded and formerly oppositional leaders become newly-seated elites, their reliance on the patronage of the masses does not wither and is, in fact, in most instances accentuated. Their mandate is no longer to oppose the regime but to make good on the numerous promises they gave before the revolution's success. The viability of the fledgling post-revolutionary order depends on a continuation of the mass patronage that the revolutionaries acquired before they attained formal political power. To sustain power, they now need to deliver the goods which they promised, or at least to divert attention from them by fomenting popular anger against enemies of the new order, real or imagined.

Diverting attention they indeed do, as the many instances of politically sanctioned post-revolutionary violence, wars and other international disputes, and purges and the elimination of 'counter-revolutionaries' demonstrate. But even if only symbolic, a token delivery of the goods promised is necessary to maintain the viability of the new system. The result is populist and politically inclusionary regimes, regimes that in one way or another allow greater participation in the body politic if not in the actual decision-making process itself.

It is here in these inclusionary, post-revolutionary regimes that revolutions meet an embryonic death. Various means of patronage such as economic reforms, programmes for public welfare, and greater political participation, no matter how farcical and marginal, heighten the new regime's sense of legitimacy among the population and, at least so long as that legitimacy lasts, make it immune from another revolution. Moreover, post-revolutionary regimes, which in any event owe their very genesis to violence, feel less inhibited to use coercion in order to preserve their newly-acquired powers than would otherwise be the case. The constant identification of counter-revolutionary elements as the prime public enemy, the perpetual sense of besiegement and threat from outside forces, and the un-ending rhetoric of denouncing the morbid past all make post-revolutionary regimes more prone to using violence against actual or perceived sources of opposition. Crushing those who oppose the new order is indeed one of the very sources upon which its legitimacy is based. Interconnected as they often are, post-revolutionary legitimacy and violence are the most potent preservers of Third World political systems. Otherwise, in the many instances where normative means of political competition are absent, the tendency toward violence and revolutions remain an endemic probability. Whether the new wave of emerging democracies in the Third World prove capable of stemming the tide of engendered instability remains to be seen. What is certain is the enduring likelihood of further revolutionary eruptions in narrowly based, delegitimised regimes promoting rapid social change and industrial development in the face of non-responsive and unchangeable political structures.

NOTES

1 For an examination of the concept of revolution see, James Farr. 'Historical Concepts in Political Science: The Case of "Revolution"'. *American Journal of Political Science*. vol. 26, no. 4, (November 1982), pp.

688–708, and John Dunn. 'Revolution', in T. Ball, J. Farr, and R. Hanson, eds. *Political Innovation and Conceptual Change*. (Cambridge: Cambridge University Press, 1988), pp. 133–56.

2 John Dunn. *Modern Revolutions: An Introduction to the Analysis of a Political Phenomenon*. 2nd edn. (Cambridge: Cambridge University Press, 1989), p. xvi.

3 Ibid.

4 Peter Calvert. *Politics, Power, and Revolution: An Introduction to Comparative Politics*. (London: Wheatsheaf, 1983), p. 163.

5 See, for example, Laszlo Bruszt. '1989: The Negotiated Revolution in Hungary'. *Social Research*. vol. 57, no. 2, (Summer 1990), pp. 365–87.

6 Ibid. p. 386.

7 Mehran Kamrava. 'Causes and Leaders of Revolution'. *Journal of Social, Political, and Economic Studies*. vol. 15, no. 1, (Spring 1990), p. 84.

8 A few examples of works on revolutions include: Michael Freeman. 'Review Article: Theories of Revolution'. *British Journal of Political Science*. vol. 2, 1972, pp. 339–59; Rod Aya. 'Theories of Revolution: Contrasting Models of Collective Violence'. *Theory and Society*. vol. 8, no. 1, (July 1979), pp. 39–99; Perez Zagorin. 'Theories of Revolution in Contemporary Historiography'. *Political Science Quarterly*. vol. LXXXVIII, no. 1, (March 1973), pp. 23–52; Theda Skocpol. *States and Social Revolutions*. (Cambridge: Cambridge University Press, 1979), Chapter 1; Issac Kromnick. 'Reflections on Revolution: Definition and Explanation in Recent Scholarship'. *History and Theory*. Vol. XI, no. 1, (1972), pp. 22–63; J.M. Maravall. 'Subjective Conditions and Revolutionary Conflicts: Some Remarks'. *British Journal of Sociology*. vol. 27, no. 1, (March 1976), pp. 21–34; and, L. Stone. 'Theories of Revolution'. *World Politics*. vol. 18. (1966), pp. 159–76.

9 See, especially, Barbara Salert. *Revolutions and Revolutionaries*. (New York: Elsevier, 1976); and Rod Aya. 'Theories of Revolution: Contrasting Models of Collective Violence'.

10 James Farr. 'Historical Concepts in Political Science: The Case of "Revolution"'. p. 706.

11 Ibid.

12 John Dunn. *Rethinking Modern Political Theory*. (Cambridge: Cambridge University Press, 1985), p. 77.

13 Mehran Kamrava. 'Causes and Leaders of Revolutions'. p. 84.

14 The Third World is inundated with examples of movements which embrace foreign ideologies and import them with little alteration to fit local conditions. 'Maoist' groups across the Middle East and Latin America, especially the Shining Path in Peru, are a prime example.

15 Chalmers Johnson. *Revolutionary Change*. (London: Longman, 1983).

16 James Davies. 'Toward a Theory of Revolution'. *American Sociological Review*. vol. 27, no. 1, (February 1962), pp. 7–19; and Tedd Gurr. *Why Men Rebel?* (Princeton, NJ: Princeton University Press, 1970).

17 Samuel Huntington. *Political Order in Changing Societies*. (New Haven, Conn.: Yale University Press, 1968).

18 Jerrold Green. 'Countermobilization as a Revolutionary Form'. *Comparative Politics*. vol. 16, no. 2, (January 1984), pp. 153–69.

19 Theda Skocpol. *States and Social Revolutions*.
20 Mehran Kamrava. 'Causes and Leaders of Revolutions'. pp. 80–1.
21 See, for examle, Theda Skocpol. 'Rentier State and Shi'a Islam in the Iranian Revolution'. *Theory and Society*. vol. 11, no. 3, (May 1982), pp. 265–83.
22 Diplomatic pressures and conditional relations with the United States were highly instrumental in the direction and success of revolutions in Iran and the Philippines, as were relations between the Soviet Union and those governments which fell to revolutions in eastern Europe in the late 1980s.
23 Samuel Huntington. *Political Order in Changing Societies*. pp. 4–5.
24 Huntington calls these states 'praetorian'. See Ibid. p. 168; also see above, Chapter 1.
25 See above, Chapter 4.
26 Edmond Keller. 'Revolution and the Collapse of Traditional Monarchies: Ethiopia', in Barry Schutz and Robert Slater, eds. *Revolution and Political Change in the Third World*. (Boulder, Colo.: Lynne Rienner, 1990), p. 87.
27 Lucian Pye. 'Legitimacy Crisis', in Lucian Pye *et al. Crises and Sequences in Political Development*. (Princeton, NJ: Princeton University Press, 1971), p. 183.
28 Chalmers Johnson. *Revolutionary Change*. p. 65.
29 Lucian Pye. 'Legitimacy Crisis'. p. 138.
30 Samuel Huntington. *Political Order in Changing Societies*. p. 31.
31 Lucian Pye. 'Legitimacy Crisis'. p. 141.
32 Barry Schultz and Robert Slater. 'A Framework for Analysis', in Barry Schultz and Robert Slater, eds. *Revolution and Political Change in the Third World*. p. 5.
33 Lucian Pye. 'Legitimacy Crisis'. p. 150.
34 Samuel Huntington. *Political Order in Changing Societies*. p. 275.
35 Jeff Goodwin and Theda Skocpol. 'Explaining Revolutions in the Contemporary Third World'. *Politics and Society*. vol. 17, no. 4, (December 1989), p. 498.
36 See above, Chapter 1.
37 Jeff Godwin and Theda Skocpol. 'Explaining Revolutions in the Contemporary Third World'. pp. 498–9.
38 Ibid. p. 500.
39 See above, Chapter 1.
40 Barry Schultz and Robert Slater. 'A Framework for Analysis'. p. 7.
41 Barry Schultz and Robert Slater. 'Patterns of Legitimacy and Future Revolutions in the Third World', in Barry Schultz and Robert Slater, eds. *Revolution and Political Change in the Third World*. p. 248.
42 See above, Chapter 2.
43 Theda Skocpol. *States and Social Revolutions*. p. 286.
44 Barry Schultz and Robert Slater. 'A Framework for Analysis'. p. 5.
45 James Davies. 'Toward a Theory of Revolution'. p. 17.
46 Ted Gurr. *Why Men Rebel?* pp. 121–2.
47 R. Ben Jones. *The French Revolution*. (London: Hodder & Stoughton, 1967), p. 16.

48 Richard Charques. *The Twilight of the Russian Empire*. (Oxford: Oxford University Press, 1965), p. 204.
49 Pedro Perez Sarduy. 'Culture and the Cuban Revolution'. *The Black Scholar*. vol. 20, nos. 5–6, (Winter 1989), p. 18.
50 Mehran Kamrava. *Revolution in Iran: Roots of Turmoil*. (London: Routledge, 1990), p. 68.
51 Laszo Bruszt. '1989: The Negotiated Revolution in Hungary'. p. 386.
52 R. Ben Jones. *The French Revolution*. p. 15.
53 Pedro Perez Sarduy. 'Culture and the Cuban revolution'. p. 19.
54 Mehran Kamrava. *Revolution in Iran*. p. 66.
55 Theda Skocpol. *States and Social Revolutions*. p. 17.
56 John Dunn. *Modern Revolutions*. p. xxi.
57 Theda Skocpol. *States and Social Revolutions*. p. 31.
58 Ibid. p. 47.
59 See, especially, Samuel Huntington. *Political Order in Changing Societies*. Chapter 4, and Jeff Goodwin and Theda Skocpol. 'Explaining Revolutions in the Contemporary Third World'. pp. 498–9.
60 Jeff Goodwin and Theda Skocpol. 'Explaining Revolutions in the Contemporary Third World'. p. 504.
61 Ibid. p. 496.
62 T. David Mason. 'Indigenous Factors', in Barry Schultz and Robert Slater, eds. *Revolution and Political Change in the Third World*. p. 40.
63 Jeff Goodwin and Theda Skocpol. 'Explaining Revolutions in the Contemporary Third World'. p. 500.
64 David Mason. 'Indigenous Factors'. p. 33.
65 Mehran Kamrava. 'Causes and Leaders of Revolutions'. pp. 83–4.
66 See Mehran Kamrava. *Revolution in Iran*. pp. 30–2 and 40–5; and Laszlo Bruszt. '1989: The Negotiated Revolution In Hungary'. pp. 381–2.
67 Jeff Goodwin and Theda Skocpol. 'Explaining Revolutions in the Contemporary Third World'. p. 501.
68 Barry Schultz and Robert Slater. 'Patterns of Legitimacy and Future Revolutions in the Third World'. p. 248.
69 Jeff Goodwin and Theda Skocpol. 'Explaining Revolutions in the Contemporary Third World'. p. 502.
70 William Foltz. 'External Causes', in Barry Schultz and Robert Slater, eds. *Revolution and Political Change in the Third World*. pp. 54–9.
71 Girard Chaliand. *Revolution in the Third World: Myths and Prospects*. (New York: Viking Press, 1977, p. 40.
72 William Foltz. 'External Causes'. p. 63.
73 See Bruce Miroff. *Pragmatic Illusions: The Presidential Politics of John F. Kennedy*. (New York: David McKay, 1976), especially pp. 110–66. A more up-to-date discussion of US foreign policy toward Latin America can be found in, Thomas Paterson, J. G. Clifford, and Kenneth Hagan. *American Foreign Policy: A History*. (Lexington, Mass: D.C. Heath & Co., 1991), pp. 588–90, 627–32.
74 Quoted in Clifford Krauss. 'Revolution in Central America?' *Foreign Affairs*. vol. 65, no. 3, (1987), p. 564.
75 Ibid. pp. 564–5.

76 Thomas Paterson, J. G. Clifford, and Kenneth Hagen. *American Foreign Policy.* p. 588.
77 Samuel Huntington. *Politcal Order in Changing Societies.* p.34.
78 See above, Chapter 1.
79 Samuel Huntington. *Political Order in Changing Societies.* p. 37.
80 Ibid. p. 56.
81 Ibid. p. 403.
82 Ibid. p. 21.
83 Irma Adelman and Jarius Hihn. 'Crisis Politics in Developing Countries'. *Economic Development and Cultural Change.* vol. 33, no. 1, (October 1984), p. 20.
84 Elbaki Hermassi. *The Third World Reassessed.* (Berkeley, Calif.: University of California Press, 1980), pp. 59–60.
85 Ibid. p. 44.
86 See above, Chapter 1.
87 For a discussion of 'corporatism' see, Rod Hague and Martin Harrop. *Comparative Politics and Government: An Introduction.* (Atlantic Highlands, NJ: Humanities Press, 1987), pp. 134–7. See also above, Chapter 1.
88 Jeff Goodwin and Theda Skocpol. 'Explaining Revolutions in the Contemporary Third World'. p. 500.
89 John Dunn. *Rethinking Modern Political Theory.* p. 77.
90 John Dunn. *Modern Revolutions.* p. 236.
91 In *Political Order in Changing Societies*, Samuel Huntington classifies revolutions into 'Eastern' and 'Western' ones (p. 266).
92 Planned revolutions correspond closely to the variety Robert Dix calls 'Latin American'. Such revolutions occur, he writes, 'in regimes that have been narrow, modernizing, military-based dictatorships rather than, say, weak monarchies. They have not simply collapsed, almost of their own weight, as in the Western style of revolution. Instead, they have had to be overthrown and their supporting armed forces defeated or demoralized in combat with those bent on revolution'. Robert Dix. 'Varieties of Revolution'. *Comparative Politics.* vol. 15, no. 3, (April 1983), p. 283.
93 Jeff Goodwin and Theda Skocpol. 'Explaining Revolutions in the Contemporary Third World'. p. 492.
94 Carlos Vilas. 'Popular Insurgency and Social Revolution in Central America'. *Latin American Perspectives.* vol. 15, no. 1, (Winter 1988), p. 69.
95 Ibid. p. 70.
96 James Scott. 'Hegemony and the Peasantry'. *Politics and Society.* vol. 17, no. 3, (1977), p. 294.
97 Theda Skocpol. 'What Makes Peasants Revolutionary?' *Comparative Politics.* vol. 14, no. 3, (April 1982), p. 364.
98 James Scott. 'Hegemony and the Peasantry'. p. 295.
99 Girard Chaliand. *Revolution in the Third World.* p. 48.
100 Ibid. pp. 42–3.
101 Samuel Huntington. *Political Order in Changing Societies.* p. 290.
102 Jeff Goodwin and Theda Skocpol. 'Explaining Revolutions in the Contemporary Third World'. p. 496.

103 Girard Chaliand. *Revolution in the Third World*. p. 35.
104 Stuart Schram. *The Political Thought of Mao Tse Tung*. (New York: Praeger, 1972), p. 253. See also, ibid. pp. 236–64.
105 James Scott. 'Hegemony and the Peasantry'. p. 289.
106 Eric Wolf. *Peasant Wars of the Twentieth Century*. (New York: Harper & Row, 1969), p. 276.
107 Ibid. p. 279. Also see Theda Skocpol. 'What Makes Peasants Revolutionary?'.
108 Jeff Goodwin and Theda Skocpol. 'Explaining Revolutions in the Contemporary Third World'. p. 497.
109 T. David Mason. 'Indigenous Factors'. p. 42.
110 Jeff Goodwin and Theda Skocpol. 'Explaining Revolutions in the Contemporary Third World'. p. 493.
111 Ibid.
112 Jerrold Green. 'Countermobilization as a Revolutionary Form'. p. 147.
113 Ibid. pp. 160–1.
114 Chalmers Johnson. *Revolutionary Change*. p. 101.
115 This was precisely the case in the revolutions that occurred in France, Iran, and in Eastern Europe in the end of the 1980s. In the Russian revolution, however, the soviets played an important organisational role.
116 Girard Chaliand. *Revolution in the Third World*. p. 40.
117 See Mehran Kamrava. *Revolution in Iran* Chapter 5, esp. pp. 128–30; for eastern Europe, see the special edition on eastern European revolutions in *Social Research*. vol. 57, no. 2, (Summer 1990).
118 Gerald Greene. *Comparative Revolutionary Movements*. (Englewood Cliffs, NJ: Prentice-Hall, 1974), p. 57.
119 This was particularly the case in the Cuban and the Ethiopian revolutions, where the ideological orientations of post-revolutionary political leaders did not fully become apparent until some time after their success.
120 Jeff Goodwin and Theda Skocpol. 'Explaining Revolutions in the Contemporary Third World'. p. 494.
121 Samuel Huntington. *Political Order in Changing Societies*. pp. 300–1.
122 Gerald Greene. *Comparative Revolutionary Movements*. p. 63.
123 T. David Mason. 'Indigenous Factors'. p. 48.
124 Ibid. p. 44.
125 Barrington Moore. *Injustice: The Social Base of Obedience and Revolt*. (London: Macmillan, 1978), p. 459.
126 Peter Calvert. *Politics, Power, and Revolution*. p. 168.
127 See above, Chapter 2.
128 Ted Gurr. *Why Men Rebel?* pp. 121–2.
129 James Davies. 'Toward a Theory of Revoltion'. p. 8.
130 Ted Gurr. *Why Men Rebel?* p. 46. For a full analysis of relative deprivation see, ibid. pp. 46–56.
131 Ibid. p. 37.
132 Ibid. p. 205.
133 Manus Midlarsky. 'Rulers and the Ruled: Patterned Inequality and the Onset of Mass Political Violence'. *American Political Science Review*. vol. 82, no. 2, (June 1988), p. 492.
134 Ibid. p. 493.

135 See Jack Goldstone. 'State Breakdown in the English Revolution: A New Synthesis'. *American Journal of Sociology*. vol. 92, no. 2, (September 1986), pp. 257–322.

136 Ibid. pp. 310–11.

137 Manus Midlarsky. 'Scarcity and Inequality: Prologue to the Onset of Mass Revolution'. *Journal of Conflict Resolution*. vol. 26, no. 1, (March 1982), p. 34.

138 Manus Midlarsky. 'Rulers and the Ruled: Patterned Inequality and the Onset of Mass Political Violence'. pp. 493–4.

139 Jerome Himmelstein and Michael Kimmel. 'Review Essay: States and Revolutions: The Implications and Limits of Skocpol's Structural Model'. *American Journal of Sociology*. vol. 86, no. 5, (March 1981), p. 1147. Also see Theda Skocpol. 'What makes Peasants Revolutionary?'.

140 Jeffrey Paige. *Agrarian Revolution: Social Movements and Export Agriculture in the Underdeveloped World*. (New York: Free Press, 1975), p. 41.

141 Val Moghadam. 'Industrial Development, Culture, and Working Class Politics: A Case Study of Tabriz Industrial Workers in the Iranian Revolution'. *International Sociology*. vol. 2, no. 2, (June 1987), pp. 164–5.

142 Chalmers Johnson. *Revolutionary Change*. p. 62.

143 See above, Chapter 2.

144 Samuel Huntington. *Political Order in Changing Societies*. p. 290.

145 See John Dunn. *Modern Revolutions*.

Chapter 7

Conclusion

The Third World is a battlefield. It is a battlefield of forces clashing with each other head-on, brutal in their confrontation, naked in their defence. It is where dramas unfold constantly, unravelling themselves and in their midst political, economic, social, and cultural dynamics which traumatise the region and its inhabitants. It is a dynamic arena, changeable and in constant flux.

It is this quality of metamorphosis which has endowed the Third World with as much enigma for students and observers as agony and trial for its citizens. The Third World keeps changing faster than academics can understand and theorise about it, and even faster than its people can become accustomed to its transient socio-political and cultural forms. A mutually reinforcing puzzlement has resulted, with academics not understanding the predicaments and the peoples of the Third World, and the peoples of the Third World not understanding themselves and their own predicaments. A multiplicity of forces, meanwhile, keeps up a barrage of the region with unabated strength and frequency. Political systems evolve and collapse; industrial projects are launched, revised, abrogated, and launched again; populations shift and gravitate toward existing centres; cherished values are ridiculed and the ridiculous cherished; political religions and prophets come and go; and people rise up, but are subdued again – all in the name of state-building, all the inevitable trials of national growth and development.

Nowhere have the painful reverberations of the Third World's dramas been so vocally and publicly played out as in the political arena. As if stricken with a pathological disease, Third World politics has become a field plagued by violence and instability, greed and corruption, avarice and malice. To this day, imbedded ethnic and tribal nuances tear nations apart, segregating and separating their peoples along the lines of racial, tribal, and linguistic differences. While the process of state building may have for the most part given birth to structurally viable systems, such states have been unable to devise polities capable of overwhelming centrifugal forces engendered through centuries of cleavages. The Nigeria of the 1970s or the Lebanon of the 1980s may no longer be the norm, but the pushes and pulls of non-state loyalties are still strong enough to spark mass protests at the death of a tribal notable or the vitriolic speeches of a separatist leader. From among these torn societies come personalist leaders, claiming to be the one and only holders of a saving vision, men whose continued hold on power is indispensable to national unity, cohesion, and progress. Many are soldiers in mufti, generals who like to be presidents, men who think their military background and discipline provides the panacea their country needs. Some are aspiring civilians, either thrust on the national scene during the struggle for liberation or having risen through the ranks of the bureaucracy. A few, as of late, are turbaned, believing their righteous ways offer both political and sociocultural salvation.

Despite their garb, however, few Third World leaders have withstood the temptations associated with their office. Tanzania's Julius Nyerere, who in 1985 voluntarily gave up political office, is indeed a rare breed. Some have dispensed with pretensions and declared themselves President for Life, and those who maintain a semblance of electoral accountability act as if ending their tenure would usher in disaster and catastrophe. The Third World is a land of many presidents but few elections. In their different ways, leaders cling on to office as if there were no tomorrow, often placing themselves at the centre of a stale and inherently fragile political universe. Whether by patrimonial or clientalist manipulations, or by the sheer brutality of military force, or by rigging elections and intimidating voters, they remain in office until forced out by powers more brutal than their own. Coups and assassinations are endemic, fear and suspicion ever-present, instability brewing just beneath the surface. In some cases, it takes nothing short of full-scale revolutions and civil wars to force self-declared saviours out of office. Even the seemingly peaceful democratisation of Latin America was not that peaceful considering that misguided economic policies brought Latin American societies close to falling apart at the seams. For its part, the Argentine junta had to deal with the additional burden of a humiliating defeat at the hands of the British Navy after the Falklands fiasco.

The political drama is played out within the context of changing norms, fluctuating classes and groups, disjointed cultures, and fractured traditions. The many consequences of change – demographic, economic, industrial, and cultural change – torment Third World societies just as much as they throw its political world into chaos and confusion. The problem of figuring out how to survive in the world of international economy, never mind getting ahead, is just one dilemma. At least, economic issues create tangible problems, those of unemployment and hyperinflation, international indebtness and budget deficits. That such shortcomings have become lingering features of Third World economies doesn't necessarily mean they cannot be solved; perhaps the political will is lacking, perhaps the problems are too deep to be solved by the current cosmetic reforms. But the problems of social and cultural malady are much less easily discernible and mostly intangible. They are, however, equally fierce in afflicting Third World societies and their peoples, their ways of life, and their spirits and cultures. Countercultures and escapism may not be as hard on the stomach as are poverty and unemployment, but they are psychologically as debilitating as the former are physically. To cry over drowning in the shifting of cultural sands shows a sentimental twitch for nostalgia, not the stuff of which academic analysis is made. But to overlook the dramatic ramifications of ailments resulting from social and cultural change, the alienating effects of sudden changes in one's environment, the demoralizing consequences of being told what to read and what to think, and the strength of the energy released when there is an opportunity for self-expression, would be as unforgivably shortsighted.

Where the Third World is heading is not fully clear. Only ideological diehards dare make predictions and back them up with conviction and moral force. Had Regis Debray and Che Guevara been alive today they would most likely be leading intellectually distraught lives, disillusioned because the revolutions that they advocated for Latin America and elsewhere never materialised, and the one that did take place, Iran's Islamic revolution, occurred under religious auspices. Communism saw its stronghold of eastern Europe turn into its own burial ground in the 1980s, and with that its chances of growth in the Third World grew even dimmer than the time when powerful international patrons like Mao exported it. Third Worldism, meanwhile, which was so noisily hailed in the 1960s by the likes of Tito, Nehru, and Sukharno, has long been dead, having succumbed early on to long-standing national enmities, competition over scarce resources, and the intricacies of international diplomacy.

But it is inaccurate to assume that the failure of non-Western 'isms' in the Third World is tantamount to a victory for Western ways and means for the region. To the contrary, imported Western models are as likely to crumble under the weight of indigenous conditions as Eastern imports faltered some time ago. Iraq's invasion of Kuwait in 1990, to take a random example, is as shattering to the dogma of Ronald Reagan as it is to that of the late Nasser.[1] Reagan was hardly alone among Western leaders who saw in Saddam Hussein a secular, 'Westernized' alternative to Iran's revolutionary, 'barbaric' leaders.[2] Africa has already taught us that emulating Western institutions and practices invariably leads to a mockery of their underlying principles and beliefs. From east Asia to the Middle East and Africa, and even in Latin America, imported Western institutions frequently cast a thin mask over what are in reality tailor-made political systems and offices.

Where the Third World goes is not determined by any grand and universal processes or by an overwhelming movement in one specific direction. The region's future direction is, rather, dependent on the initiatives and policies of its individual leaders and the particular social and cultural characteristics of the countries they lead. It is their ability in not just surviving the tumults of the political arena but in stewarding their nations toward specific ends which ultimately determine their success or failure. It is hard not to set ideal goals: balanced opportunities for economic prosperity; greater attention to rural areas and the economic well-being of their inhabitants; advancements in education, not just in literacy but in nurturing intellectual independence; and, perhaps prerequisites to all, political systems and cultures in which liberties are safeguarded and security assured. Enumerating on these and many other ideal goals is easy; the challenge lies in getting them implemented. To assert that the success of their implementation depends solely on the intentions of politicians would be to reduce the level of analysis to unforgivably reductionist proportions. But the centrality of human agency to the political drama is irrefutable. Clearly, the international political, military, and economic frameworks within which states operate determine a good measure of their domestic characteristics, a factor of which most eastern Europeans would these days happily remind the rest of us. Also determinant are domestic conditions, those

INTERNATIONAL PEOPLE'S HEALTH COUNCIL

The struggle for health is a struggle for liberation from poverty, hunger, and unfair socio-economic structures.

What is it?

The International People's Health Council is a world-wide coalition of people's health initiatives and socially progressive health groups and movements committed to working for the health and rights of disadvantaged people ... and, ultimately, of all people. The vision of the IPHC is to advance toward health for all people -- viewing health in the broad sense of physical, mental, social, economic and environmental well-being. We believe that:

* "Health for all" can only be achieved through PARTICIPATORY DEMOCRACY (decision-making power by the people), EQUITY (in terms of equal rights and satisfaction of everyone's basic needs) and ACCOUNTABILITY of government and leaders to the people.the strong participation of people in the decisions that affect their lives.

* The policies of today's dominant power structures -- tied as they are to powerful economic interests -- have done much to precipitate and worsen humanity's present social, economic, environmental, and health crises. Those who prosper from unfair social structures are resistant to change. They also have vast power and global reach. So today, changes leading toward a healthier world order must be spearheaded through a world-wide grassroots movement that is strong and well coordinated enough so it can force the dominant power structures to listen and finally to yield.

The IPHC intends to facilitate sharing of information, experiences, methods, and resources among a wide range of persons, and coalitions involved in community health work oriented toward empowerment and self-determination.

ingrained practices validated by decades (at times centuries) of social acceptance and experience. Brutal as they were, the efforts of 'modernising' dictators such as Turkey's Ataturk, Iran's last Shah, and the many juntas of Latin America have hardly left an imprint except on the most superficial aspects of their societies. All tried to do away with tradition, viewing it as *the* obstacle to progress and modernisation. All failed in their efforts, neither eradicating traditions completely nor implanting lasting legacies of modernity.

Writing on the American experience nearly two hundred years ago, de Tocqueville claimed that 'the causes which mitigate the government are to be found in the circumstances and the manners of the country more than in its laws'.[3] His words could not have been more prophetic for today's Third World, given the plethora of democratic constitutions there in the face of non-democratic systems. To accuse Third World cultures of fostering anti-democratic principles finds uncomfortable parallels with the claims of modern-day Rudyard Kiplings for whom 'we told you so' has become a favourite phrase. But it is true none the less. Democracy will not appear in the Third World unless many national cultural foundations are changed or reconstructed anew. Much social engineering has and continues to occur in the region, most of it directed by leaders seeking to appease their own vanity and enhance their personal tenure. The direction of these engineering efforts needs to change, as do some of the institutional means through which they are instilled. At the same time, ignoring indigenous social and cultural circumstances for the sake of higher ideals would be to fall into the very same traps that the Ataturks and the Shahs have fallen into.

NOTES

1 Gamal Abdul Nasser, the late president of Egypt, was a staunch advocate of Arab unity. Even after Egypt's defeat by Israel in the 1967 war, Nasser remained greatly popular through the Arab world, the hero of the youth who saw in his ideas visions of grandeur and power. See Fouad Ajami. *The Arab Predicament: Arab Political Thought and Practice since 1967.* (Cambridge: Cambridge University Press, 1981), pp. 84–94.

2 James Bill. *The Eagle and the Lion: The Tragedy of American-Iranian Relations.* (New Haven, Conn.: Yale University Press, 1988), p. 307. For Reagan's pre-Iraqi sympathies see, ibid. pp. 306–7.

3 William Ebenstein. *Great Political Thinkers: From Plato to the Present.* 4th edn. (New York: Holt, Rinehart & Winston, 1951), p. 549.

Bibliography

Abrams, Charles. 'Squatting and Squatters', in Janet Abu-Lughod and Richard Hay, eds. *Third World Urbanization*. Chicago: Maaroufa Press, 1977, pp. 293–99.

Adelman, Irma and Jairus Hihn. 'Crisis Politics in Developing Countries'. *Economic Development and Cultural Change*. vol. 33. no. 1, (October 1984), pp. 1–22.

Aguirre, B.E. 'The Conventionalization of Collective Behavior in Cuba'. *American Journal of Sociology*. vol. 90, no. 3, (1984), pp. 541–66.

Ahmad, Zakaria. 'The Evolution and Development of the Political System in Malaysia'. R. Scalapino, S. Sato and J. Wanandi, eds. *Asian Political Institutionalization*. Berkeley, Calif.: Institute of East Asian Studies, 1986, pp. 221–40.

Ajami, Fouad. *The Arab Predicament: Arab Political Thought and Practice since 1967*. Cambridge: Cambridge University Press, 1981.

Alatas, Syed Hussein. *Modernization and Social Change*. London: Angus & Robertson, 1972.

Al-Haj, Majid. 'The Changing Arab Kinship Structure: The Effects of Modernization in an Urban Community'. *Economic Development and Cultural Change*. vol. 36, no. 2, (January 1988), pp. 237–58.

Almond, Gabriel and G. Bingham Powell. *Comparative Politics: Systems, Processes and Policy*. Boston: Little, Brown, 1978.

Almond, Gabriel and Sidney Verba. *The Civic Culture*. London: Sage, 1989.

Altbach, Philip and S. Gopinathan. 'Textbooks in the Third World: Challenge and Response', in P. Altbach, A. Arboleda and S. Gopinathan, eds. *Publishing in the Third World: Knowledge and Development*. London: Mansell, 1985.

Anderson, Lisa. *The State and Social Transformation in Tunisia and Libya, 1830–1980*. Princeton, NJ: Princeton University Press, 1986.

Armstrong, Warwick and T.G. McGee. *Theatres of Accumulation: Studies in Asian and Latin American Urbanization*. London: Methuen, 1985.

Arrington, Leonard and Davis Bitton. *The Mormon Experience: A History of the Latter-day Saints*. New York: Vintage, 1980.

Ashford, Douglas. 'Attitudinal Change and Modernization', in Chandler

Morse, Douglas Ashford, Frederick Bent, William Friedland, John Lewis and David Macklin. *Modernization by Design: Social Change in the Twentieth Century*. London: Cornell University Press, 1969, pp. 147–88.

Aya, Rod. 'Theories of Revolution Reconsidered: Contrasting Models of Collective Violence'. *Theory and Society*. vol. 8, no. 1, (1979), pp. 39–99.

Ayubi, Nazih. 'The Politics of Militant Islamic Movements in the Middle East'. *Journal of International Affairs*. vol. 36, no. 2, (Fall/Winter 1982–83), pp. 271–87.

Bakhash, Shaul. *The Reign of the Ayatollahs: Iran and the Islamic Revolution*. London: I.B. Tauris, 1985.

Becker, Charles and Andrew Morrison. 'The Determinants of Urban Population Growth in Sub-Saharan Africa'. *Economic Development and Cultural Change*. vol. 36, no. 2, (January 1988), pp. 259–78.

Bent, Frederick. 'A Comparative Analysis of Public Adminstration in Modern, Traditional, and Modernizing Societies', in Chandler Morse, ed. *Modernization by Design: Social Change in the Twentieth Century*. Ithaca, NY: Cornell University Press, 1969, pp. 189–237.

Berg-Schlosser, Dirk. 'African Political Systems: Typology and Performance'. *Comparative Political Studies*. vol. 17, no. 1, (1984), pp. 121–51.

Berry, Brian. *Comparative Urbanization: Divergent Paths in the Twentieth Century*. New York: St Martin's, 1981.

Berry, Sara. 'Work, Migration, and Class in Western Nigeria: A Reinterpretation', in Fredrick Cooper, ed. *Struggle for the City: Migrant Labor, Capital, and the State In Urban Africa*. London: Sage, 1988, pp. 247–73.

Bigo, Pierre. *The Church and Third World Revolution*. Jeane Marie Lyons, trans. New York: Orbis, 1977.

Bill, James. *The Eagle and the Lion: The Tragedy of American-Iranian Relations*. New Haven, Conn.: Yale University Press, 1988.

Bill, James and Robert Springborg. *Politics in the Middle East*. Glenview, Ill. and Boston: Scott, Foresman/Little, Brown, 1990.

Birand, Mehmet Ali. *The Generals' Coup in Turkey*. Trans. M.A. Dikerdem. London: Bramssey's, 1987.

Biswas, Basudeb and Rati Ram. 'Military Expenditure and Economic Growth in Less Developed Countries: An Augmented Model and Further Evidence'. *Economic Development and Cultural Change*. vol. 34, no. 2, (January 1986), pp. 361–72.

Blumer, Herbert. *Industrialization as an Agent of Social Change: A Critical Analysis*. Hawthorne, NY: Aldine de Gruyter, 1990.

Boyd, Douglas and Joseph Straubhaar. 'Developmental Impact of Home Video Cassette Recorders on Third World Countries.' *Journal of Broadcasting and Electronic Media*. vol. 29, no. 1, (Winter 1985), pp. 5–21.

Brandt, Vincent and Man-gap Lee. 'Community Development in the Republic of Korea', in Ronald Dore and Zoe Mars, eds. *Community Development*. London: Croom Helm, 1981, pp. 49–136.

Braveboy-Wagner, Jacqueline. *Interpreting the Third World: Politics, Economics, and Social Issues*. New York: Praeger, 1986.

Brekelbaum, Trudy. 'The Use of Paraprofessionals in Rural Development'. *Community Development Journal*. vol. 19, (October 1984), pp. 232–45.

Bromley, Ray. 'Working in the Streets: Survival Strategy, Necessity, or Unavoidable Evil?', in Josef Gugler, ed. *The Urbanization of the Third World*. Oxford: Oxford University Press, 1988, pp. 161–82.

Bruneau, Thomas and W.E. Hewitt. 'Patterns of Church Influence in Brazil's Political Transition'. *Comparative Politics*. vol. 22, no. 1, (October 1989), pp. 39–61.

Bruszt, Laszlo. '1989: The Negotiated Revolution in Hungary'. *Social Research*. vol. 57, no. 2, (Summer 1990), pp. 365–87.

Butterworth, Charles. 'State and Authority in Arabic Political Thought', in Ghassan Salame, ed. *The Foundations of the Arab State*. London: Croom Helm, 1987, pp. 91–111.

Calvert, Peter. *Politics, Power and Revolution: An Introduction to Comparative Politics*. London: Wheatsheaf, 1983.

Calvez, Jean-Yves. *Politics and Society in the Third World*. Trans. M.J. O'Connell. Maryknoll, NY: Orbis, 1973.

Cammack, Paul, David Pool, and William Tordoff. *Third World Politics: A Comparative Introduction*. Baltimore, Md: Johns Hopkins University Press, 1988.

Castelli, Manuel. 'Squatters and the State in Latin America', in Josef Gugler, ed. *The Urbanization of the Third World*. Oxford: Oxford University Press, 1988. pp. 338–66.

Chaliand, Girard. *Revolution in the Third World: Myths and Prospects*. New York: Viking Press, 1977.

Charques, Richard. *The Twilight of the Russian Empire*. Oxford: Oxford University Press, 1965.

Chazan, Naomi. 'The New Politics of Participation in Tropical Africa'. *Comparative Politics*. vol. 14, no. 2, (January 1982), pp. 169–90.

Chilcote, Ronald. 'Introduction: Dependency or Mode of Production? Theoretical Issues', in Ronald Chilcote and Dale Johnson, eds. *Theories of Development: Mode of Production or Dependency?* London: Sage, 1983, pp. 231–55.

Chileshe, Jonathon. *Third World Countries and Development Options: Zambia*. New Delhi: Vikas, 1986.

Chilton, Stephen. 'Defining Political Culture'. *Western Political Quarterly*. vol. 41, no. 3, (September 1988), pp. 419–45.

Chin-wee, Chung. 'The Evolution of Political Institutions in North Korea', in R. Scalapino, S. Sato, and J. Wanandi, eds. *Asian Political Institutionalization*. Berkeley, Calif.: Institute of East Asian Studies, 1986, pp. 18–41.

Claessen, Henri. 'Changing Legitimacy', in R. Cohen and J. Toland, eds. *State Formation and Political Legitimacy*. New Brunswick, NJ: Transaction Books, 1988, pp. 23–44.

Clements, Kevin. *From Right to Left in Development Theory: An Analysis of the Political Implications of Different Models of Development*. Singapore: The Institute of Southeast Asian Studies, 1980.

Cohen, Abner. 'The Politics of Ethnicity in African Towns', in Josef Gugler, ed. *The Urbanization of the Third World*. Oxford: Oxford University Press, 1988, pp. 328–37.

Cohen, Youssef. 'The Impact of Bureaucratic-Authoritarian Rule on Economic Growth'. *Comparative Political Studies*. vol. 18, no. 1, (April 1985), pp. 122–36.

Conway, M. Margaret. 'The Political Context of Political Behavior'. *Journal of Politics.* vol. 51, no. 1, (February 1989).

Cooper, Frederick. 'Urban Space, Industrial Time, and Wagelabor in Africa', in Fredrick Cooper, ed. *Struggle for the City: Migrant Labour, Capital, and the State in Urban Africa.* London: Sage, 1988, pp. 7–50.

Cornelius, Wayne A. 'The Political Sociology of Cityward Migration In Latin America: Towards Empirical Theory', in Janet Abu-Lughod and Richard Hay, eds. *Third World Urbanization.* Chicago: Maaroufa Press, 1977, pp. 213–24.

Cosio, Ignacio Algara. 'Community Development in Mexico', in Ronald Dore and Zoe Mars, eds. *Community Development.* London: Croom Helm, 1981, pp. 337–432.

Cotton, J. 'From Authoritarianism to Democracy in South Korea'. *Political Studies*, vol. 37, (June 1989), pp. 244–59.

Davies, James. 'Toward a Theory of Revolution'. *American Sociological Review.* vol. 27, no. 1, (February 1962), pp. 7–19.

Decalo, Samuel. 'African Personal Dictatorships'. *The Journal of Modern African Studies.* vol. 23, no. 2, (1985), pp. 209–37.

de Gennaro, Bruno Musti. 'Ujamaa: The Aggrandizement of the State', in Rosemary Galli, ed. *The Political Economy of Rural Development: Peasants, International Capital, and the State.* Albany, NY: SUNY, 1981, pp. 111–55.

Dhaouadi, Mahmoud. 'An Operational Analysis of the Phenomenon of the Other Underdevelopment in the Arab World and in the Third World'. *International Sociology.* vol. 3, no. 3, (September 1988), pp. 219–34.

Dix, Robert. 'The Varieties of Revolution'. *Comparative Politics.* vol. 15, no. 3, (April 1983), pp. 281–94.

Dror, Yehezkel. 'Public-Policy-Making in Avant-Garde Developing States', in Harvey Kebschull, ed. *Politics in Transitional Societies.* New York: Appleton-Century-Crofts, 1973, pp. 278–86.

Dube, S.C. *Modernization and Development: The Search for Alternative Paradigms.* Tokyo: United Nations University, 1988.

Dunn, John. *Modern Revolutions: An Introduction to the Analysis of a Political Phenomenon.* 2nd edn. Cambridge: Cambridge University Press, 1989.

——. 'Revolution', in T. Ball, J. Farr, and R. Hanson, eds. *Political Innovation and Conceptual Change.* Cambridge: Cambridge University Press, 1988.

——. *Rethinking Modern Political Theory.* Cambridge: Cambridge University Press, 1985.

Ebenstein, William. *Great Political Thinkers: From Plato to the Present.* 4th edn. New York: Holt, Rinehart and Winston, 1951.

Eckstein, Harry. 'A Culturalist Theory of Political Change'. *American Political Science Review.* vol. 82, no. 3, (September 1988).

Eckstein, Susan. 'Politics of Conformity in Mexico City', in J. Gugler, ed. *The Urbanization of the Third World.* Oxford: Oxford University Press, 1988, pp. 294–307.

Edwards, Sebastian and Simon Teitel. 'Introduction to Growth, Reform, and Adjustment: Latin America's Trade and Macroeconomic Policies in the 1970s and the 1980s'. *Economic Development and Cultural Change.* vol. 34, no. 3, (April 1986), pp. 423–31.

Eisenstadt, S.N. 'Problems of Emerging Bureaucracies in Developing Areas and New States', in Harvey Kebschull, ed. *Politics in Transitional Societies.* New York: Appleton-Century-Crofts, 1973, pp. 286–93.

Ellul, Jacques. *Propaganda: The Formation of Men's Attitudes.* Konrad Kellen and Jean Lerner, trans. New York: Vintage, 1973.

Enayat, Hamid. *Modern Islamic Political Thought.* London: Macmillan, 1982.

Epstein, Edward. 'Legitimacy, Institutionalization, and Opposition in Exclusionary Bureaucratic Authoritarian Regimes: The Situation in the 1980s'. *Comparative Politics.* vol. 17, no. 1, (1984), pp. 37–54.

Eun Sung, Chung. 'Transition to Democracy in South Korea'. *Asian Profile.* vol. 17, no. 1, (February 1989), pp. 25–37.

Fanon, Frantz. *Black Skin, White Mask.* Trans. Charles Lam Markmann. New York: Grove Press, 1967.

Farhi, Farideh. 'State Disintegration and Urban-Based Revolutionary Crisis: A Comparative Analysis of Iran and Nicaragua'. *Comparative Political Studies.* vol. 21, no. 2, (July 1988), pp. 231–56.

Farr, James. 'Historical Concepts in Political Science: The Case of Revolution'. *American Journal of Political Science.* vol. 26, no. 4, (November 1982), pp. 688–708.

Feder, Ernest. 'The World Bank–FIRA Scheme in Action in Temporal, Veracruz', in Rosemary Galli, ed. *The Political Economy of Rural Development.* Albany, NY: SUNY Press, 1981.

Feit, Edward. *The Armed Bureaucrats: Military Administrative Regimes and Political Development.* Boston, Mass: Houghton Mifflin, 1973.

Fields, Gary. 'Place to Place Migration in Colombia'. *Economic Development and Cultural Change.* vol. 30, no. 3, (April 1982), pp. 539–58.

Findlay, Allen and Anne Findlay. *Population and Development in the Third World.* London: Methuen, 1987.

Foltz, William. 'External Causes', in Barry Schultz and Robert Slater, eds. *Revolution and Political Change in the Third World.* Boulder, Colo.: Lynne Rienner, 1990, pp. 54–68.

Foster, Phillip. 'The Educational Policies of Postcolonial States', in Anderson, Lascelles and Douglas Windham, eds. *Education and Development: Issues in the Analysis and Planning of Postcolonial Societies.* Lexington, Mass: Lexington Books, 1982, pp. 3–25.

Frank, Andre Gunder. 'Crisis and Transformation of Dependency in the World-System', in Ronald Chilcote and Dale Johnson, eds. *Theories of Development: Mode of Production or Dependency?* London: Sage, 1983, pp. 181–200.

Freeman, Michael. 'Review, Article: Theories of Revolution'. *British Journal of Political Science.* vol. 2, 1972, pp. 339–59.

Friedland, William. 'A Sociological Approach to Modernization', in Chandler Morse, *et al. Modernization by Design: Social Change in the Twentieth Century.* London: Cornell University Press, 1969, pp. 34–84.

Gaikwad, V.R. 'Community Development in India', in Ronald Dore and Zoe Mars, eds. *Community Development.* London: Croom Helm, 1981.

Galli, Rosemary, ed. *The Political Economy of Rural Development: Peasants, International Capital, and the State.* Albany, NY: SUNY Press, 1981.

Gareau, Fredrick. 'Another Type of Third World Dependency: The Social Sciences'. *International Sociology.* vol. 3, no. 2, (June 1988), p. 173.

Ghai, Dharam and Cynthia Hewitt de Alcantara. 'The Crisis of the 1980s in Sub-Saharan Africa, Latin America and the Caribbean: Economic Impact, Social Change and Political Implications'. *Development and Change*. vol. 12, (1990), pp. 389–426.

Gilbert, Alan and Josef Gugler. *Cities, Poverty, and Development: Urbanization in the Third World*. Oxford: Oxford University Press, 1982.

Goldstone, Jack. 'State Breakdown in the English Revolution: A New Synthesis'. *American Journal of Sociology*. vol. 92, no. 2, (September 1986), pp. 257–322.

Goldthrope, J.E. *The Sociology of the Third World, Disparity and Development*. Cambridge: Cambridge University Press, 1984.

Goodwin, Jeff and Theda Skocpol. 'Explaining Revolutions in the Contemporary Third World'. *Politics and Society*. vol. 17, no. 2, (December 1989), pp. 489–509.

Green, Jerrold. 'Countermobilization as a Revolutionary Form'. *Comparative Politics*. vol. 16, no. 2, (January 1984), pp. 153–69.

Greene, Gerald. *Comparative Revolutionary Movements*. Englewood Cliffs, NJ: Prentice-Hall, 1974.

Gugler, Josef. 'Overurbanization Reconsidered', in Josef Gugler, ed. *The Urbanization of the Third World*. Oxford: Oxford University Press, 1988, pp. 74–92.

——. 'The Urban Character of Contemporary Revolutions', in Josef Gugler, ed. *The Urbanization of the Third World*. Oxford: Oxford University Press, 1988, pp. 399–412.

Gurr, Ted Robert. 'War, Revolution, and the Growth of the Coercive State'. *Comparative Political Studies*. vol. 21, no. 1, (April 1988), pp. 45–65.

——. *Why Men Rebel?* Princeton, NJ: Princeton University Press, 1970.

Hague, Rod and Martin Harrop. *Comparative Politics and Government: An Introduction*. Atlantic Highlands, NJ: Humanities Press, 1987, pp. 134–7.

Han, S.J. 'South Korea in 1988: Revolution in the Making'. *Asia Survey*. vol. 29, (January 1989), pp. 29–38.

Hansen, Klaus. *Mormonism and the American Experience*. Chicago: University of Chicago Press, 1981.

Harris, John and Alden Speare. 'Education, Earnings, and Migration in Indonesia'. *Economic Development and Culture Change*. vol. 34, no. 2, (January 1986), pp. 223–44.

Hartmann, Elizabeth, and James Boyce. 'Needless Hunger: Poverty and Power in Rural Bangladesh', in Rosemary Galli, ed. *The Political Economy of Rural Development: Peasants, International Capital, and the State*. Albany, NY: SUNY Press, 1981, pp. 175–210.

Hay, Richard. 'Patterns of Urbanization and Socio-economic Development in the Third World: An Overview', in Janet Abu-Lughod and Richard Hay, eds. *Third World Urbanization*. Chicago: Maaroufa Press, 1977, pp. 71–101.

——. 'Rural–Urban Mobility in South and Southeast Asia, Different Formulations . . . Different Answers?', in Janet Abu-Lughod and Richard Hay, eds. *Third World Urbanization*. Chicago: Maaroufa Press, 1977, pp. 196–212.

Herbert, John. *Urban Development in the Third World: Policy Guidelines*. New York: Praeger, 1979.

Hermassi, Elbaki. *The Third World Reassessed*. Berkeley, Calif.: University of California Press, 1980.

Hernandez, Gloria. 'Political Institution Building in the Philippines', in R. Scalapino, S. Sato, and J. Wanandi, eds. *Asian Political Institutionalization*. Berkeley, Calif.: Institute of East Asian Studies, 1986.

Higgot, Richard. *Political Development Theory: The Contemporary Debate*. London: Croom Helm, 1983.

Hillmann, Michael, ed. *Iranian Society: An Anthology of Writings by Jalal Al-e Ahmad*. Lexington, Ky: Mazda Press, 1982.

Himmelstein, Jerome and Michael Kimmel. 'Review Essay: States and Revolutions: The Implications and Limits of Skocpol's Structural Model'. *American Journal of Sociology*. vol. 86, no. 5, (March 1981), pp. 1145–54.

Hinnebusch, Raymond. 'Charisma, Revolution, and State Formation: Qaddafi and Libya'. *Third World Quarterly*. vol. 7, no. 1, (January 1984), pp. 59–73.

Hintzen, Percy. 'Bases of Elite Support for a Regime: Race, Ideology, and Clientalism as Bases for Leaders in Guyana and Trinidad'. *Comparative Political Studies*. vol. 16, no. 3, (October 1983), pp. 363–91.

Horowitz, Dan. 'Dual Authority Politics'. *Comparative Politics*. vol. 14, no. 3, (April 1982), pp. 329–49.

Howe, Elizabeth. 'Responsive Planning and Social Development Programs in the Third World'. *Journal of Planning Literature*. vol. 2, no. 4, (Autumn 1987), pp. 384–404.

Hoy, Terry. 'Octavio Paz: The Search for Mexican Identity'. *Review of Politics*. vol. 44, no. 3, (July 1982), pp. 370–85.

Hsu, Immanuel. *The Rise of Modern China*. Oxford: Oxford University Press, 1990.

Huntington, Samuel. *Political Order in Changing Societies*. New Haven, Conn.: Yale University Press, 1968.

——. 'Social and Institutional Dynamics of One-Party Systems', in S. Huntington and C. Moore, eds. *Authoritarian Politics in Modern Society*. London: Basic Books, 1970, pp. 3–47.

Inglehart, Ronald. 'The Renaissance of Political Culture'. *American Political Science Review*. vol. 82, no. 4, (December 1988), pp. 1203–30.

Jackson, Robert, and Carl Rosberg. 'Personal Rule: Theory and Practice in Africa'. *Comparative Politics*. vol. 16, no. 4, (1984), pp. 421–42.

Jellinek, Lea. 'The Changing Fortunes of a Jakarta Street-Trader', in Josef Gugler, ed. *The Urbanization of the Third World*. Oxford: Oxford University Press, 1988, pp. 220–3.

Jimenez, Emmanuel. 'The Value of Squatter Dwellings in Developing Countries'. *Economic Development and Cultural Change*. vol. 30, no. 4, (July 1982), pp. 739–52.

Johnson, Carlos. 'Ideologies in Theories of Imperialism and Dependency', in Ronald Chilcote and Dale Johnson, eds. *Theories of Development: Mode of Production or Dependency?* London: Sage, 1983, pp. 75–104.

Johnson, Chalmers. *Revolutionary Change*. London: Longman, 1983.

Johnson, Dale. 'Class Analysis and Dependency', in Ronald Chilcote and Dale Johnson, eds. *Theories of Development: Mode of Production or Dependency?* London: Sage, 1983, pp. 231–55.

Jones, R. Ben. *The French Revolution*. London: Hodder & Stoughton, 1967.

Kamrava, Mehran. *Revolution in Iran: Roots of Turmoil*. London: Routledge, 1990.

——. 'Causes and Leaders of Revolution'. *Journal of Social, Political, and Economic Studies*. vol. 15, no. 1, (Spring 1990), pp. 79–89.

——. 'Intellectuals and Democracy in the Third World'. *Journal of Social, Political and Economic Studies*. vol. 14, no. 2, (Summer 1989).

Kavanagh, Denis. *Political Culture*. London: Macmillan, 1972.

Keesing, Donald. 'Small Population as a Political Handicap to National Development', in Harvey Kebschull, ed. *Politics in Transitional Societies*. New York: Appleton-Century-Crofts, 1973, pp. 318–26.

Keller, Edmond. 'Revolution and the Collapse of Traditional Monarchies: Ethiopia', in Barry Schutz and Robert Slater, eds. *Revolution and Political Change in the Third World*. Boulder, Colo.: Lynne Rienner, 1990, pp. 81–98.

Kelley, Allen and Jeffrey Williamson. 'The Limits to Urban Growth: Suggestions for Macromodeling Third World Economies'. *Economic Development and Cultural Change*. vol. 30, no. 3, (April 1982), pp. 595–623.

Keyfitz, Nathan. 'Development and the Elimination of Poverty'. *Economic Development and Cultural Change*. vol. 30, no. 3, (April 1982), pp. 649–70.

Kim, Hyung-Chang. 'The Americanization of Higher Education in Korea'. *Asian Profile*. vol. 17, no. 2, (April 1989).

Krauss, Clifford. 'Revolution in Central America?' *Foreign Affairs*. vol. 65, no. 3, (1987), pp. 564–81.

Koreber, A.L. 'Diffusionism', in Edwin R.A. Feligman and Alvin Johnson, eds. *The Encyclopedia of the Social Sciences III*. New York: Macmillan, 1937.

Kromnick, Issac. 'Reflections on Revolution: Definition and Explanation in Recent Scholarship'. *History and Theory*. vol. XI, no. 1, 1972, pp. 22–63.

Kuyunsa, Bidum. 'The Priest as a Change Agent'. *Community Development Journal*. vol. 19, (October 1984), pp. 252–60.

Laite, Julian. 'The Migrant Response in Central Peru', in Josef Gugler, ed. *The Urbanization of the Third World*. Oxford: Oxford University Press, 1988.

Landim, Leilah. 'Non-governmental Organizations in Latin America'. *World Development*. vol. 15, Supplement, (1987), pp. 29–38.

Ledent, Jacques. 'Rural–Urban Migration, Urbanization, and Economic Development'. *Economic Development and Cultural Change*. vol. 30, no. 3, (April 1982), pp. 507–38.

Leeds, Anthony. 'Housing-Settlement Types, Arrangements for Living, Proletarianization, and the Social Structure of the City', in Janet Abu-Lughod and Richard Hay, eds. *Third World Urbanization*. Chicago: Maaroufa Press, 1977, pp. 330–7.

Le Grande, William. 'Central America', in B. Schultz and R. Slater, eds. *Revolution and Political Change in the Third World*. Boulder, Colo.: Lynne Rienner, 1990, pp. 142–60.

Levine, Daniel. 'Religion and Politics in Contemporary Historical Perspective'. *Comparative Politics*. vol. 19, no. 1, (October 1986).

——. 'Assessing the Impact of Liberation Theology in Latin America'. *Review of Politics*. vol. 50, no. 2, (Spring 1988).

Levy, Daniel. 'Comparing Authoritarian Regimes in Latin America: Insights from Higher Education Policy'. *Comparative Politics.* vol. 14, no. 1, (October 1981), pp. 31–52.

Linn, Johannes. 'The Cost of Democracy in the Developing Countries'. *Economic Development and Cultural Change.* vol. 30, no. 3, (April 1982), pp. 625–48.

Lipton, Michael. 'Why Poor People Stay Poor: Urban Bias in World Development', in Josef Gugler, ed. *The Urbanization of the Third World.* Oxford: Oxford University Press, 1988, pp. 40–51.

Litwak, Robert. *Detente and the Nixon Doctrine: American Foreign Policy and the Pursuit of Stability.* Cambridge: Cambridge University Press, 1984.

Liviga, Athumani, and Jan Kees van Donge. 'Tanzanian Political Culture and the Cabinet'. *The Journal of Modern African Studies.* vol. 24, no. 4, (1986), pp. 619–39.

Lomnitz, Larissa. 'The Social and Economic Organization of a Mexican Shantytown', in Josef Gugler, ed. *The Urbanization of the Third World.* Oxford: Oxford University Press, 1988, pp. 242–63.

McCormick, Gordon. 'The Shining Path and Peruvian Terrorism'. *The Journal of Strategic Studies.* vol. 10, no. 4, (December 1987), pp. 109–26.

McDermott, Anthony. *Egypt from Nasser to Mubarak: A Flawed Revolution.* London: Croom Helm, 1988.

McDonough, Peter. 'Repression and Representation in Brazil'. *Comparative Politics.* vol. 15, no. 1, (October 1982), pp. 73–99.

McGee, T.G. *The Urbanization Process in the Third World: Explorations in Search of a Theory.* London: G. Bell & Sons, 1971.

McGee, T.G. 'The Persistence of the Proto-Proletariat: Occupational Structures and Planning of the Future of the Third World Cities', in Janet Abu-Lughod and Richard Hay, eds. *Third World Urbanization.* Chicago: Maaroufa Press, 1977, pp. 257–70.

Macklin, David. 'A Social-Psychological Perspective on Modernization', in Chandler Morse, *et al. Modernization by Design: Social Change in the Twentieth Century.* London: Cornell University Press, 1969, pp. 85–146.

Ma'oz, Moshe. *Syria Under Hafiz Al-Asad: New Domestic and Foreign Policies.* Jerusalem: Hebrew University Press, 1975.

Maravall, J.M. 'Subjective Conditions and Revolutionary Conflicts: Some Remarks'. *British Journal of Sociology.* vol. 27, no. 1, (March 1976). pp. 21–34.

Marcos, Ferdinand. *Notes on the New Society of the Philippines.* Manila: Marcos Foundation, 1973.

——. *Five Years of the New Society.* Manila: Marcos Foundation, 1978.

Marenin, Otwin. 'Policing African States: Toward a Critique'. *Comparative Politics.* vol. 14, no. 4, (July 1982), pp. 379–96.

Marshall, Susan. 'Politics and Female Status in North Africa: A Reconsideration of Development Theory'. *Economic Development and Cultural Change.* vol. 32, no. 3, (April 1984), pp. 499–524.

Marton, Katherin. *Multinationals, Technology, and Industrialization: Implications and Impact in Third World Countries.* Lexington, Va: Lexington Books, 1986.

Mason, T. David. 'Indigenous Factors', in B. Schultz and R. Slater, eds.

Revolution and Political Change in the Third World. Boulder, Colo.: Lynne Rienner, 1990, pp. 30–53.

Mattelart, Armand. *Transnationals and the Third World: The Struggle for Culture.* David Buxton, trans. South Hadley, Mass: Bergin & Garvey, 1983.

Mecham, J. Lloyd. 'Latin American Constitutions: Nominal or Real', in Harvey Kebschull, ed. *Politics in Transitional Societies.* New York: Appleton-Century-Crofts, 1973, pp. 219–27.

Midlarsky, Manus. 'Scarcity and Inequality: Prologue to the Onset of Mass Revolution'. *Journal of Conflict Resolution.* vol. 26, no. 1, (March 1982), pp. 3–38.

——. 'Rules and the Ruled: Patterned Inequality and the Onset of Mass Political Violence'. *American Political Science Review.* vol. 82, no. 2, (June 1988), pp. 491–509.

Migdal, Joel. *Peasants, Politics, and Revolution: Pressures Toward Political and Social Change in the Third World.* Princeton, NJ: Princeton University Press, 1974.

Miroff, Bruce. *Pragmatic Illusions: The Presidential Politics of John F. Kennedy.* New York: David McKay, 1976.

Moghadam, Val. 'Industrial Development, Culture and Working Class Politics: A Case Study of Tabriz Industrial Workers in the Iranian Revolution'. *International Sociology.* vol. 2, no. 2, (June 1987), pp. 151–75.

Moore, Barrington. *Injustice: The Social Base of Obedience and Revolt.* London: Macmillan, 1978.

Moore, Clement. 'The Single Party as a Source of Legitimacy', in S. Huntington and C. Moore, eds. *Authoritarian Politics in Modern Society.* London: Basic Books, 1970, pp. 48–72.

Moore, Wilbert. *Social Change.* Englewood Cliffs, NJ: Prentice-Hall, 1963.

Moore, Sally Falk. 'Legitimation as a Process: The Expansion of Government and Party in Tanzania', in R. Cohen and J. Toland, eds. *State Formation and Political Legitimacy.* New Brunswick, NJ: Transaction Books, 1988, pp. 156–60.

Mushi, Samuel. 'Community Development in Tanzania', in Ronald Dore and Zoe Mars, eds. *Community Development.* London: Croom Helm, 1981, pp. 139–242.

Nash, Manning. *Unfinished Agenda: The Dynamics of Modernization in Developing Nations.* Boulder, Colo.: Westview, 1984.

Nelson, Joan. *Access to Power: Politics and the Urban Poor in Developing Nations.* Princeton, NJ: Princeton University Press, 1979.

Nettl, J.P. 'Ideas, Intellectuals, and Structures of Dissent', in Philip Rieff, ed. *On Intellectuals.* Garden City, NY: Anchor Books, 1970.

Nkrumah, Kwame. *Consciencism.* London: Heinemann, 1964.

Nordlinger, Eric. *Soldiers in Politics: Military Coups and Governments.* Englewood Cliffs, NJ: Prentice-Hall, 1977.

——. 'Soldiers in Mufti: The Impact of Military Rule Upon Economic and Social Change in the Non-Western States', in Harvey Kebschull, ed. *Politics in Transitional Societies.* New York, NY: Appleton-Century-Crofts, 1973, pp. 250–61.

Nwabueze, B.O. *The Presidential Constitution of Nigeria.* London: C. Hurst & Co., 1982.

Ogburn, W.F. *Social Change with Respect to Culture and Original Nature*. New York: Viking, 1950.

O'Kane, Rosemary. 'A Probabilistic Approach to the Causes of Coups d'Etat'. *British Journal of Political Science*. vol. 11, (1981), pp. 287–398.

Onibokun, Adepoju G. 'Urban Growth and Urban Management in Nigeria', in Richard Stern and Rodney White, eds. *African Cities in Crisis: Managing Rapid Urban Growth*. Boulder, Colo.: Westview, 1989, pp. 69–111.

Ortega, Marvin. 'The State, the Peasantry and the Sandanista Revolution'. *Journal of Development Studies*. vol. 26, no. 4, (1990), pp. 122–42.

Pahlavi, Mohammad Reza. *Mission for My Country*. New York: McGraw Hill, 1960.

——. *Answer to History*. New York: Stein & Day, 1980.

Paige, Jeffrey. *Agrarian Revolution: Social Movement and Export Agriculture in the Underdeveloped World*. New York: Fress Press, 1975.

Parker, Richard. 'Anti-American Attitudes in the Arab World'. *Annals of the American Academy of Political and Social Sciences*. vol. 497 (May 1988).

Parsa, Misagh. 'Theories of Collective Action and the Iranian Revolution'. *Sociological Forum*. vol. 3, no. 1, (Winter 1988), pp. 41–71.

Paterson, Thomas, J.G. Clifford and Kenneth Hagan. *American Foreign Policy: A History*. Lexington: Mass: D.C. Heath, 1991.

Paz, Octavio. *The Labyrinth of Solitude: Life and Thought in Mexico*. Trans. Lysander Kemp. London: Evergreen, 1961.

Philips, George. 'Military-Authoritarianism in South America: Brazil, Chile, Uruguay and Argentina'. *Political Studies*. vol. 32, (1984), pp. 1–20.

Portis, E.B. 'Charismatic Leadership and Cultural Democracy'. *Review of Politics*. vol. 41, no. 2, (Spring 1987), pp. 231–50.

Preston, Samuel. 'Urban Growth in the Developing Countries: A Demographic Reappraisal', in Josef Gugler, ed. *The Urbanization of the Third World*. Oxford: Oxford University Press, 1988, pp. 211–31.

Pye, Lucian. 'Identity and Political Culture', in Lucian Pye, Leonard Binden, James Coleman, Joseph La Palombara, Sidney Verba and Myron Weiner. *Crises and Sequences in Political Development*. Princeton, NJ: Princeton University Press.

——. 'The Legitimacy Crisis', in Lucian Pye *et al. Crises and Sequences in Political Development*. Princeton, NJ: Princeton University Press, 1971.

——. 'The Non-Western Political Process', in Harvey Kebschull, ed. *Politics in Transitional Societies*. New York: Appleton-Century-Crofts, 1973, pp. 21–31.

——. 'The Concept of Political Development', in Harvey Kebschull, ed. *Politics in Transitional Societies*. New York: Appleton-Century-Crofts, 1973, pp. 49–52.

——. 'Political Development and Political Decay', in Harvey Kebschull, ed. *Politics in Transitional Societies*. New York: Appleton-Century-Crofts, 1973, pp. 53–60.

Randall, Vicky and Robin Theobald. *Political Change and Underdevelopment: A Critical Introduction to Third World Politics*. London: Macmillan, 1985.

Ranger, Terence. 'Religion, Development, and African Christian Identity', in Kirsten H. Petersen, ed. *Religion, Development and African Identity*. Uppsala: The Scandinavian Institute for African Studies, 1987.

Remmer, Karen. 'Redemocratization and the Impact of Authoritarian Rule in Latin America'. *Comparative Politics*. vol. 17, no. 3, (April 1985), pp. 253–76.

Richards, Gordon. 'Stabilization Crisis and the Breakdown of Military Authoritarianism in Latin America'. *Comparative Political Studies*. vol. 18, no. 4, (January 1986), pp. 449–85.

Robert Bryan. *Cities of Peasants: The Political Economy of Urbanization in the Third World*. London: Sage, 1978.

Roett, Riodan. 'Anti-Americanism in the Southern Cone of Latin America'. *Annals of the American Academy of Political and Social Sciences*, vol. 497 (May 1988), p. 71.

Rogers, Andrei. 'Sources of Urban Population Growth and Urbanization, 1950–2000: A Demographic Accounting'. *Economic Development and Cultural Change*. vol. 30, no. 3, (April 1982), pp. 483–506.

Rogers, Andrei and Jeffrey Williams. 'Migration, Urbanization, and Third World Development: An Overview'. *Economic Development and Cultural Change*. vol. 30, no. 3, (April 1982), pp. 463–82.

Rohrer, Wayne. 'Developing Third World Farming: Conflict between Modern Imperatives and Traditional Ways'. *Economic Development and Cultural Change*. vol. 34, no. 2, (January 1986), pp. 299–314.

Rondinelli, Denis. *Secondary Cities in Developing Countries: Policies for Diffusing Urbanization*. London: Sage, 1983.

Rosenbaum, Walter. *Political Culture*. New York: Praeger, 1975.

Rubin, Barry. *Modern Dictators: Third World Coup Makers, Strongmen, and Populist Tyrants*. New York: McGraw-Hill, 1987.

Rubenstein, Alvin and Donald Smith. 'Anti-Americanism in the Third World'. *Annals of the American Academy of Social and Political Sciences*. vol. 497 (May 1988), p. 35.

Rustow, Dankwart. 'Ataturk's Political Leadership', in R. Winder, ed. *Near Eastern Round Table 1967–68*. New York: NYU Press, 1969, pp. 143–55.

Sabot, Richard. 'Migration and Urban Surplus Labor: Policy Options', in Josef Gugler, ed. *The Urbanization of the Third World*. Oxford: Oxford University Press, 1988, pp. 93–108.

Salert, Barbara. *Revolutions and Revolutionaries*. New York: Elsevier, 1976.

Samudamanija, Chai-Anan. 'Political Institutionalization in Thailand: Continuity and Change', in R. Scalapino, S. Sato, and J. Wanandi, eds. *Asian Political Institutionalization*. Berkeley, Calif.: Institute of East Asian Studies, 1986, pp. 241–60.

Sandbrook, Richard. 'The State and Economic Stagnation in Tropical Africa'. *World Development*. vol. 14, no. 3, (1986), pp. 319–32.

Sarduy, Pedro Perez. 'Culture and the Cuban Revolution'. *The Black Scholar*. vol. 20, nos. 5–6, (Winter 1989), pp. 17–23.

Scalapino, Robert. 'Legitimacy and Institutionalization in Asian Socialist Societies', in R. Scalapino, S. Sato, and J. Wanandi, eds. *Asian Political Institutionalization*. Berkeley, Calif.: Institute of East Asian Studies, 1986, pp. 59–94.

Schahgaldian, Nikola. *The Clerical Establishment in Iran*. Santa Monica, Calif.: Rand Corporation, 1989.

Schram, Stuart. *The Political Thought of Mao Tse Tung*. New York: Praeger, 1972.

Schultz, Barry and Robert Slater. 'A Framework for Analysis', in B. Schultz and R. Slater, eds. *Revolution and Political Change in the Third World*. Boulder, Colo.: Lynne Rienner, 1990, pp. 3–18.

——. 'Patterns of Legitimacy and Future Revolutions in the Third World'. B. Schultz and R. Slater, eds. *Revolution and Political Change in the Third World*. Boulder, Colo.: Lynne Rienner, 1990, pp. 247–50.

Scott, James. 'Hegemony and the Peasantry'. *Politics and Society*. vol. 7, no. 3, (1977), pp. 267–96.

Scruton, Roger. *A Dictionary of Political Thought*. London: Macmillan, 1982.

Seligson, Mitchell. 'Democratization in Latin America: The Current Cycle', in J. Malloy and M. Seligson, eds. *Authoritarians and Democrats: Regime Changes in Latin America*. Pittsburg: University of Pittsburg Press, 1987, pp. 3–12.

Simmons, Ozzie. *Perspectives on Development and Population Growth in the Third World*. London: Plenum, 1988.

Skocpol, Theda. *States and Social Revolutions*. Cambridge: Cambridge University Press, 1979.

——. 'Social Revolutions and Mass Military Mobilization'. *World Politics*. vol. XL, no. 2, (January 1988), pp. 147–68.

——. 'What Makes Peasants Revolutionary?' *Comparative Politics*. vol. 14, no. 3, (April 1982), pp. 351–375.

——. 'Rentier State and Shi'a Islam in the Iranian Revolution'. *Theory and Society*. vol. 11, no. 3, (May 1982), pp. 265–83.

Spalding, Rose. 'State Power and its Limits: Corporatism in Mexico'. *Comparative Political Studies*. vol. 14, no. 2, (July 1981), pp. 139–61.

Speare, Alden and John Harris. 'Education, Earnings, and Migration in Indonesia'. *Economic Development and Cultural Change*. vol. 34, no. 2, (January 1986), pp. 223–44.

Stark, Oded and Robert Lucas. 'Migration, Remittances, and the Family'. *Economic Development and Cultural Change*. vol. 36, no. 3, (April 1988), pp. 465–82.

Stark, Oded and David Lavhari. 'On Migration and Risk in LDCs'. *Economic Development and Cultural Change*. vol. 31, no. 1, (October 1982), pp. 191–6.

Stern, Richard. 'The Administration of Urban Services', in Richard Stern and Rodney White, eds. *African Cities in Crisis: Managing Rapid Urban Growth*. Boulder, Colo.: Westview, 1989, pp. 37–63.

——. 'Urban Local Government in Africa', in Richard Stern and Rodney White, eds. *African Cities in Crisis: Managing Rapid Urban Growth*. Boulder, Colo.: Westview, 1989, pp. 20–36.

Stokes, Randall and David Jaffee. 'Another Look at the Export of Raw Materials and Economic Growth'. *American Sociological Review*. vol. 47, no. 3, (June 1982), pp. 402–7.

Stone, L. 'Theories of Revolution'. *World Politics*. vol. 18, 1966, pp. 159–76.

Strasser, Hermann and Susan Randall. *An Introduction to Theories of Social Change*. London: Routledge & Kegan Paul, 1981.

Stultz, Newell. 'Parliaments in Former British Black Africa', in Harvey Kebschull, ed. *Politics in Transitional Societies*. New York: Appleton-Century-Crofts, 1973, pp. 262–77.

Sung-joo, Han. 'Political Institutionalization in South Korea, 1961–1984', in R. Scalapino, S. Sato, and J. Wanandi, eds. *Asian Political Institutionalization*. Berkeley, Calif.: Institute for East Asian Studies, 1986, pp. 116–37.

Tachau, Frank and Metin Heper. 'The State, Politics, and the Military in Turkey'. *Comparative Politics*. vol. 16, no. 1, (October 1983), pp. 17–37.

Timothy, Bankole. *Kwame Nkrumah from Cradle to Grave*. Dorchester: Gavin Press, 1981.

Torp, Jens Erik. *Industrial Planning and Development in Mozambique*. Uppsala, Sweden: The Scandinavian Institute of African Studies, 1979.

Vacs, Aldo. 'Authoritarian Breakdown and Redemocratization in Argentina', in J. Malloy and M. Seligson, eds. *Authoritarians and Democrats: Regime Transition in Latin America*. Pittsburg: University of Pittsburg Press, 1987, pp. 15–42.

Veltmeyer, Henry. 'Surplus Labor and Class Formation on the Latin American Periphery', in Ronald Chilcote and Dale Johnson, eds. *Theories of Development: Mode of Production or Dependency?* London: Sage, 1983, pp. 201–30.

Vilas, Carlos. 'Popular Insurgency and Social Revolution in Central America'. *Latin American Perspectives*. vol. 15, no. 1, (Winter 1988), pp. 55–77.

Watson, Keith. 'Educational Neocolonialism – The Continued Legacy', in Keith Watson, ed. *Education in the Third World*. London: Croom Helm, 1982, p. 184.

Weiner, Myron. 'Institution Building in South Asia', in R. Scalapino, S. Sato, and J. Wanandi, eds. *Asian Political Institutionalization*. Berkeley, Calif.: Institute of East Asian Studies, 1986, pp. 288–312.

——. 'Political Participation: Crisis of the Political Process', in Lucian Pye, et al. *Crises and Sequences in Political Development*. Princeton, NJ: Princeton University Press, 1971.

Weinstein Jay. 'The Third World and Developmentalism: Technology, Morality, and the Role of Intellectuals', in Raj Mayhan, ed. *The Mythmakers: Intellectuals and the Intelligentsia in Perspective*. Westport, Conn.: Greenwood, 1987.

White, Rodney. 'The Influence of Environmental and Economic Factors on the Urban Crisis', in Rodney White and Richard Stern, eds. *African Cities in Crisis: Managing Rapid Urban Growth*. Boulder, Colo.: Westview, 1989.

Whyte, Martin King. 'Social Control and Rehabilitation in Urban China', in Josef Gugler, ed. *The Urbanization of the Third World*. Oxford: Oxford University Press, 1988, pp. 246–86.

Wiarda, Howard. 'Political Culture and the Attraction of Marxist-Leninism: National Inferiority Complex as an Explanatory Factor'. *World Affairs*. vol. 151, no. 3, (Winter 1988–89).

Willner, Ann Ruth and Dorothy Willner. 'The Rise and Role of Charismatic Leaders', in Harvey Kebschull, ed. *Politics in Transitional Societies*. New York: Appleton-Century-Crofts, 1973, pp. 227–36.

Wolpin, Miles. 'Sociopolitical Radicalism and Military Professionalism in the Third World'. *Comparative Politics*. vol. 15, no. 2, (January 1983), pp. 203–21.

Wolf, Eric. *Peasant Wars of the Twentieth Century*. New York: Harper & Row, 1969.

World Bank. *World Development Report 1990*. Oxford: Oxford University Press, 1990.

Zagorin, Perez. 'Theories of Revolution in Contemporary Historiography'. *Political Science Quarterly*. vol. LXXXVIII, no. 1, (March 1973), pp. 23–52.

Index